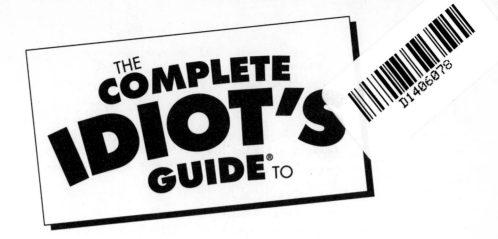

Jesus

by James Stuart Bell and Tracy Macon Sumner

ALPHA

A member of Penguin Group (USA) Inc.

To my friend Rick Richardson—priest, evangelist, and Cardinals fan—who is dedicated to reaching a postmodern world with the message of Jesus.—JB

To all those who have encouraged me and helped me shape my faith in Jesus over the years.—TMS

ALPHA BOOKS

Published by the Penguin Group

Penguin Group (USA) Inc., 375 Hudson Street, New York, New York 10014, U.S.A.

Penguin Group (Canada), 10 Alcorn Avenue, Toronto, Ontario, Canada M4V 3B2 (a division of Pearson Penguin Canada Inc.)

Penguin Books Ltd, 80 Strand, London WC2R 0RL, England

Penguin Ireland, 25 St Stephen's Green, Dublin 2, Ireland (a division of Penguin Books Ltd)

Penguin Group (Australia), 250 Camberwell Road, Camberwell, Victoria 3124, Australia (a division of Pearson Australia Group Pty Ltd)

Penguin Books India Pvt Ltd, 11 Community Centre, Panchsheel Park, New Delhi—110 017, India

Penguin Group (NZ), cnr Airborne and Rosedale Roads, Albany, Auckland 1310, New Zealand (a division of Pearson New Zealand Ltd)

Penguin Books (South Africa) (Pty) Ltd, 24 Sturdee Avenue, Rosebank, Johannesburg 2196, South Africa

Penguin Books Ltd, Registered Offices: 80 Strand, London WC2R 0RL, England

Most Alpha books are available at special quantity discounts for bulk purchases for sales promotions, premiums, fundraising, or educational use. Special books, or book excerpts, can also be created to fit specific needs.

For details, write: Special Markets, Alpha Books, 375 Hudson Street, New York, NY 10014.

Publisher: *Marie Butler-Knight*
Product Manager: *Phil Kitchel*
Senior Managing Editor: *Jennifer Bowles*
Senior Acquisitions Editor: *Renee Wilmeth*
Development Editor: *Michael Hall*
Senior Production Editor: *Billy Fields*

Copy Editor: *Jennifer Connolly*
Cartoonist: *Jody Schaeffer*
Cover/Book Designer: *Trina Wurst*
Indexer: *Angela Bess*
Layout: *Ayanna Lacey*
Proofreading: *John Etchison*

Contents at a Glance

Contents

Foreword

Long ago, when I was in grade school, I was told that the secret of successful writing is to know your ideal reader, the person at the receiving end with whom you want to communicate. This was sound wisdom, and I have tried to keep the maxim in mind throughout the half-century of my own writing career. So, I confess, it "gave me furiously to think," as the French say, when I was asked to write a foreword to a *Complete Idiot's Guide*. What job, I wondered, was the adjective doing? Was it announcing the book as a complete idiot on its subject, as in fact it is, or was it saying that the ideal reader would be a complete idiot—which is, perhaps, the more natural way to read it. Just the sort of question, you might think, that a prissy English expat like me would choke on.

But wait a minute. That word "idiot" has come down in the world. It did not start as a negation of brain power, like the English "booby" and the American "klutz." It transcribes the Greek "idiotēs," which means an ordinary private person as distinct from a public officer or performer. And this, as I take it, is the sort of complete idiot for whom this book is written—an honest and as yet uncommitted nonspecialist, who nonetheless is open to be interested in anything important.

Is Jesus important? He is the most unique and influential person who ever lived. It cannot reasonably be denied that he came into and exited from this world miraculously, by virginal conception and bodily ascension. He left behind him a group of youngish Jews, including his own family, who were sure they had seen him alive and well after his execution and burial (his tomb was found empty), and over the next generation they established a worldwide church, international and multinational, that worshipped him. In his earthly lifetime he had spoken and behaved as if he were God incognito, and his followers were convinced that he was precisely that. From his day to ours he has been turning human lives upside down (or rather, since they are upside down already, right way up), and something like a third of the world's population today will testify that he still does this. The New Testament tells in detail how it all began. Modern America knows in a general way that our culture and heritage are what they are because Jesus was what he was, but we have forgotten most of the facts about him and need to be reminded of them. Here, now, they are served up to complete idiots as it were, on a plate.

Books about persons of religious significance are expected to be dull; but not this one. The author appears as a cross between Jim Lehrer and Dr. Seuss, and his well-informed presentation of Jesus is witty and sharp all the way. Try it—you will, I believe, like it and find it interesting, compelling even, whoever you are, and end up telling your friends that it was a fun read. O happy idiot, to have the old, old story made so wonderfully fresh and tasty for you! May the full benefit of it soon be yours.

Dr. J. I. Packer

Regent College
Vancouver, B.C.

Introduction

The life and death of Jesus of Nazareth was a pivotal point in human history; so much so that we date our years as C.E. (Common Era) and B.C.E. (before Common Era) from the time of the birth of Jesus. Many of the historical figures and events that we are so familiar with, at least until the eighteenth century (and after to a lesser degree), have a component of the Christian religion closely tied in.

One need only look at significant periods—the Middle Ages, the Renaissance, and the Reformation, for instance—to see the centrality of the Christian church in the wars, politics, and overall culture of the time. One sees kings and commoners bowing to the wishes of priests, pastors, and popes. And although that extreme may not be the case today, and some call this a post-Christian era, Western values, laws, and social structures echo this past legacy laid out by Jesus.

One may argue that this is the legacy of an institution, the Christian church. True, but their laws and structures stem from the life, death, and teachings of Jesus the Christ, or the Messiah and Savior of the world, as his followers called him, as found in the four gospels of the New Testament part of the Bible.

This book is meant to be more of a biography introducing you to a person in his historical context than a book about doctrine or devotion. We're not psychologists trying to set up a personality profile or scholars in quest of the historical Jesus. We'll leave the technical details and debates to them. We are simply trying to get you more familiar with the greatest figure of all time, through the eyes of reliable eyewitnesses in documents not that far removed from his lifetime.

We could have chosen a number of primary sources, but have gone with presenting the *biblical* Jesus as found in the New Testament accounts of four writers, three who were eyewitnesses. Even then, we couldn't cover all the stories Jesus told or people he met. Yet we certainly feel that we covered what was important for you, the reader, to know. We follow the life of Christ roughly chronologically, and create a tapestry based on four different, but complementary, perspectives of his close followers.

We begin by laying out the cultural and religious background of the Jewish and Roman world at the time of Jesus' birth and then look at what the Jews were expecting in terms of a Messiah, or Ruler-Savior, from centuries past. This will give you a better understanding of where he fulfilled their expectations and where he caught them off guard. We don't want the action to be slow, but we do want to give you a sense of movement and context, because Jesus was an itinerant preacher who was on a mission to accomplish certain things, even his own death on a cross.

We describe and explain things as they happened, taking them at face value, whether they be demons, miracles, or the event of the Resurrection of Jesus itself. This was the successful formula for my (Jim's) *The Complete Idiot's Guide to the Bible* and I'm emulating it here. We both encourage you to evaluate the claims of Jesus and the Bible in which he appears, and pursue sources that deal with these truth claims. Based on the absolutes, warnings, and rewards found in the life of Jesus, it's worth the effort.

As you'll discover, most people who encountered Jesus in the gospel accounts were deeply affected, one way or another. We can't guarantee that will happen to you, but we hope it will, and for the better.

Extras

There are three sidebars in this book, identified by an appropriate icon, that will provide supplemental information that adds to the understanding of the main text, or allows for interesting little side trips. We felt the following three were critical areas that were necessary to give sufficient background to the story line of the life and ministry of Jesus.

Let's Come to Terms

These are explanations of terms that you may be unfamiliar with, mainly from a religious or cultural root. These sidebars can cover anything from religious celebrations to explaining the names of coins used at the time. It will help you keep from stumbling over terminology you may not recognize.

W.W.J.K. (What Would Jesus Know?)

These sidebars are bits of background information that stem from the time of Jesus. He would have been familiar with most of the religious, cultural, and political material covered here, but it is unfamiliar to a lot of us today. These are a little twist on W.W.J.D., or the "What Would Jesus Do?" fad.

His Name Is Jesus, a.k.a.

These are explanations of the different roles and names given to the coming Messiah in the Old Testament of the Bible, names Jesus designated to himself, and finally, names the Christian church gave him after he left this Earth—the latter two found in the New Testament. After reading these you will have a much better understanding of the significance attributed to the Messiah and all he is and does in terms of what Christians believe.

Acknowledgments

To Renee Wilmeth, who has given me the opportunity to do five *Complete Idiot's Guides* as well as manage the *Christian Family Guides*. I want to reach those who may be just beginning in these spiritual areas and this has been a great medium. To my wife, Margaret, who has encouraged me throughout this process to make Jesus accessible to everyone.—JB

Just about any project worth pursuing is a team effort, and this book is certainly no exception. I would like to thank my partner in this project, Jim Bell, for giving me constant encouragement and guidance during its early and middle stages. Special thanks to the good people at Alpha Books for their hard work in helping make this project all that it could be. Thanks to our editor, Michael Hall, for his hard and painstaking work in helping us craft this book through its final stages.—TMS

Trademarks

All terms mentioned in this book that are known to be or are suspected of being trademarks or service marks have been appropriately capitalized. Alpha Books and Penguin Group (USA) Inc. cannot attest to the accuracy of this information. Use of a term in this book should not be regarded as affecting the validity of any trademark or service mark.

Part 1

Setting the Stage for the Messiah

No great movement—be it a religious, social, or political one—"just happens." It takes a lot of preparation to get people ready for something "new."

In the case of Jesus' coming, the Jewish people of first-century Palestine had long held to the hope offered by Old Testament prophecies that their deliverer, or "Messiah," would come from God to free them from generations of oppression.

Jesus came into a world of incredible turmoil, a world in which many of the Jewish people had come to a point where they could no longer endure life as it was. The stage was set for something "new."

The Man Who Would Be King (of Kings)

In This Chapter

- ◆ The claims Jesus made … and how he backed them up
- ◆ Jewish prophecies of the coming Messiah
- ◆ Jesus in Old Testament prophecy

History is filled with accounts of people who have claimed to be sent from God and who had large followings, even after their deaths. Mohammed, the founder of the religion of Islam, claimed to be sent from God, as did Buddha, whose teachings were the basis of the religion of Buddhism. Men like Plato, Confucius, Zoroaster, and literally thousands of others also claimed to have God-inspired messages for humankind.

Jesus Christ, a Jewish carpenter and teacher who lived early in the first century C.E. in what was then called Palestine, also claimed to be sent from God and also had a large following of people. The difference is, he claimed to *be* God in the flesh, whereas the others only claimed to be prophets and philosophers pointing to concepts of God that were very different.

We can read in the Bible of Jesus' incredible and, to some of the people around him, provocative and scandalous claims.

You're Telling Us You're *Who?*

Jesus couldn't have been clearer about who he believed sent him and what his coming meant. Over and over again, he told the people around him, including the religious authorities, that God had personally sent him into the world as the long-awaited Messiah.

Jesus identified himself in a variety of ways and a variety of settings. He was identified in the Bible as the Messiah not just through his own words and actions, but also through the words of many people who knew him.

What Others Were Saying

One day Jesus asked his disciples who people believed he was. There had been a lot of talk among the people in the area where Jesus lived about who he was, so he asked the disciples what they had been hearing. After they told him what people had been saying about him, he asked them what *they* thought. One of those disciples, a man named Simon Peter, responded, "You are the Messiah, the Son of the living God." Jesus not only affirmed Peter's words but told him he was blessed because he recognized that Jesus was the Messiah (Matthew 16:13–20).

> **His Name Is Jesus, a.k.a.**
>
> "The Lion of the Tribe of Judah/ The Lamb" (Revelation 5:5). Jesus was descended from the tribe of Judah and is seen here at the end of all things in both his ruling strength and power as well as his submission and weakness from the Cross.

In another incident, Jesus talked with a woman in Galilee about who he was. The woman knew that a Messiah was coming, one who would be called "Christ." Jesus wasted no time telling her, "I am the Messiah!" (John 4:4–26).

Yes, I'm *His* Son!

As if saying that he was the Messiah sent from God wasn't enough, Jesus shook up the religious establishment of his day even further by claiming to be the Son of God himself: "… why do you call it blasphemy when the Holy One who was sent into the world by the Father says, 'I am the Son of God'?" (John 10:36). But he went even a step further by saying that he was the one and only way to God: "I am the way, the truth, and the life. No one can come to the Father except through me" (John 14:6).

Here are just a few of Jesus' other amazing claims:

◆ "I assure you, those who listen to my message and believe in God who sent me have eternal life. They will never be condemned for their sins, but they have already passed from death into life" (John 5:24).

◆ "But I have a greater witness than John—my teachings and my miracles. They have been assigned to me by the Father, and they testify that the Father has sent me. And the Father himself has also testified about me. You have never heard his voice or seen him face to face, and you do not have his message in your hearts, because you do not believe me—the one he sent to you" (John 5:36–38).

◆ "I don't speak on my own authority. The Father who sent me gave me his own instructions as to what I should say" (John 12:49).

◆ "Anyone who has seen me has seen the Father!" (John 14:9).

So Where's the Proof?

If you're going to make claims like the ones Jesus made, you'd better be ready to back them up. If you don't, you'll just be added to the list of thousands in history who claimed to have some special connection to God.

Jesus did just that!

Jesus' approach to backing up his claims was a simple one. Basically, he said that he would fulfill all of the Old Testament prophecies concerning the promised coming of the Messiah. One day, he very boldly told a group of Jewish leaders, "You search the Scriptures because you believe they give you eternal life. But the Scriptures point to me!" (John 5:39).

Indeed, Jesus fulfilled literally hundreds of Old Testament predictions concerning the coming of the Messiah. What's more, some of those prophecies were ones that only the Messiah could have fulfilled. (In Appendix B, you will see that he fulfilled *all* of the messianic prophecies listed.)

Before we move on to the specific prophecies Jesus fulfilled, let's take a look at what the Jewish people were looking for when it came to their Messiah.

A "Garden-Variety" Messianic Prophecy

You don't have to read far in the Bible before you see the first promise of a Messiah. The scene was the Garden of Eden, and human life had just taken a drastic turn for

Let's Come to Terms

Original Sin is a belief in Christianity that refers to how sin (that is, rebellion against God) began in the Garden of Eden, where Adam and Eve disobeyed God and ate the fruit of the tree he told them to stay away from. This doctrine says that the sin of these two people would be passed down to every generation of humans who followed them.

the worse. Adam and Eve had disobeyed God by eating fruit from the tree he had warned them to stay away from.

Without getting too theological here, we'll just tell you that the result of their disobedience, what has come to be known as the *"Original Sin,"* polluted the entire human race. Because of that, God and mankind were now separated and it would be up to God to do what no human could do: provide a way for sin to be forgiven. That's exactly what he promised to do when he told the devil-in-snake's clothing, "From now on, you and the woman will be enemies, and your offspring and her offspring will be enemies. He will crush your head, and you will strike his heel" (Genesis 3:15).

There's a lot more to this promise than women not liking snakes. What it meant, in a nutshell, was that one day a woman would give birth to a son who would "crush the head" of the devil once and for all. That wouldn't come without the devil gaining what he thought would be something of a victory; the Messiah would have to be bruised before everything was completed.

That was the first of hundreds of "Messianic prophecies"—in other words, the predictions of a coming Messiah. The Old Testament, from the third chapter of Genesis to the last chapter of the book of Malachi, is filled with promises of his arrival and of what his arrival would mean to the entire human race.

We can't cover all of these prophecies in this chapter (for a more comprehensive list, see Appendix B), so for now, we'll just give you an overview of what the Old Testament had to say about the coming Messiah.

He's a Prophet, He's a Priest, He's a King!

For several centuries prior to the birth of Jesus, the Jewish people had been looking and longing for the coming of a Messiah. They weren't looking for much—just someone to serve as a prophet, priest, and king ... all at once! In short, they wanted a Messiah who would tell them what God wanted them to hear, minister to them as only a priest can, and rule over them with kindness. It shouldn't come as a surprise that the Jews were looking for such a Messiah. After all, that is exactly the kind of deliverer they had been promised in their holy books!

The Promise of a Prophet

Long before Jesus came on the scene, God made this promise to the people of Israel: "I will raise up a prophet like you from among their fellow Israelites. I will tell that prophet what to say, and he will tell the people everything I command him" (Deuteronomy 18:18).

The Promise of a Priest

King David was the writer of most of the Psalms, many of which contained prophecies of the coming Messiah. In one of his Psalms, David wrote this of the coming Messiah: "The Lord has taken an oath and will not break his vow: "You are a priest forever in the line of Melchizedek'" (Psalm 110:4).

This meant that the Messiah would be a leader much like *Melchizedek*, who is mentioned in the book of Genesis as the king of what would become Jerusalem and a "priest of God Most High."

> **Let's Come to Terms**
>
> The name **Melchizedek**, which appears in Psalm 110:4, a well-known Messianic prophecy, literally means "righteous king," suggesting that the Jews were looking for a righteous leader as their Messiah.

The Promise of a King

The Jewish people were looking for a king along the lines of David, the great military, political, and spiritual leader who helped establish Israel as a great nation during his reign. The Old Testament contains several prophecies of a "Messiah king," one of which was Psalm 2:6, which reads, "For the Lord declares, 'I have placed my chosen king on the throne in Jerusalem, my holy city.'" Another "Messiah-king" prophecy is found in the book of Genesis: "The scepter will not depart from Judah, nor the ruler's staff from his descendants, until the coming of the one to whom it belongs, the one whom all nations will obey" (Genesis 49:10).

The Old Testament contains literally hundreds of prophecies of the coming Messiah, but one book is known to contain the most prophecies—and the most-detailed prophecies—of his coming.

Isaiah's Messianic Message

More than 700 years before Jesus' birth, there was a Jewish prophet by the name of Isaiah, who wrote the Old Testament book that bears his name. Isaiah's writings include prophecies of God's judgment on humanity, but they also contain a lot of hope, especially when it comes to his predictions concerning the Messiah.

Here are a few of those very specific prophecies:

> **His Name Is Jesus, a.k.a.**
>
> "Jesus Christ" (Matthew 1:21/ John 6:16). Jesus comes from the name "Joshua," which means savior or captain of the armies of God. "Christ" means the Anointed One or Messiah.

- ◆ **He would be born as a man:** "For a child is born to us, a son is given to us …" (9:6).

- ◆ **His mother would be a virgin:** "All right then, the Lord himself will choose the sign. Look! The virgin will conceive a child! She will give birth to a son and will call him Immanuel— 'God is with us'" (7:14).

- ◆ **He would be a descendant of King David:** "… then David's throne will be established by love. From that throne a faithful king will reign, one who always does what is just and right" (16:5).

- ◆ **His ministry would include miracle healings:** "And when he comes, he will open the eyes of the blind and unstop the ears of the deaf. The lame will leap like a deer, and those who cannot speak will shout and sing! Springs will gush forth in the wilderness, and streams will water the desert" (35:5–6).

- ◆ **He would be the Messiah for Jews and non-Jews alike:** "You will do more than restore the people of Israel to me. I will make you a light to the Gentiles, and you will bring my salvation to the ends of the earth" (49:6).

- ◆ **He would come to bring news of healing and freedom:** "The Spirit of the Sovereign Lord is upon me, because the Lord has appointed me to bring good news to the poor. He has sent me to comfort the brokenhearted and to announce that captives will be released and prisoners will be freed" (61:1).

> **Let's Come to Terms**
>
> **Messianic prophecies** is a very biblical-sounding term for Old Testament prophecies that predict the arrival of the Jewish Messiah as well as details about his life and work on earth.

The Messiah Is Coming, but First …

Isaiah also predicted the arrival of someone who would prepare the way for the coming of the Messiah: "Listen! I hear the voice of someone shouting, 'Make a highway for the Lord through the wilderness. Make a straight, smooth road through the desert for our God'" (Isaiah 40:3). The Old Testament prophet Malachi echoes this prophecy: "'Look! I am sending my messenger, and he will prepare the way before me. Then the Lord you are seeking will suddenly come to his Temple.

The messenger of the covenant, whom you look for so eagerly, is surely coming,' says the Lord Almighty" (Malachi 3:1).

These prophecies mean that there would be a "forerunner" or "announcer" for the coming Messiah, one who would prepare the people of Israel for his arrival. This forerunner, it turns out, would be John the Baptist, who began his ministry prior to that of Jesus' and who made it perfectly clear that he was not the Messiah but the one who would prepare the world for his coming (more on John the Baptist's ministry in Chapter 8).

> **W.W.J.K. (What Would Jesus Know?)**
>
> The Old Testament prophet Isaiah, whose name literally means "Salvation of Jehovah," lived and worked during the reigns of several kings of Judah. His prophecies included many warnings of coming judgment from God on his people, but they also included predictions of a Messiah and an outpouring of God's Spirit on his people.

Although the Old Testament prophecies tell us of a coming Messiah who would be a "prophet, priest, and king," they also contain predictions of a Messiah who would suffer and die on behalf of his people.

The "Other Side" of the Messiah

Isaiah paints a beautiful word picture of the prophet, priest, and king who would serve as Israel's Messiah. But that's only half of the picture. The other half is the one of the *"Suffering Servant."* Isaiah tells us that the Messiah would endure rejection, persecution, and hatred at the hands of his enemies. Furthermore, he would be judged as a common criminal and beaten and whipped before being "pierced" or crucified. Then, he would die and be buried.

Here are some of Isaiah's "Suffering Servant" prophecies:

- **He was rejected by the Jews:** "But my work all seems so useless! I have spent my strength for nothing and to no purpose at all. Yet I leave it all in the Lord's hand; I will trust God for my reward" (49:4).

- **He suffered:** "He was despised and rejected—a man of sorrows, acquainted with bitterest grief. We turned our backs on him and looked the other way when he went by. He was despised, and we did not care" (53:3).

> **W.W.J.K. (What Would Jesus Know?)**
>
> Isaiah's *"Suffering Servant,"* which is found mostly in chapters 52 and 53 of the book of Isaiah, describes with amazing detail and accuracy the persecution, arrest, trial, and death of Jesus. The term "Suffering Servant" is used to describe the "other side" of the Messiah, who would also be a prophet, priest, and king for his people.

◆ **He was persecuted:** "From prison and trial they led him away to his death. But who among the people realized that he was dying for their sins—that he was suffering their punishment?" (53:8).

Okay, but *Why* Did He Have to Suffer?

Isaiah and others (we'll get to them in a minute) describe a horrible scene of torture and death for the Messiah. But why did that scene have to take place? Why did the Messiah have to suffer and die? Isaiah answers those questions this way:

> Yet it was our weaknesses he carried; it was our sorrows that weighed him down. And we thought his troubles were a punishment from God for his own sins! But he was wounded and crushed for our sins. He was beaten that we might have peace. He was whipped, and we were healed! All of us have strayed away like sheep. We have left God's paths to follow our own. Yet the Lord laid on him the guilt and sins of us all.
>
> Isaiah 53:4–6

In other words, the coming Messiah would be one who would not only serve as a prophet, priest, and king, but one who would suffer and die on behalf of sinners so that God could forgive their sins.

While Isaiah gives us a very vivid and detailed "big picture" of the coming Messiah, he and the rest of the Old Testament writers also give us some details of his life on earth.

It's All in the Details

The most amazing thing about the Old Testament prophecies about Jesus is that there is so much detail about him. The Old Testament is chock-full of details about the Savior's birth, early life, ministry, arrest, and death. There are prophecies that foretold what Jesus said and did, as well as what those around him said and did.

Here are some of them:

Oh Little Town of Bethlehem ...

You don't have to be an authority on all things biblical to know that Jesus was born in Bethlehem, a tiny village in the part of the world where Jesus lived. But what you may not know is that the birthplace of the Messiah was foretold in Old Testament prophecy.

Around 700 B.C.E. there lived an obscure Jewish prophet by the name of Micah. You'll find his Old Testament book wedged in between the books of Jonah and Nahum. In that book, you'll find an incredible prophecy about the birthplace of the Messiah: "But you, O Bethlehem Ephrathah, are only a small village in Judah. Yet a ruler of Israel will come from you, one whose origins are from the distant past" (Micah 5:2). The Gospel of John reports an incident in Jesus' life that tells us a lot about the Jewish expectation of the Messiah, namely that not all of them knew all of the prophecies of his coming. In that account, some people in Jerusalem said, "For we know where this man comes from. When the Messiah comes, he will simply appear; no one will know where he comes from" (John 7:27). However, it's right there in writing! The prophet Micah predicted that the Messiah would be born in Bethlehem!

A King Riding on a Donkey

The Gospel of Matthew tells us that when Jesus made his final entrance into the holy city of Jerusalem—in what is called the "Triumphal Entry"—he came riding on a donkey while being hailed as a king. Crowds of people lined the road, which they had covered with their cloaks and with branches cut from the trees, crying out "Praise God for the Son of David! Bless the one who comes in the name of the Lord! Praise God in highest heaven!" (Matthew 21:9).

> **W.W.J.K. (What Would Jesus Know?)**
>
> Experts believe that Jesus' arrival into Jerusalem on a donkey was symbolic of the nature of his "kingship." Jesus wasn't coming to bring forceful overthrow of the Roman rule of Palestine, as many Jews believed the Messiah would do. Rather, he was coming to bring peace to all humankind.

Matthew records that this episode in the life of Jesus was the fulfillment of this Old Testament prophecy: "Rejoice greatly, O people of Zion! Shout in triumph, O people of Jerusalem! Look, your king is coming to you. He is righteous and victorious, yet he is humble, riding on a donkey—even on a donkey's colt" (Zechariah 9:9).

Betrayed ... for Silver

As you will read in more detail later on, one of Jesus' disciples, Judas Iscariot, betrayed him. In fact, the Gospel of Matthew records that Judas betrayed Jesus for exactly 30 pieces of silver, which Judas would later, in a fit of remorse, return to those who gave it to him in the first place. They, in turn, used it to buy a potter's field, where foreigners would be buried.

Around 500 years before these events took place, the prophet Zechariah foretold them exactly as they would happen: "And I said to them, 'If you like, give me my wages, whatever I am worth; but only if you want to.' So they counted out for my wages thirty pieces of silver. And the Lord said to me, 'Throw it to the potters'—this magnificent sum at which they valued me! So I took the thirty coins and threw them to the potters in the Temple of the Lord'" (Zechariah 11:12–13).

A Kangaroo Court Trial and Sentencing

As you will read later on, the trial of Jesus before his death sentence was a great example of a "kangaroo court." He faced trumped-up charges and there was no defense offered, even by Jesus himself. The Old Testament contains many prophecies about this trial and sentence. Here are just a few of them:

◆ **He was accused based on the lies of his opponents:** "… while the wicked slander me and tell lies about me. They are all around me with their hateful words, and they fight against me for no reason" (Psalm 109:2–3).

◆ **He offered no defense against the accusations:** "He was oppressed and treated harshly, yet he never said a word. He was led as a lamb to the slaughter. And as a sheep is silent before the shearers, he did not open his mouth" (Isaiah 53:7).

◆ **Though he was innocent, he was sentenced to death:** "He had done no wrong, and he never deceived anyone. But he was buried like a criminal; he was put in a rich man's grave" (Isaiah 53:9).

Let's Come to Terms

Crucifixion was a form of capital punishment used by the Roman Empire during, before, and after the time of Jesus. In it, the victim was nailed by the hands and feet to a cross made of wood. We'll include a more detailed description of crucifixion in Chapter 23.

Seeing the Crucifixion

Isaiah wasn't the only Old Testament figure to write of the "Suffering-Servant" Messiah. The Psalms also foretold in great detail the actual crucifixion scene. Psalm 22, for example, includes these words of Jesus from the cross: "My God, my God! Why have you forsaken me?" (verse 1). This Psalm also included this description of the *crucifixion* itself: "They have pierced my hands and feet" (verse 16).

Psalm 22 also says, "They divide my clothes among themselves and throw dice for my garments" (verse 18). The Gospel of Mark records the fulfillment of this prophecy: ""Then they [the Roman soldiers] nailed him to the cross. They gambled for his clothes, throwing dice to decide who would get them" (Mark 15:24).

Sound Like Anyone You Know?

While we haven't come even close to listing all the "Messianic prophecies" in the Old Testament, we've covered enough to show you that they point to one person, and that's Jesus. While Jesus was far from the only one in human history to claim to be sent from God, he was the only one who was foretold in prophecy.

The Least You Need to Know

- ◆ Jesus made some incredible claims about himself, many of which shook up the religious establishment of his day.

- ◆ The Old Testament contains literally hundreds of prophecies concerning the coming Messiah.

- ◆ The Old Testament prophecies painted a very detailed picture of the Messiah as both a conquering king and a suffering servant.

2

The World Jesus Came Into

In This Chapter

- ◆ The "look" of Palestine (Israel) at Jesus' arrival
- ◆ The establishment of the Jewish nation and culture
- ◆ The Jewish legacy of oppression and occupation
- ◆ Political and economic life under King Herod the Great

Jesus was born in, lived in, and ministered in first-century Palestine, or Israel as it is called today. Palestine was a tiny country—only slightly larger in area than the state of Vermont—located on the eastern shore of the Mediterranean Sea.

In ancient (Old Testament) times, this area was referred to as "the land of the Amorites," after its original inhabitants. After the Israelites took control of the area, around 1200 B.C.E., they renamed it "Canaan," after the grandson of Noah. Today, Christians refer to this part of the world as "the Holy Land," simply because it is the place where Jesus was born and lived.

Let's Come to Terms

Palestine was part of what is now called the **Fertile Crescent,** a term coined by James Henry Breasted, a University of Chicago (Illinois) archeologist. The Fertile Crescent, so called because it is very rich farming land with a good supply of water, includes much of present-day Israel, the West Bank, Lebanon, and parts of Jordan, Syria, Iraq, and southeastern Turkey.

The Geography of Palestine 101

Geographically, the land then called Palestine looked today pretty much like it does today. Palestine stretched about 270 miles north to south along the Mediterranean Sea and 100 to 170 miles west to east. Its western boundary was the Mediterranean Sea and its eastern boundary was the Syrian-Arabian desert. The northern boundary was the Lebanon Mountain range, and the southern boundary was Idumea and the deserts near the Dead Sea.

The 200-mile-long Jordan River cuts through the country, with a slightly larger amount of land on the west side than on the east. During Jesus' time, the area east of the Jordan River was part of Palestine, though today it is the country Jordan.

Who Lived Where in Palestine

Historians estimate that around the time of Jesus' birth, there were just under three million Jews living in Palestine. Most of the rest of the population was composed of "Gentiles"—Greeks and Romans who had settled there over the previous centuries. Palestine at that time was controlled by the Roman Empire, which had installed Herod the Great to rule over the country.

In those days, Palestine was split into several regions, each of which was divided into local territories. Each of the local territories was divided into towns and villages.

Here is a quick rundown of the provinces that were key in Jesus' life and the people who lived in them:

Let's Come to Terms

The word **Gospel** literally means "Good News," or "Truth" and that is certainly fitting, as all four of the books tell the good news of Jesus' story, including his life, death, and resurrection—all of which were a part of God's plan to save humankind from sin.

Galilee

This is where Jesus spent most of his early life. It was located in the southern part of Palestine and bordered the Sea of Galilee. Nazareth, Jesus' hometown, and Capernaum, where he spent most of his adult life, were both located there. Galilee was home to a mixture of Jews, Greeks, and Romans, but the great majority of the people who lived there were Jewish.

Perea

Don't bother looking for the name "Perea" anywhere in the Bible. In the gospels (Matthew, Luke, Mark, and John), Perea is referred to as "the land beyond the Jordan." It is a narrow strip of land east of the Jordan River, directly across from Judea and Samaria. Jesus spent a lot of time in this area, which had a large population of Jews, and many of his followers lived there. The area is now the Arab Kingdom of Jordan.

Judea

The province of Judea, which was mostly Jewish as far as its human population was concerned, included the city of Jerusalem, which was the capital of Palestine and the "hub" for the religious life of the Jews and the scene of some of the most important events in Jewish history. In the minds of the Jews, including Jesus himself, this was a holy place, as it was the site of the Jewish Temple.

During Old Testament times, Judea was known as the Kingdom of Judah. Judea was divided into 11 local territories, each governed by a Roman commissioner at the time of Christ. Pontius Pilate, who played a key role in the life of Christ (more about that in Chapter 20), was the best known of those Roman commissioners.

Samaria

Wedged in between Judea and Galilee, on the west side of the Jordan River, was the province called Samaria. Today, this area is referred to as the "West Bank." The people who lived here were descendants of colonists who had come after the fall of the Northern Kingdom of Israel around 722 B.C.E. as well as a remnant of Jews.

Although there were many Jews living in Samaria—many of whom were of "mixed blood," meaning they were the offspring of marriages between Jews and Gentiles—there was great hatred between them and the "orthodox" Jews from other parts of Palestine. In fact, most Jews would go out of their way to avoid traveling through Samaria.

Decapolis

East of the Sea of Galilee is an area called "Decapolis," which is Greek for "10-part city," or "10 cities." Decapolis was inhabited mostly by Greeks who had settled there after the time of Alexander the Great, and it was the scene of a number of events in the life of Jesus.

So What's the Problem?

Prior to the birth of Jesus Christ, there were within the hearts of most of the Jews feelings of discontent and longing—discontent over the fact that they were not, as a nation, independent of the influence or control of outside powers and longing for the time when their Messiah would arrive and reestablish the rule of God over their homeland.

To understand why the Jewish people at the time of Jesus were so eagerly and longingly awaiting the arrival of their Messiah, you need to understand a little something about Jewish history from the time of the Exodus from Egypt up to the beginning of the first century C.E.

The story of Israel was one that included settlements and resettlements, divisions and subdivisions, invasions and occupations. There were times when the Jews enjoyed a measure of independence, but by the time Jesus was born, the Jews had endured several centuries of domination and sometimes mistreatment at the hands of occupiers.

Stepping Back ... Just a Few Thousand Years

The Old Testament book of Exodus tells the story of a Jewish people held in slavery by Egypt. But under the leadership of Moses, who the Jews believed God had called to deliver them from the hands of their oppressors, they left Egypt around 1445 B.C.E. to begin their journey to the "Promised Land."

W.W.J.K. (What Would Jesus Know?)

Just about everyone in the Jewish culture at the time of Jesus knew what the term "Exodus" meant. In fact, the Jews had long hoped for a "deliverer" who would stand up to their oppressors and free them, just like Moses had stood up to Pharaoh and freed the people of Israel from Egyptian bondage.

Some 600,000 Jewish families left Egypt at that time, and embarked on a 40-year journey through the Red Sea (literally, as the account in Exodus tells us), deserts, mountains, and wilderness. Finally, four decades later, under the leadership of Moses' successor, Joshua, the children of Israel, as the Bible calls them, settled in the Promised Land.

The Jews' settlement in the Promised Land was followed by what is called the era of the Judges, which was a time when Israel was ruled by a series of 14 warrior/prophets and a time when Israel was invaded several times by a series of outside forces. Eventually, the people of Israel, ever mindful of outside threats, wanted to centralize their government under the leadership of a king, the first of which was Saul, who took the throne in roughly 1020 B.C.E.

The nation reached its height of power, prosperity, and influence in the era from around 1000 B.C.E. and 922 B.C.E. This was the time of Israel's two greatest kings: David (yes, the same David who, as a teenager, fought a winning battle with a giant Philistine by the name of Goliath) and his son and predecessor, Solomon.

> **W.W.J.K. (What Would Jesus Know?)**
>
> It was under the leadership of King Solomon that the Jews constructed the first Temple on Mount Moriah in Jerusalem, a project that took many thousands of artisans and labors seven and a half years to complete.

Under the reign of Solomon, the nation of Israel was riding high. Israel had the respect, admiration, and even fear of the rest of the known world, and the result was a 40-year period of uninterrupted peace and incredible economic expansion.

It seemed nothing could stop Israel. But the good times came to an end almost as soon as Solomon died.

All Good Kingdoms Must Come to an End

Solomon was succeeded by his son, Rehoboam, in about 922 B.C.E. Unfortunately for the nation of Israel, Rehoboam lacked his father's wisdom, and most of the nation rejected his leadership. The end result of all this was that Israel, which had been so magnificently united under David and Solomon, split into two nations: the *Northern Kingdom*, called "Israel," and the *Southern Kingdom*, called "Judah." That marked the beginning of a long period of mistrust and conflict between the two kingdoms.

> **Let's Come to Terms**
>
> The **Northern Kingdom** of what was once the nation of Israel was composed of the Jewish tribes of Reuben, Simeon, Levi, Dan, Nathtali, Gad, Asher, Issachar, Zebulun, and Joseph, while the **Southern Kingdom** was composed of the Jewish tribes of Judah and Benjamin. Each was ruled by a series of kings who, with few exceptions, were terrible leaders.

But the situation got worse for what used to be the nation of Israel. In around 725 B.C.E., the rapidly growing Assyrian Empire, under King Shalmaneser V, savagely—we're talking torture and decapitation—attacked the Northern Kingdom. The siege was completed in 722 B.C.E., under King Sargon II, leaving Judah as

Let's Come to Terms

Lamentations is the name of a book in the Old Testament that mourns the aftermath of the Babylonian conquest of the Southern Kingdom and the destruction of Jerusalem and of the holy Temple. It was written by the prophet Jeremiah, who had previously warned his people of coming judgment from God.

the world's sole Jewish kingdom. Many from the Northern Kingdom were either killed or driven from their homeland or taken to other parts of the Assyrian Empire.

Around a century and a quarter later, in 595 B.C.E., the Babylonians, under King Nebuchadnezzar, attacked Judah and replaced King Jehoiachin with a man named Zedekiah, who would serve as their "puppet" king. At that time, some 10,000 Jews were taken into captivity.

When Zedekiah rebelled, the Babylonians attacked again. This time, they laid waste to the city of Jerusalem, destroyed the Temple, and took all but the very poorest Jews into captivity. Their destination was the great ancient Mesopotamian city of Babylonia, which stood on the banks of the Euphrates River near the present-day city of Al Hillah, Iraq.

Now, This Is Our Kind of Conqueror!

The destruction of Jerusalem and the Temple and the Babylonian captivity that followed was, to say the least, a blow to the Jews. Most of them knew about the Egyptian captivity of their forefathers and of the exodus led by Moses, and they longed for a liberator of their own.

That liberator—Cyrus the Great, the founder and king of the Media-Persia Empire—arrived on the scene in around 537 B.C.E., after the Persians overthrew the Babylonian Empire. The captive Jews cheered Cyrus, who they saw as anointed of God to free them. In return, Cyrus showed great respect toward the cultures and religious beliefs of the people who had suffered under the captivity of Nebuchadnezzar and his successors.

W.W.J.K. (What Would Jesus Know?)

King Cyrus of Persia was not a Jew, but he was still seen as a liberating hero among the Jews at Jesus' time. He was remembered for paying great respect to the Jewish people and to their God: "The Lord, the God of heaven has given me all the kingdoms of the earth. He has appointed me to build him a Temple in Jerusalem in the land of Judah. All of you who are the Lord's people may return to Israel for this task. May the Lord your God be with you!" (2 Chronicles 36:23)

Cyrus decreed that the Jews be allowed to return to their homeland and that they be allowed to reinstitute and practice their own culture and belief systems. He even went so far as to raise finances for their journey home and to help locate the Temple artifacts that Nebuchadnezzar's boys had taken from the Temple. While not all of the Jews returned to their homeland, some 40,000 of them began their journey home.

Over the century that followed their liberation from Babylon, the Jews went about rebuilding their city, their culture, their economy, and their religious institutions. They even built a new Temple to replace the one destroyed when the Babylonians overran Jerusalem. By the time the Persian Empire came to an end, Jerusalem was a thriving and mostly independent city.

This Hellenization Thing: It's All Greek to Us!

In the mid-fourth century B.C.E., in what historians consider one of the greatest military campaigns in history, Alexander the Great of Macedonia overran the Persian Empire and seized control of the entire civilized world, including Palestine. This was the beginning of nearly two centuries of Greek rule over Palestine.

Under Alexander and his predecessors, the Jews were allowed to maintain their traditions and a measure of national independence, but Jewish culture and religion were greatly changed by this Greek influence. This is what is commonly called "Hellenization."

In many ways, it was an "East meets West" situation. This continued well after Alexander's death in 323 B.C.E.

The Ptolemies

When Alexander died, there was no heir to his throne, so a period of intense struggle for control of the empire ensued among his four generals. This continued until 315 B.C.E., when the kingdom was split among them. Still, the fight for control continued, and in 323 the Ptolemies, under the leadership of Soter Ptolemy I, established control of Palestine.

For the most part, the Ptolemaic Dynasty treated their Jewish subjects well. Although the Jews were taxed very heavily, they were allowed to live and worship according to their own culture and religion. But near the end of the dynasty's control of Palestine, there were some exceptions, most notably under the rule of Philoprater (Ptolemy IV), a tyrant who hated the Jews and persecuted them mercilessly. Naturally, the Jews hated the man, and they celebrated wildly at his death in 203 B.C.E.

The last of the Ptolemaic rulers to hold control over Palestine was Epiphanes (Ptolemy V). In 198 B.C.E., the Seleucids, under the leadership of Antiochus III, the king of Syria, took control of Palestine in the Battle of Panion in the Jordan Valley.

The Seleucids

At first the Jews were fairly pleased with life under the Seleucids. If nothing else, the constant battles between the Ptolemies and Seleucids had come to an end in Palestine. Antiochus also reconfirmed their religious and national independence. But that all changed with the ascension to the throne of Antiochus IV Epiphanes.

Jewish Life Under the Cruelest of the Cruel Tyrants

Antiochus murdered his predecessor, Seleucus IV, in 175 B.C.E. and took the throne as king of Syria. He was determined to make Judah truly "Greek"—in culture, in government, and in religion—and to that end, he did everything he could to put an end to all Jewish religious practices. His cruelty in accomplishing that goal seemed to know no bounds. He committed atrocity after atrocity in an effort to suppress the practice of the Jewish religion.

> ### His Name Is Jesus, a.k.a.
>
> "The Resurrection and the Life" (John 11:25). Jesus proved that he could resurrect the dead when he raised his friend Lazarus out of a tomb. But he told Martha, the sister of Lazarus, that he himself was the cause and effect of resurrection. He was the eternal life that made this happen—not just another miracle that he performed.

Naturally, the resentment over Antiochus's iron-fisted rule grew steadily. Finally, one day in 167 B.C.E., Antiochus put the proverbial "last straw" on the backs of the Jewish people when he entered the Temple, set up an altar to the pagan god Zeus, and sacrificed a pig on it.

That, history records, was the beginning of the end of outside rule over the Jews in Palestine—at least for a time.

We're Mad As Heck, and We're Not Gonna Take It Anymore!

Antiochus's actions so outraged the Jews that they rebelled violently against Seleucidian rule. This uprising—led by Judah Maccabeus, the son of an aging Jewish priest named Mattathias—has come to be known as the Maccabean Revolt.

Antiochus sent out his troops to try to put down the revolt, but that would prove to be no easy matter. The "Maccabees," another name for the Jewish rebels, knew the country well and were able to hide out in the deserts and mountains—tough terrain for most armies.

An Uphill Battle, but a Successful One

Some of the battles went to the Greeks, and some went to the rebels. But Judah, who turned out to be a fine military leader in his own right, wouldn't allow the Jews to give up but encouraged them to fight on until they reached their objective: the liberation of Jerusalem and the Temple.

Despite being outnumbered and badly "outgunned," the Maccabees eventually prevailed. In 165 B.C.E., three years after the start of the rebellion, these brave Jewish fighters beat back Antiochus's forces and retook Jerusalem.

> **W.W.J.K. (What Would Jesus Know?)**
>
> The Jewish Feast of Dedication began after the Jews captured Jerusalem and rededicated the Temple, which had been defiled by the Syrians. It was held around what is now December 25 and commemorated that rededication following the Maccabean Revolt.

Let the Good Times Roll ... but Not for Long

The Maccabees' incredible military victory marked the beginning of a period of Jewish independence called the Hasmonean Dynasty. But this time of Jewish autonomy lasted just over a century before corruption and a sibling rivalry combined to bring the Jewish homeland back into captivity.

Following the death of Hasmonean Queen Alexandra-Salome, two of her sons, Hyrcanus and Aristobulus, vied for the throne in Jerusalem. Hyrcanus, the elder of the two, was the rightful heir, but Aristobulus wasn't going to settle for being second banana. The conflict between the two escalated, and by 67 B.C.E., Palestine was in the midst of civil war. With all this internal bickering going on, the Jews and their land were ripe for the picking.

The Romans, who for the previous century had been advancing eastward in expansion of their empire, took advantage of the situation.

Haven't We Been Here Before?

In 67 B.C.E., the Roman general Gaius Pompeius (Pompey) received two messages—one from Hyrcanus and one from Aristobulus—asking for help in defeating one another. The High Priest of the Jews was a man named Antipater, who very opportunistically sided with Hyrcanus and persuaded him to appeal to Rome for help. Hyrcanus agreed, and Pompey was happy to oblige.

But under Pompey's leadership, the Roman forces did more than assist: They defeated the Maccabees and took possession of Jerusalem. This spelled the end of the Maccabean dynasty and Jewish independence.

Life Under a Puppet King

Part of the Roman Empire's "foreign policy" was to install kings who were friendly to Caesar and who could be controlled. The Romans referred to them as "client kings," but today we might call them "puppets."

The Romans gave Hyrcanus a small territory to rule, but the real ruler of Palestine—at least at first—was Antipater, the son of parents who had converted to Judaism and a ruler who was loyal to the Roman Empire. Antipater didn't believe that Hyrcanus was the right man to rule in Judea, so he took matters into his own hands and appointed one of his sons, Phasael, as governor of Jerusalem and another of his sons, Herod, as governor of Galilee.

In 40 B.C.E., Rome installed Herod as king of Judea. Three years later, a young man named Octavian became Emperor of Rome under the title Augustus Caesar and confirmed Herod as king of the Jews. Herod captured Jerusalem by force, and from there, he ruled Palestine until 4 B.C.E.

Herod took the throne in Palestine during a time of great turmoil. The Jewish people didn't want to be subjects of Rome, and there were several bloody uprisings as a result. More than 100,000 Jews had died in various resistance movements just three years prior to Herod's rise to power.

Just What's So "Great" About This Herod?

Herod the Great was half Jew/half Arab (Jewish only on his father's side), but his loyalty was with Rome. For these reasons and others, he was unable to fully win over the Jewish population in Palestine.

During the first third of Herod's reign, he concentrated on improving the domestic situation in Palestine, a country that had been in chaos for centuries, and on consolidating his power. It was during this time that Herod initiated massive building programs. But at the same time, Herod damaged his standing in the eyes of many, if not most, of the Jews. First, he tried protecting his position as king by ordering the assassinations of many of his Hasmonean rivals. Second, he confiscated the property and possessions of the "upper crust" of the Jewish community in Jerusalem so that he could pay off his war debts. He married a Jewish woman named Mariamne, a Hasmonean princess, but that didn't help his standing with the Jews.

Even the Worst Despot Has His Good Side

Herod tried to win over the Jews by beginning the reconstruction of the Temple in Jerusalem, the most ambitious of his many building projects. His plan was to replace the small Temple built when the Jews returned from Babylon to Jerusalem.

But the Jews were reluctant to allow Herod, a man they saw as a foreigner and a false king, to take on such a project. It was only after Herod laid the materials required for the construction of the Temple at the foot of Mount Moriah and trained about 10,000 priests as builders that the Jews agreed to allow him to move forward with the project.

The Temple was magnificent. In *The Jewish War*, Jewish historian Flavius Josephus described it like this: "Viewed from without, the Sanctuary had everything that could amaze the mind or eyes. Overlaid all round with stout plates of gold, the first rays of the sun it reflected so fierce a blaze of fire that those who endeavored to look at it were forced to turn away as if they had looked straight at the sun."

When Things Headed Downhill

Around the middle of Herod's reign, Palestine was a relatively peaceful and prosperous place to live in. Many were employed through Herod's building projects, and Palestine's fertile farmlands were producing well. People had jobs and were relatively content. But during the latter third of Herod's reign, things went downhill. Instead of prosperity and contentment, there was economic decline and dissatisfaction among the people. This timing couldn't have been worse for Herod's kingdom.

Herod's building programs were at a point when he needed more money to continue them, but his finances were drying up. To continue financing his building programs, he increased the taxation on the people, many of whom weren't working at all. When he could not raise enough through taxation, he resorted to forced labor to complete his projects.

Who's Next?

If that weren't enough, questions began to arise about Herod's successor. His wives plotted behind his back to secure power for their sons. One of them even plotted against Herod himself.

Herod knew no bounds when it came to protecting himself against those who challenged

> **W.W.J.K. (What Would Jesus Know?)**
>
> **Caesar Augustus** was the first of two Caesars to hold that position during Jesus' lifetime. The other was Tiberius, who was Roman emperor from 14–37 C.E., which was during the time of Jesus' public ministry.

his rule. He executed several members of his family, including Mariamne, his mother, and three of his own sons. All of this from a guy who followed Mosaic law to the letter, including the prohibition against eating pork. This led Augustus to jest, "I would rather be Herod's pig than Herod's son."

Nobody Knows the Troubles I've Seen ...

It wasn't a pleasant experience to be the average Jew living in Palestine during the final third of Herod the Great's reign, and that meant ever-increasing discontent on their part. In a nation full of intensely independent people whose ancestors had endured horrific treatment at the hands of one occupier or conqueror after another, the Romans were not particularly popular rulers.

Herod, like many rulers before him, had slaughtered many people, and the Jews resented him for it. But what made things worse during the final third of his reign was the difficult economic times the Jews had to endure in their own homeland.

Jesus came into a world of political, social, and economic difficulty and discontentment on the part of many of the Jewish people. They were ready for the arrival of the deliverer, the Messiah their Scriptures and religious tradition had long promised them would come. This Messiah would return them to the "glory days"—the kingdom enjoyed under David and Solomon.

The Least You Need to Know

- ◆ Jesus lived and served in a place called Palestine (modern-day Israel), which was under the control of the Roman Empire.

- ◆ Part of the Jewish legacy was a long history of oppression and occupation at the hands of outside forces.

- ◆ Jesus was born near the end of the reign of King Herod the Great.

- ◆ The political, social, and economic atmosphere in Palestine raised within the Jews a longing for the Messiah.

Chapter 3

The Jewish Religion of Jesus' Time

In This Chapter

◆ The expectation of the Messiah among the Jews

◆ "Outside" influences on the Jewish faith

◆ Pharisees, Sadducees, and other Jewish "sects" at the time of Jesus

In the last chapter, we discussed the political and economic conditions in early first-century C.E. Palestine. Now, we want to look at the religion of the Jewish people in Palestine at that time and how it further prepared the way for the coming of the Messiah.

Late first-century B.C.E. was a time of great division in Palestine, and it ran across political, racial, and religious lines. There were Jews, Greeks, and Romans living there, in addition to the hated Samaritans (see Chapter 2) as well as the "half Jews" (Herod, for example). There was also division within the Jewish community itself, especially when it came to how they practiced their faith.

This Is Not Our Fathers' Faith!

By the first century B.C.E., there were Jews living all over the then-known world. These "foreigners," as many of the Jews in Palestine saw them, had received a very "Greek" education and had adopted much of the Greek culture, with its emphasis on philosophy and the arts. When they returned to their homeland—if only to attend one of the many Jewish festivals of the time—they brought with them that Greek influence.

W.W.J.K. (What Would Jesus Know?)

Herod the Great, while he practiced a form of Judaism, was not actually of Jewish blood at all. Kyprose, Herod's mother, was an Arab and Antipater, his father, was an Idumaean who came from a family who had been forced to convert to Judaism.

On top of that, Greek and Roman domination of Palestine over the course of hundreds of years had altered the way many of the Jews practiced their religion. This "Hellenism," as historians call it, brought about in Palestine and the rest of the Jewish world a mixture of Jewish and Gentile cultures and religious practices.

This Hellenism Isn't So Bad ... or Is It?

Some of the Jews in Palestine liked the influences of outside cultures, especially the Greek and Roman ones. But most of them were offended by what the influence of those cultures had done and were doing to their own culture and religion. They resented especially the introduction of images of the many Greek deities into Palestine.

By the time of Jesus, the Romans had given King Herod almost total authority over Palestine, and in return he was careful to honor the Empire in every way. Although he tried in many ways not to offend the religious sensibilities of the Jews, he often failed. He authorized the reconstruction of the Temple in about 20 B.C.E. (although the whole of the Temple wasn't completed until 64 B.C.E., but was in use in Jesus' time) and the construction of many synagogues.

In the Jews' minds, though, this was nothing but an attempt to make up for the offenses many of Herod's projects represented to them. For example, Herod had a sports center built near the Temple that was often the venue for nude wrestling. Many of the Jewish people wanted to rid their homeland of these and many other affronts to their faith. For that reason, they further longed and hoped for the time when God, and no outside earthly "ruler," would hold power over them.

We Know He's Coming, but *When?*

The Jews who lived in the "Promised Land" prior to the birth of Jesus believed that God was still with them and that they were still his "chosen people." But many of them felt as though they as a people were still in exile. At that time, there were still many Jews living in foreign lands. Also, they didn't see themselves as truly free because they had to answer to yet another foreign power, namely Rome.

But there was more: The Jews saw their own high priests and other religious leaders as corrupt. The reason? Traditionally, the office of Jewish high priest was hereditary, meaning that high priests had to be from a certain family lineage. But that changed during the days of Antiochus Epiphanes, when the Syrian court began appointing the high priest.

This continued under King Herod, meaning that the top figure in the Jewish religion at that time was appointed by "outsiders." The authorities could replace the high priest for any reason they saw fit, or for no reason at all, and that created a situation where the high priests were a little too "cozy" with the rulers.

> **His Name Is Jesus, a.k.a.**
>
> "The Great High Priest" (Hebrews 4:14). The high priest in the Old Testament offered sacrifices for the sins of the Jewish people. Jesus is both the sacrifice (a.k.a. Lamb of God) and the high priest who offers himself to the Father to cleanse us of our sins. In heaven he's like a mediator between a sinful world and a holy God, pointing to what he himself has done on our behalf to make us acceptable to the Father.

God, Come Down, It's a Mess

The Jews believed that there was only one way these problems could be solved, and that was for God to come personally and deliver them and reestablish his kingdom on earth. And they believed that God would do just that. After all, through the words of the prophets centuries before, he had promised them deliverance from all earthly powers.

The Jews in Palestine prior to Jesus' arrival held out hope that a yet-to-come deliverer, or Messiah, would be a part of that plan and that he would come during their lifetimes. When that happened, it would be the beginning of a renewal of the kingdom as they had known it under David and Solomon.

Phonies, Fakers, and Posers

The longing on the part of the Jews for a deliverer created a vacuum in the Jewish culture that impostors were all too happy to fill—or at least *try* to fill. Throughout

Jewish history, there have been many supposed "messiahs" who claimed that they were the promised deliverer, all of whom turned out to be frauds.

Around the time of Jesus and even before, the sad lives most of the Jews lived put them in an especially vulnerable state, and many charismatic leaders tried to convince them that they were the messiah. Unfortunately, some of the Jews actually followed these "false messiahs," and many paid for it with their lives.

Now let's take a look at the inner workings of the Jewish religious world in early first-century Palestine.

Jerusalem: Many Reasons to Party!

Jerusalem, which was the site of the second Temple (the first, as you may recall from the last chapter of this book, was destroyed when the Babylonians sacked the city and took many of the Jews into captivity), was the center of the Jewish religious world—even for the Jews living outside Palestine. Many from outside Palestine would travel to Jerusalem several times a year to major festivals, or "feasts." These festivals included:

- **Passover,** which celebrated the exodus from Egypt.

- **Pentecost,** a harvest festival which was a time to recognize God's giving of the Law of Moses to his people.

- **Tabernacles,** which commemorated God's provision and care for the Jews during their travels in the wilderness.

- **Dedication,** which commemorated the rededication of the Temple following the Maccabean Revolt.

- **Purim,** which recognized the victory for the Jews over Haman, as recorded in the Old Testament book of Esther.

W.W.J.K. (What Would Jesus Know?)

Before and during the time of Jesus, the Jews used a calendar much different from the one we use today. The Jewish year began with the month of *Tishri,* around September or October according to our calendar, and ended with the month of *Adar,* around our February/March. The Passover feast was held in days 14–21 of the month of *Nisan* (our March/April). Pentecost was held on the sixth day of *Sivan* (our May/June). Tabernacles was held on days 15–21 of *Tishri.* Dedication was held on *Kislev* 25 (our November/December). Purim was held on *Adar* 14–15.

Before the Babylonian Exile, the one and only place the Jews could worship was in the Temple in Jerusalem. That changed when the Jews returned to their homeland, as synagogues started to appear. The synagogues didn't replace the Temple, but served as centers of prayer and instruction and interpretation of the Law of Moses. There was only one Temple but many synagogues.

The New Testament of the Bible calls the teachers in the synagogues "Scribes." Regular meetings were held in the synagogues on the Sabbath (from sundown Friday through sundown Saturday) and on Mondays and Tuesdays.

In addition to being home to the Temple, Jerusalem was also home to a religious/political body that held a lot of control over how Jews conducted themselves.

Let's Come to Terms

The **Temple** in Jerusalem was the center of Jewish worship. After the Jews had settled in the Promised Land, under the leadership of King Solomon, they built the Temple, which replaced the Tabernacle (a portable tent used as the place of worship during their pilgrimage from Egypt). King David conceived the plan for the Temple, but was forbidden to build it because he was a warrior and not a priest.

Who's in Charge Here?

Part of the Jewish anticipation of the arrival of the Messiah centered on the formation of the Great *Sanhedrin*, or "Council of Elders." The Great Sanhedrin was a body of Jewish religious leaders responsible for governing the city, both as legislators and as that culture's version of a "supreme court."

The Jews believed that the Sanhedrin was the "rebirth" of a similar council during the time of Moses and that it would play a part of the Messiah's arrival.

There were smaller versions of the Sanhedrin in almost every city and village in Palestine, but the Sanhedrin in Jerusalem was the one that heard cases from around Palestine and the rest of the Jewish world.

Let's Come to Terms

The **Sanhedrin**, which literally means "a sitting together" or "council," was a 71-member (70 members with 1 high priest) judicial and administrative body that oversaw the religious affairs of the Jews at the time of Jesus. It is believed to have gotten its start at the time of the Maccabees. Jesus was tried by the Sanhedrin on charges of blasphemy for claiming to be the Messiah.

Our Customized Messiah?

The Jews all believed in and served the same God—the God of Abraham, Moses, and David—but they were anything but unified when it came to how to serve him and how to herald in the long-awaited Messiah.

Because of that, by the time of Jesus' birth many divisions, or sects, of the Jewish religion had arisen in Palestine. The two best known and most influential of these sects were the Pharisees and the Sadducees, both of whom played big parts in the Sanhedrin and both of whom would play a major part in Jesus' story.

> **His Name Is Jesus, a.k.a.**
>
> "Prince of Peace" (Isaiah 9:6). Jesus will bring in the total external peace among his people in the Kingdom of God, and also an internal spiritual peace that is described in the Bible as a peace that is beyond our understanding.

The Pharisees, I See

The Pharisees are believed to have gotten their start during the Maccabean Revolt, which started in 167–168 B.C.E. It was then that the "Pious Ones" or "*Hasidim*"—Jewish leaders who were willing to die rather than adopt the Greek religions and ways of life as decreed by Antiochus Epiphanes—fought on behalf of Judas Maccabeus.

As you may remember from Chapter 2, the Maccabean Revolt was ultimately successful and led to the founding of a Jewish government called the Hasmonean Dynasty. It was under this government that the *Hasidim* received the privilege of teaching at the Temple in Jerusalem. It is believed that the *Hasidim* were the forerunners to the Pharisees.

Pharisees, Holier Than Thou

The Pharisees were what we might call "separatists," in that they wanted to keep their culture and religion free from outside influences. They had a more liberal view of what was "God's word" than did the Sadducees. The Pharisees held to the written Scriptures—the *Torah*, or the written Jewish law—and the Old Testament prophets, as well as unwritten traditional teachings of Moses that had been passed through the centuries by the Jewish rabbis.

> **Let's Come to Terms**
>
> The **Torah** is a collection of Jewish laws preserved in the original Hebrew language and handwritten on parchment scrolls.

While the Pharisees were more liberal when it came to what they believed constituted the law of God, they were anything but liberal when it came to living by that law. They were devoted to the daily application and observance of both the written Torah and the *Oral Torah.* The Pharisees lived by the very strictest interpretations of the Torah and the tradition, and they expected others to do the same. The Pharisees believed that strict adherence to the law would make people holy and hasten the advent of the Messiah.

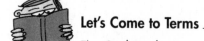

Let's Come to Terms

The **Oral Torah,** or *"Pirke Aboth,"* was the source of the traditional teaching that the Pharisees adopted into their system of beliefs. It is believed that much of the Oral Torah came before the written Torah that God gave Moses on Mount Sinai some 3,300 years ago.

There's a Whole New World Beyond

The Pharisees lived and worked in Palestine, but they didn't see it, or any other earthly place, as their home. They fully expected that the world as they knew it would end soon and that the Messiah would lead only the most devoted Jews against their earthly enemy, the Roman Empire. They believed that when their deliverer came, he would found a Jewish kingdom that would last 1,000 years. At the end of that time, this kingdom—along with the rest of the world—would be destroyed and replaced by an eternal kingdom, where God's people would live after being raised from the dead.

The Pharisees believed in the free will of humans but also in a God who was willing to intervene on our behalf. They believed in the resurrection from the dead and in the existence of spiritual beings—angels, who served God, and demons, who served the devil. They believed in an eternal soul and that when a man or woman died, he or she would be rewarded or punished in the afterlife, depending on what kind of life he or she lived.

Jesus: Way Too Liberal and Free

The first mention of the Pharisees, as well as the Sadducees, in the New Testament appears in Matthew 3:7–10, where we read of John the Baptist challenging their ideas concerning the true identity of the people of God. John suggested that being a descendent of Abraham didn't necessarily make one a true Jew. That identity, he told them, came from a heart that loved and obeyed God. It is also in this passage that we read of John's announcement to these religious leaders of the soon—very soon—to come Messiah.

Later on in the gospels, we see several confrontations between Jesus and the Pharisees, most of whom didn't like his teachings when it came to what he believed about the law, which they believed were far too liberal and free.

A *Few* Friends in High Places

While the gospels don't paint a very flattering picture of the Pharisees, there were those among their ranks who seemed to sympathize with Jesus. For example, the Gospel of John tells the story of Nicodemus, a Pharisee who carried on a lengthy conversation with Jesus about who he was, who had sent him, and why he had come.

During the course of that conversation, Jesus said something that would become what is probably the best-known verse in the Bible: "For God so loved the world that he gave his only Son, so that everyone who believes in him will not perish but have eternal life" (John 3:16). Later on, Nicodemus argued with his fellow Sanhedrin members that Jesus deserved to be treated fairly (John 7:50–52).

> **Let's Come to Terms**
>
> The **Mosaic Law** is the law God gave Moses at the time of the Jewish Exodus from Egypt concerning how the Jewish people were to live and worship. God gave Moses the law on Mount Sinai (Exodus 20–24).

While the Pharisees served in the same Sanhedrin as the Sadducees, there were some huge differences between the two concerning the *Mosaic Law*, what part the Romans should play in Jewish life, and the Messiah.

The Sadducees: Who Dies with the Most Toys Wins

The Sadducees rejected the traditional teachings embraced by the Pharisees and accepted only *the Pentateuch* as their standard for religious life. They rejected the writings of the prophets as a basis for their beliefs. They also held some very different views from the Pharisees when it came to spiritual beliefs.

> **W.W.J.K. (What Would Jesus Know?)**
>
> The **Pentateuch** is the books of Jewish Law, or what we now know as the first five books of the Bible—Genesis, Exodus, Leviticus, Deuteronomy, and Numbers.

The Sadducees believed that God created people to live lives of service and praise for him, but that there was nothing after that. In other words, they didn't believe in an eternal soul but believed that when the body dies, so does the soul. They didn't believe in eternal rewards for the righteous or eternal punishment for sinners. They also didn't believe that God was interested in day-to-day human affairs or willing to act on behalf of the people. They didn't believe in the resurrection of the dead, and they didn't buy into the existence of spiritual beings—angels or demons.

There's Strength in (Lesser) Numbers

The Sadducees held the majority in that body. That meant that the Sadducees, who aligned themselves more with the Roman government than with the common people, were the party with the political power.

What they didn't have, however, was the support of the Jewish people, most of whom didn't accept their teachings or like their cozy relationship with the Romans. In fact, most of the Jews *hated* the Sadducees, and for that reason they seldom passed legislation in the Sanhedrin without the support and approval of the Pharisees.

Pharisees and the Great Class Warfare

The party who enjoyed the support of the masses and who had the most influence over them was the Pharisees. The Pharisees seemed to have their fingers on the pulse of the average Jew. That only makes sense, as Pharisees were from more "middle-class" backgrounds, while most of the Sadducees were from the wealthiest and most influential of families.

For that reason, the Sadducees had no choice but to give in to the Pharisees when it came to religious issues. That influence put the Pharisees in a place where they could instruct the people on all matters of the Jewish religion. As we pointed out in Chapter 2, when Herod the Great took the throne, one of the first things he did was try to eliminate any kind of religious or political opposition to his rule. One of his programs to that end was to attempt to lessen the influence and power the Pharisees had over the Jews.

Smaller Parties, but Still Big Players

There were other religious parties in Palestine at the time of Jesus, some of which were smaller but still played a big part in his story.

Essenes, the Jewish "Monks" of Jesus' Time

The Essenes, whose origins, like those of the Pharisees, are thought to go back to the *Hasidim* (remember, the *Hasidim* were the Jewish leaders who fought on behalf of Judas Maccabeus in the Maccabean Revolt), were a group of Jews who lived very much as Catholic monks live in monasteries to this day.

The Essenes practiced self-denial to the extreme and lived in colonies away from the cities. The Pharisees wanted to keep the Jewish faith and culture separate from the outside world, but the Essenes took that way of thinking and living even further than the Pharisees. The Essenes believed that the entire religious system was corrupt and wanted all of it replaced. That would happen, they believed, when God himself did it.

Zealots with a Capital Z

When we think of the word *zealot*, we usually think of someone who stands strong for what he or she believes in, no matter what it takes. The Zealots in Jesus' day fit that description to the extreme. They refused to give any kind of allegiance to the Romans who occupied their land. The Zealots held that God and God alone was king, and at times they resorted to violence—against fellow Jews and Romans alike—to throw off Roman rule. In the gospels (Matthew, Mark, Luke, and John), at least 1 of Jesus' 12 apostles—a man named Simon—was called a Zealot.

The Herodians: We Can Make This Work

Not all Jews in Jesus' day were all that eager to be rid of the Roman occupation of Palestine. Some of them—and they were a minority—welcomed the Roman domination of their land.

The Herodians, so named because of their allegiance to Herod the Great and his successors, were among this group. The Herodians believed that rule by Herod and his successors was the last best hope for the Jewish people retaining any kind of independence.

Ascribe to the Scribes the Name of "Rabbi"

The Scribes weren't really a religious party in the same sense that the Pharisees, Sadducees, Essenes, and Zealots were. Rather, they were the scholars of Jewish religious writings whose job it was to teach the people to read and understand them. Most of the Scribes were Pharisees, but the Sadducees and Zealots also had Scribes in their ranks. There were always Scribes, or "teachers of the law" as the gospels call them, in the Sanhedrin.

Setting Straight Those Crazy, Mixed-up Kids

The world of the Jewish religion in Palestine was full of conflict and division as the day of Jesus' arrival approached. The Jews believed that the Messiah would one day come and that someone would come to prepare the way for him. But there was plenty they didn't know for sure.

The Jewish people didn't know when the deliverer would arrive, and they were divided on what they needed to do in order to hasten his appearance. It was a world of despair and confusion, expectation and hope, conflict and division. Into this world full of longings and questions came Jesus, who was about to give answers unlike any the Jews had expected.

The apostle Paul, in his letter to the Galatians, wrote, "But when the right time came, God sent his Son, born of a woman, subject to the law" (Galatians 4:4). Indeed, the right time had come, and Jesus would come upon the scene of early first-century Palestine, where he would rock the thinking and faith of the religious establishment of the day.

The Least You Need to Know

- At the time of Jesus, the Jews looked forward with great expectancy to the arrival of a Messiah.

- The Jewish religion was influenced—some say "corrupted"—by the influence of outside cultures.

- The Jewish people were divided on what they needed to do to hasten the coming of the Messiah.

- There were several "sects" in Judaism at that time, the most influential and powerful being the Pharisees, followed by the Sadducees.

4

The Gospels: Four "Snapshots" of Jesus' Life

In This Chapter

♦ Where we read of Jesus' life: in the gospels

♦ The same story, told four different ways

♦ The writers of the four gospels

♦ The differences between and similarities of the four gospels

Just about everything we know about the life of Jesus on Earth is found in the Bible, specifically in first four books of the New Testament: the "gospels"—Matthew, Mark, Luke, and John.

Yes, the other books of the New Testament expound on and explain the meanings of Jesus' teachings and give the reader practical ways to apply them. But only those four books say anything about the actual words and deeds of Jesus.

The *gospels* bear the names of the four men who wrote them, each of whom had a different perspective of the same events, namely the life and work of Jesus. Each of the writers had his own unique background, and each of these backgrounds is reflected in how each gospel is written. (More on that later.)

Not a Loose Canon

There were many other accounts of Jesus' life written in the first century C.E., but only the four now in the Bible were accepted into what is called the "canon" of Scripture, meaning the books that were accepted as part of the Bible.

That began happening in the second century C.E. when church leadership started to weed out the "gospels" (and other books) that were written about Jesus but didn't pass muster.

In general, the gospels that were accepted were written by those who either knew Jesus personally during his earthly life (Matthew and John) or by people who knew people who knew him during that time (Mark and Luke).

Let's Come to Terms

The **synoptic gospels** came to be known that way after an eighteenth-century German scholar by the name of J.J. Griesbach studied the similarities of these three books by arranging them in a three-column table called a synopsis.

His Name Is Jesus, a.k.a.

"King of Kings and Lord of Lords" (Revelation 19:16). There have been throughout the ages many magnificent earthly rulers with power delegated by God. But God the Father has given ultimate cosmic authority to Jesus to judge and rule over everything in creation and establish an everlasting kingdom (of heaven) where he will be lord and king forever.

The Synopsis and the Deeper Version

The first three gospels—Matthew, Mark, and Luke—are very similar in that they share many of the same passages and accounts of the life of Jesus, often using the same words and accounts. These are called the *"synoptic gospels"* because when they are looked at together, they give us a synopsis of Jesus' life.

The fourth gospel—the Gospel of John—had a completely different tone and focus than the synoptic gospels. While the first three gospels focus on Jesus' identity, miracles, teachings, and parables, John focuses on the more "abstract" spiritual messages Jesus gave.

A Taxing Experience for the Jews

It is traditionally believed that the Gospel of Matthew was written by the same Matthew who left his life as a tax collector to serve as one of Jesus' 12 apostles. Tax collectors were despised by their fellow Jews as being greedy, dishonest puppets of the Romans. Matthew, who was called Levi before Jesus called him to follow, was the son of a man named Alphaeus. Bible scholars are split when it comes to the date of the writing of Matthew's gospel. Some believe it was written between the years 60 and 65 C.E., while others think it was as late as 85 C.E.

W.W.J.K. (What Would Jesus Know?)

As you read the gospel accounts of Jesus' life, you'll notice that some events seem to be in a different order. There are two theories as to why this is. The first is that during the course of Jesus' life, he probably said and did some of the same things in different settings, much like an evangelist might preach the same message in every city he visits. The other theory is that some of the gospel writers were more "topical" than "chronological" in their telling of Jesus' story.

Matthew's Messianic Message for the (Jewish) Masses

Remember in Chapters 1–3, where we talked about how the Jewish people in Jesus' time were longing for and looking for the promised coming of the Messiah? Well, Matthew's gospel, although it contains a great message for everyone, was written especially for them. Matthew's message in a nutshell was this: Jesus is the Messiah we Jews have been waiting for, and we know that because he was everything God said the Messiah would be.

Why do we say that? Well, as you read the Gospel of Matthew, you'll notice that it's full of references to Old Testament Messianic prophecies and how Jesus fulfilled them. There are more than 60 Old Testament references in the Gospel of Matthew, and more than 40 of those are direct quotations of ancient prophecies of the coming Messiah.

A Very "Fulfilling" Gospel Message

You'll also see the word *fulfilled* over and over in the Gospel of Matthew, and most of the time it refers to Jesus' fulfillment of Messianic prophecies. Here are just a few examples:

- ◆ "Then what was said through the prophet Jeremiah was *fulfilled:* 'A voice is heard in Ramah, weeping and great mourning, Rachel weeping for her children and refusing to be comforted, because they are no more'" (Matthew 2:17–18).

- ◆ "… and he went and lived in a town called Nazareth. So was *fulfilled* what was said through the prophets: 'He will be called a Nazarene'" (Matthew 2:23).

- ◆ "So was *fulfilled* what was spoken through the prophet: 'I will open my mouth in parables, I will utter things hidden since the creation of the world'" (Matthew 13:35).

Back to the Roots of the Family Tree???

Matthew's gospel starts out with the genealogy of Jesus, calling him "the son of David." This "family tree" starts out "Abraham was the father of Isaac ..." goes to "David, the father of Solomon," then proceeds all the way to "Joseph, the husband of Mary, of whom was born Jesus, who is called Christ." This in itself was a reference to the fulfillment of the prophecy that the Messiah would be a descendant of David and an heir to his throne of Israel.

This is just the kind of message that would appeal to the average Jewish person wondering whether or not Jesus really was the promised Messiah.

Making a "Mark" for the Gospel Message

The second of the four gospels was penned by Mark, who was referred to in the book of Acts as "John Mark." Not a lot is known about the man who wrote the Gospel of Mark. The Bible tells us that he was associated with the apostle Paul and his partner-in-missions Barnabas—himself the cousin of Mark's mother—and that he accompanied them on a missionary journey to Antioch, a large city on the Orontes River in Syria.

Mark was not one of Jesus' 12 apostles. In fact, his name isn't mentioned in the text of any of the gospels. Some believe that Mark was one of Jesus' many disciples—those who followed him and listened to his teaching and saw his work—and that he was therefore an eyewitness to a lot of the things Jesus said and did.

Tradition has it that Mark was at one time very close to Peter, one of Jesus' closest disciples, and that he based his gospel account largely on Peter's teaching and accounts. In fact, some ancient writers refer to the Gospel of Mark as "Peter's Gospel."

Let's Hire a Ghostwriter

Some believe that Mark was something of a "ghostwriter" for Peter, who was the actual eyewitness to the accounts written in the gospel and who gave Mark all the information he needed to write it down accurately.

Mark's Gospel is believed to be the first written of the four (around 60 to 70 C.E., according to many scholars) and that Matthew and Luke both incorporated much of the material in his gospel into their own.

It's Not All Greek, but a Lot Is

The Gospel of Mark is believed to have been written especially for the Greek and Roman Christians of the first century C.E. That's because he never quoted Jewish law, which would be a necessity for a gospel account written for Jewish people.

Mark quoted the Old Testament only twice in the whole book, the first time to announce the coming of John the Baptist as recorded in Isaiah 40:3. He also very often took the time to translate Aramaic words and phrases into Greek, his target audience's own language.

That is very much in contrast to Matthew, whose book is very heavy with references to Jewish law and to Old Testament prophecies of the coming Messiah. Rather than focusing on the fulfillment of those prophecies, Mark attempted to show that Jesus was the Messiah by focusing on the words he spoke and the work he did while on Earth.

In addition to Jesus' teaching, Mark lists 19 of Jesus' miracles in this book. In short, he didn't want to tell us who Jesus was, he wanted to show us!

To Mark, Brevity Was a Virtue

Mark is the shortest of the four gospels, and that is partly due to what he left out of his account. For example, unlike Matthew and Luke, the other two "synoptic" gospels, Mark makes no reference to the genealogy of Jesus and there is no mention of the virgin birth. Also left out is the famous "Sermon on the Mount," which Matthew covered in three chapters.

> **W.W.J.K. (What Would Jesus Know?)**
>
> It's not known for certain if Mark was a personal acquaintance of Jesus' during his ministry. It is, however, widely believed that Jesus' meeting with his 12 disciples in the upper room in Jerusalem prior to his arrest and crucifixion was held in the home of Mark's mother.

> **His Name Is Jesus, a.k.a.**
>
> "Image of God" (Colossians 1:15). In the book of Colossians it states that not only is Jesus the exact representation of God but in Jesus himself all things are created. This includes his creating everything in the visible universe as well as the invisible "powers" in the heavens—the angels and archangels, whether good or fallen.

Is There a Doctor in the House?

The writer of the third of the gospel accounts was a physician named Luke, who confesses at the very beginning of his gospel that he was not one of Jesus' 12 apostles or even an eyewitness to his words and works.

There is no reference in the Bible to when Luke became a Christian, but we know that he was the only non-Jewish person to write a New Testament book. In fact, he wrote two—his gospel and the Acts of the Apostles, in which he tells the story of the beginning and expansion of Christianity into the world outside Jerusalem.

Luke is believed to have been "converted" by the apostle Paul, who he befriended and accompanied on some of his missionary journeys. In fact, late in the Acts of the Apostles, Luke writes in a first-person narrative, describing some of the events using the pronouns *we* and *us*.

No one knows for sure when Luke wrote his gospel, but most scholars believe he wrote it a few years before he wrote the Acts of the Apostles, which he wrote around 63 or 64 C.E.

Moonlighting As a Historian

Luke starts his gospel, which is written to someone named Theophilus (we have no idea who he is, but his name means "lover of God"), by explaining that he had investigated everything having to do with Jesus' story—his words *and* his actions—and had written his account based on those investigations.

Luke was apparently something of a historian, for his gospel included many details of Jesus' life left out of the other three. For example, his was the only gospel to record the account of Jesus' birth.

While Matthew makes passing mention of Jesus' birth, Luke threw in many details of that event, including the announcement to Jesus' mother, Mary, that she would give birth to the Christ. He also records the story of the conception and birth of John the Baptist. He was also the only gospel writer to include anything at all about the boyhood of Jesus.

The Stories Within *the* Story

Luke's gospel is heavy on *parables*. In all, he lists 25, 17 of which appear in his gospel only. He also lists seven of Jesus' miracles that can't be found in either of the other two synoptic gospels.

While Matthew focused on Jesus as the promised Messiah and Mark focused on the work of Jesus that proved he was Messiah, Luke focuses on Jesus the man. He presents Jesus as a man of great compassion and of intense emotions. For example, Luke alone records the instance of Jesus looking out over the holy city of Jerusalem and weeping. Luke also shows us a Jesus who had a very sympathetic attitude toward the "outcasts"—the poor, the sinners, the sick, the dying, and others.

John, and Not the Baptist

The writer of the fourth and final gospel in the Bible was John. This is the apostle John, not to be confused with John the Baptist, another character who played a big part in the life of Jesus.

This John never referred to himself by name in his gospel, instead calling himself "the disciple whom Jesus loved." John and his brother James were both among the original 12 of Jesus' apostles. Their father was Zebedee, a fairly well-to-do fisherman, and their mother was Salome. They were born in a place called Bethsaida, which was located near the northern shore of the Sea of Galilee.

Let's Come to Terms

The meaning of the word **parable**, as it appears in the gospels, literally means "a placing aside" or "a similitude." Parables were stories meant to illustrate a point of teaching. Jesus taught in parables a great deal, a common practice among Jewish rabbis. The synoptic gospels contain all of Jesus' recorded parables. John's gospel is the only one that left out what can accurately be called a parable.

W.W.J.K. (What Would Jesus Know?)

The name of the town Bethsaida literally means "House of the Fisherman." Recent research and archaeological evidence shows that Bethsaida was probably a fortified city. Jesus performed some of his best-known and important miracles in Bethsaida, including the feeding of the 5,000.

John—along with James and Peter—would become part of Jesus' "inner circle" of apostles, the three who were closest to him and who often accompanied him to places and events where the other disciples were not invited.

John was also the author of the three other New Testament books that bear his name (1 John, 2 John, 3 John), as well as the book of Revelation.

The Gospel of John was the last of the gospels written. It was completed between 80 and 100 C.E. By then, the rest of the New Testament, other than John's writings, had been completed. It is widely believed that John wrote his gospel in his old age—he was the last of the apostles still living—while living in a Greek city called Ephesus, where he served as the leader of the church there.

A Gospel with a Lot of Spirit

John's gospel is considered one the most spiritually deep books not only among the four gospels, but in the entire Bible.

It is in John's gospel where we find Jesus' repeated claims that God had not only sent him but that he was actually the Son of God. In the fifth chapter of John's gospel alone, Jesus is quoted six consecutive times as saying that God had sent him into the world. More than 30 times in this gospel, Jesus refers to God as being his Father.

Let's Come to Terms

In the Gospel of John, Jesus is referred to as "the Word." John tells us that the Word had existed alongside God and he was God in the flesh. John pointed out that although Jesus identified himself as the Messiah, his own people rejected him.

But not only does John's gospel include Jesus' claims that God sent him, it also includes several declarations of others concerning his identity. Later, John himself wrote, "But these are written that you may believe that Jesus is the Messiah, the Son of God ..." (John 20:31).

John's gospel includes a lot of Jesus' teaching not seen in the other gospels. He also lists six miracles found only in his gospel, including turning water into wine at the wedding at Cana, healing a blind man, and raising his friend Lazarus from the dead. (We'll get to those stories later in this book.)

Comparison of the Four Gospels

All four Gospels present the life and teachings of Jesus. Each book, however, focuses on a unique facet of Jesus and his character. To understand more about the specific characteristics of Jesus, read any of the four Gospels.

	Matthew	Mark	Luke	John
Jesus is	The promised King	The Servant of God	The Son of Man	The Son of God
The original readers were	Jews	Gentiles, Romans	Greeks	Christians throughout the world
Significant themes	Jesus is the Messiah because he fulfilled Old Testament prophecy	Jesus backed up his words with action	Jesus was God but also fully human	Belief in Jesus is required for salvation

	Matthew	**Mark**	**Luke**	**John**
Character of the writer	Teacher	Storyteller	Historian	Theologian
Greatest emphasis	Jesus' sermons and words	Jesus' miracles and actions	Jesus' humanity	The principles of Jesus' teaching

Do you want to know more about what Jesus was like? Read on!

The Least You Need to Know

♦ The four gospels tell the same story but with different emphases on different aspects of Jesus' life.

♦ The first three gospels—Matthew, Mark, and Luke—are what have come to be known as the "synoptic gospels" because they offer a synopsis of Jesus' life.

♦ Matthew focuses on Jesus as the fulfillment of the promise of a Messiah, Mark focuses on Jesus' work, Luke focuses on what kind of man Jesus was.

♦ The Gospel of John offers a view of Jesus greatly different from the others. John focuses on his divinity.

Part 2

Jesus' Early Life

Nearly everybody in our culture knows a little something about the birth of Jesus, even if just through singing classic Christmas songs.

But beyond the well-known Christmas story, Jesus' early life also included trips to Jerusalem, where he was dedicated at the Jewish Temple and attended his first Passover; and a trip to Egypt, where he and his family hid out to avoid threats to his life.

All of those things are recorded in the Gospels, the four books in the Bible that tell Jesus' life story, and they would later have a huge impact on Jesus as he carried out his ministry, which included preaching, teaching, and working miracles—as well as ruffling the feathers of the religious establishment.

Chapter 5

Angels We Have Heard in Unusual Places

In This Chapter

- ◆ The announcements of the births of John the Baptist and Jesus

- ◆ The births of John and Jesus

- ◆ The visit of shepherds to Jesus' birthplace

- ◆ Jesus' presentation at the Temple

Of the four gospel accounts of Jesus' life, work, and teaching, only two—Matthew and Luke—say anything about his actual birth and infancy. In fact, only the Gospel of Luke has any kind of detailed account of Jesus' birth.

After a short greeting and introduction, Luke gets his Gospel message in gear by telling us the story of an angel who had a lot of work to do to prepare the right people for the birth of Jesus. The angel Gabriel had a lot to tell Mary and Joseph, but first he had to fill the most interested parties in on the details of the one who would usher in Jesus' ministry on Earth: John the Baptist.

Better Late Than Never

There were living in Jerusalem at that time an elderly Jewish priest by the name of Zacharias and his wife Elizabeth. They were a very devout couple, but after all their years of marriage, they had no children because Elizabeth was not able to conceive.

W.W.J.K. (What Would Jesus Know?) _____

The theme of the shame of going childless is a common one in the Old Testament. The first reference to a childless couple is found in Genesis 18, which tells us of Sarah, the wife of Abraham, who was childless well into her old age. Later, in Genesis 25:21, Isaac, the son of Abraham, begged God to give him and his wife Rebekah a child. Still later in that same book, we can read of a woman named Rachel thanking God for removing the shame she felt over having no children (Genesis 30:22-23).

Let's Come to Terms ___

The name of the angel Gabriel literally means "Champion of God." Gabriel also appears in the ninth chapter of the Old Testament book of Daniel. Gabriel and another angel, Michael, were the only two angels mentioned by name in the Bible.

One day, as Zacharias was in the Temple doing his priestly duties, Gabriel sidled up to him with a rather shocking announcement: He and Elizabeth were going to be the parents of a boy named John!

This boy, the angel told him, would be the fulfillment of the Old Testament prophecy of a "forerunner" or announcer of the arrival of the Messiah: "He will be a man with the spirit and power of Elijah, the prophet of old. He will precede the coming of the Lord, preparing the people for his arrival. He will turn the hearts of the fathers to their children, and he will change disobedient minds to accept godly wisdom" (Luke 1:17).

Clam Up, Zach!

Of course, Zacharias was stunned at the announcement. In fact, he really didn't believe it. After all, he and his wife were both well along in years by this time, way too old to become first-time parents. So he asked the angel how he could know if his message was true.

Gabriel assured him that his message was from God himself, and as a sign to prove that it was true—as well as to show him what happens when people doubt God's promises—he told Zacharias that he would be unable to speak until John was born.

Just as the angel had told Zacharias, his wife Elizabeth soon became pregnant. This was incredible news for Elizabeth: "How kind the Lord is!" she exclaimed. "He has taken away my disgrace of having no children!" (Luke 1:25).

But Gabriel's work was far from finished. His next stop was the home of Mary, a young Jewish woman who just happened to be a relative of Elizabeth's and who also was about to receive some incredible news of her own.

This Child Is Everything Rolled into One (Luke 1:26–38)

Six months into Elizabeth's pregnancy with John, Gabriel visited Mary, who lived in a town in Galilee called Nazareth and who was engaged to be married to a carpenter named Joseph. What the angel had to tell her was not only huge in her own life but also the beginning of the long-awaited and hoped-for arrival of the Messiah.

Gabriel told Mary that she was highly favored by God, but she wondered and worried over what was coming next. But Gabriel told her not to worry, then gave her this incredible announcement: She would be giving birth to a child named Jesus, who would grow up to be the Son of God and King of the Jews.

W.W.J.K. (What Would Jesus Know?)

Jesus' birth through a virgin was foretold by the Old Testament prophet Isaiah, who wrote of the Messiah, "Look! The virgin will conceive a child! She will give birth to a son, and he will be called Immanuel (meaning, God is with us)" (Isaiah 7:14).

I Can't Conceive of This

That announcement made no sense to Mary, who obviously had some understanding of the process of human reproduction. She pointed out to the angel that there was no way she could be pregnant, simply because she was a virgin.

But Gabriel told Mary that nothing is impossible with God! After all, her relative Elizabeth, who was old and infertile, had also recently conceived in miraculous fashion. The angel went on to explain that it would be through the power of God that Mary would become pregnant with the one who would reign forever over the house of Jacob (or, in our words, the kingdom of Israel).

Of course, Mary agreed with the angel that she would bear the child. Right there in his presence, she said to him, "I am the Lord's servant, and I am willing to accept whatever he wants. May everything you have said come true." Then Gabriel left her.

Now *Two* Tiny Miracles (Luke 1:39–56)

Luke reports that the first thing Mary did after the angel Gabriel left her was hurry to the hill country of Judah to visit her cousin and fellow mother-to-be Elizabeth.

Let's Come to Terms

Mary's song of praise, as recorded in the book of Luke, has come to be known as **The Magnificat.** This song has become one of the best-known and best-loved Christian hymns of all time. The words of the angel to Mary are also the basis of a great hymn, the *Ave Maria*.

When Elizabeth first saw Mary and heard her voice, her baby "leaped in her womb," and she said to Mary, "You are blessed by God above all other women, and your child is blessed."

Mary, by now overcome with joy for herself and for her cousin, couldn't contain herself, and she spoke words of praise to God for what the angel Gabriel had told them both: "Oh, how I praise the Lord. How I rejoice in God my Savior! For he took notice of his lowly servant girl, and now generation after generation will call me blessed. For he, the Mighty One, is holy, and he has done great things for me."

Even a DNA Test Wouldn't Solve This One (Matthew 1:19–21)

Although Mary, Elizabeth, and Zacharias had to be in a state of euphoria over the news they had received, there was one member of the family who was none too pleased at this turn of events: Joseph, Mary's fiancé.

The Bible doesn't tell us what Mary told Joseph concerning her pregnancy. But we can safely assume that she told him exactly what the angel Gabriel had told her—that the baby she was carrying was as a result of a miracle from God and that the baby would grow up to be the promised Messiah.

But Joseph wasn't buying the story. He knew two things for certain: His fiancée was pregnant and he wasn't the father. Of course, since Joseph hadn't been told directly what the angel Gabriel had said to Mary, he suspected the worst.

What Would the Neighbors Think?

Today, a pregnancy outside of a marriage is considered by most people to be, at best, a less-than-ideal circumstance. But in those days and in that culture, it was an enormous scandal. Joseph knew that going ahead with the marriage to Mary would mean exposing himself to public disgrace and humiliation.

According to Jewish law and culture, Mary and Joseph were not yet legally married. But since they were engaged, or "pledged" to each other, they were considered husband and wife, even though their marriage had not yet been "consummated." Joseph knew that he was well within his rights to divorce Mary, and that's what he decided to do. But, being a good man who didn't want to expose Mary or her family to public shame, he decided to do it quietly and without a lot of ado.

A Strange Dream but I'll Go with It

Before Joseph could send Mary packing, yet another angelic visit—this one in a dream—confirmed Mary's story and instructed him to go forward with the marriage: He told Joseph not be afraid to go ahead with the marriage to Mary because the child she was carrying had been conceived by the Holy Spirit. He was to be named Jesus, because he would save his people from their sins. (Matthew 1:20–21).

That was just what Joseph needed to hear, and when he awoke from the dream, he did as God had instructed him and took Mary as his wife. However, Matthew tells us that they did not "consummate" the marriage until after the birth of Jesus (Matthew 1:24–25).

> **His Name Is Jesus, a.k.a.**
>
> "The Root of Jesse" (Isaiah 11:10). Jesse was the father of David. There would come a branch from the root of Jesse (a son of David) who would be a banner to the nations and gather the exiles. But complete fulfillment of this would be the eternal kingship of Jesus promised to David when he was told that his (David's) kingdom would last forever.

Being Circumspect About Circumcision (Luke 1:57–80)

Three months after Mary's arrival at their home, Zacharias and Elizabeth welcomed into their family a son, just as Gabriel had said. Eight days after his birth, Zacharias and Elizabeth took him to the Temple in Jerusalem to be circumcised.

Circumcision was a huge deal to Jewish people. It was part of what is called the *"Abrahamic Covenant"* with the people of Israel, which is found in the book of Genesis. One of Abraham's parts of that covenant was to make sure that male children from that time forward were circumcised eight days after their birth (see Genesis 17:12).

> **W.W.J.K. (What Would Jesus Know?)**
>
> The **Abrahamic Covenant** was God's promise to Abraham, the father of the Jewish nation, to make Israel a great nation and to bless all nations of the world through it (see Genesis 12:12).

It had become Jewish custom by that time for a man to give his firstborn child his name and to do it on the day of circumcision. And when Elizabeth and Zacharias's relatives, friends, and neighbors heard that they had become parents, they more or less assumed that they would name him, their only son, Zacharias.

Better Listen to Your Wife!

But with the circumcision complete, Elizabeth stunned her family, friends, and neighbors that day when she told them, "His name is John!" Wanting confirmation of this surprising decision, they all turned to Zacharias, who was still unable to speak. He motioned to them to give him a tablet so he could write down the name of the baby. To their astonishment, he wrote "His name is John!"

Immediately Zacharias was able to speak. The first words out his mouth were praises for his God, as well as these words to his son: "And you, my little son, will be called the prophet of the Most High, because you will prepare the way for the Lord" (Luke 1:76).

Let's Come to Our Census (Matthew 2:1–12, Luke 2:1–7)

In Chapter 1 of this book we listed several of literally hundreds of Old Testament prophecies concerning the coming of the Messiah. If you'll remember, we pointed out that Jewish prophet Micah wrote that the Messiah would be born in Bethlehem (Micah 5:2). That Jesus was, but it wasn't as a result of another message from God through an angel or a vision in a dream. Rather, it was as a result of the politics in the Roman Empire at that time.

> **W.W.J.K. (What Would Jesus Know?)**
>
> Christmas, the celebration of Jesus' birth, has traditionally been recognized on December 25. This tradition started in Rome in around the fourth century C.E. In the second century C.E., a man named Clement of Alexandria stated that some people thought the date of Jesus' birth was April 21, April 22, or May 20. The truth of the matter is, no one can know for certain what day of the year Jesus was born.

As Mary was getting far along in her pregnancy, Roman emperor Caesar Augustus—the nephew of Julius Caesar—decreed that a census be taken of every province of the Roman Empire, and that included all the soon-to-be-levied universal tax on all residents in every part of the empire.

In preparation for the census, Joseph and Mary traveled from Galilee to Bethlehem, a tiny village about 6 miles almost due south of Jerusalem. It was the Jewish custom at that time for people to enroll for the census in the places where their own "tribes" or families had resided. Joseph knew that he was a descendent of King David, who was born in Bethlehem. For that reason he and Mary packed up and headed there.

A Natural Birth Experience

However, when Joseph and Mary arrived in Bethlehem, the town was crowded with people who had come there for the census. Every inn, every house, every place where people could sleep for the night was filled with citizens, soldiers, and the authorities who were there to complete the census.

Let's Come to Terms

In the Old Testament, there are several Messianic prophecies stating that the Messiah would be a **descendant of David.** In his gospel, Luke underscores that Jesus was a descendant of David by tracing Joseph's family lineage clear back through David and on to Adam. Matthew, on the other hand, traces Mary's lineage back, showing that she, too, was a descendant of Israel's greatest king.

Joseph and Mary must have arrived fairly late in the census-taking process, because they couldn't find lodging. So as an alternative—apparently the only one they had—they camped out beneath the stars and among the livestock that belonged to the people of Bethlehem.

It was in this humbler-than-humble setting that Mary gave birth to what Luke calls "her first-born son" then wrapped him in "swaddling clothes" (meaning long strips of cloth wrapped tightly around the infant) and laid him in a manger, which is a feeding trough for livestock.

Today, we're used to seeing "Nativity scenes" in which the manger Jesus laid in is surrounded by a complete, free-standing stable. But the truth of the matter is that Jesus was more than likely born in a cave near the town or under an overhang outside one of the local lodges. We're also used to seeing in those scenes midwives, or someone to assist Mary in the delivery of her baby. But it's very likely that at the birth of Jesus, Mary and Joseph were alone.

However, they wouldn't be alone for long!

A Silent but Holy Night (Luke 2:8–20)

For thousands of years, the fields and hills around Bethlehem had been the workplace and home to shepherds whose job it was to keep watch over the flocks and protect them from robbers or wild animals and to keep the sheep from just wandering off. (In case you don't know, sheep aren't terribly bright animals, and they're known for wandering if someone doesn't keep an eye on them.)

The life of a shepherd was a quiet and often lonely one. Since the shepherds worked in the fields and hills, sometimes through the night, they didn't often have a lot of company. But tonight, the night of the birth of the Messiah, some shepherds working near the tiny town of Bethlehem had some company like they'd never had before.

There We Were, Just Minding Our Own Sheep ...

From out of nowhere, the shepherds' quiet night was interrupted by a terrifying spectacle: an angel from God. The angel knew immediately that the men were afraid, and he calmed them down by saying, "Do not be afraid! I bring you good news of great joy for everyone! The Savior—yes, the Messiah, the Lord—has been born tonight in Bethlehem, the city of David!" (Luke 2:10–11).

The shepherds themselves were very likely Jews who, like the rest of their brethren, had eagerly awaited the coming of the Messiah, and they were more than ready to go see him that night. But how would they know who he was? The angel told them, "And this is how you will recognize him: You will find a baby lying in a manger, wrapped snugly in strips of cloth!" (Luke 2:12).

The angel prepared to leave the shepherds, but first he was joined by a "vast host of others—the armies of heaven" (in other words, a whole lot of angels) crying out, "Glory to God in the highest heaven, and on earth peace to all whom God favors" (Luke 2:14).

His Name Is Jesus, a.k.a.
"The Head Of His Body, The Church" (Ephesians 4:15). We as the church are so closely identified in union with Jesus that we are said to corporately be his very body and he in his person is the head. Earlier in this book it says his body is filled by Christ, who fills everything everywhere with his presence (1:23).

An Angel Gave Me Permission—Honest!

When the angel and the heavenly host left the shepherds, they were again alone in the quiet of the countryside. But the message of the angel stayed with them, and it wasn't long before they figured out what to do next. The Bible says that the shepherds left their flocks of sheep and hurried— some versions of the Good Book tell us that they *ran*—to Bethlehem.

Anybody who had heard and seen what the shepherds had that night would have a story to tell. And that they did! The shepherds told anyone who would listen what the angel had told them about the newborn baby sleeping outside in a feeding trough—namely that he was the promised Messiah.

Everyone who heard what the shepherds had to say was amazed. But Luke tells us that Mary, who already had been told about the identity of her son and was no doubt still amazed at what was happening to her, "quietly treasured these things in her heart and thought about them often" (Luke 2:19).

Having seen everything the angel had told them they would, the shepherds went back to work, leaving Mary, Joseph, and the baby behind and heading back to the fields. But they didn't go quietly. Matthew says that as they left, they praised God out loud for all the things they had seen and heard that night.

Just Another Nice Jewish Boy? (Luke 2:21–40)

Eight days after the birth of their son, Mary and Joseph, being the devout Jews they were, did as Jewish law required and had their son circumcised. It was then that they named him "Jesus," just as Gabriel had told them to do. But there was more that these new parents had to do.

First Circumcised, Now Consecrated

Thirty-two days after Jesus' circumcision, it was time, according to Jewish law, for his parents to have him consecrated to God and redeemed for five shekels of silver. This was because the duties that had previously been held by firstborn sons in Israel had been, over time, taken over by the priests in the Temple. The silver was the price to be paid the priests for their service.

W.W.J.K. (What Would Jesus Know?) _____

In addition to going to the Temple to present Jesus to the priests, Mary also had to go there for herself. According to Jewish law, a woman who gives birth to a son was considered ceremonially impure for 40 days, meaning she couldn't touch anything having to do with the Temple. After those 40 days, she was to present herself at the Temple, where she presented offerings to God.

The consecration ceremony was a fairly simple process. The father formally presented the child to the priest in the Temple while he recites this prayer: "He who has sanctified us with his commandments and has commanded us to redeem the son." After the priest takes the infant, the father turns away and says, "He who has given us life," then pays the five shekels of silver. With that, the ceremony is complete.

Not everyone—even among the most devout Jews—was able to present their first-born son at the Temple. In many instances, just the sheer distance they lived from Jerusalem made that impossible. But because Bethlehem was only about 6 miles south of Jerusalem, Mary and Joseph took the relatively quick journey to present Jesus at the Temple.

I'm Dying to See This Child

When Mary and Joseph took Jesus into the Temple, they were met by a priest named Simeon, an elderly and very devout man who eagerly looked forward to the coming of the Messiah. In fact, God had told Simeon that he would see the Messiah before he died.

After Jesus' presentation to the priests, Simeon took him into his arms and blessed him. After that, he prayed this prayer that showed his awareness of Jesus' true identity: "Lord, now I can die in peace! As you promised me, I have seen the Savior you have given to all people. He is a light to reveal God to the nations and he is the glory of your people Israel!" (Luke 2:29–32).

Blessings and Heartaches

Mary and Joseph were amazed at Simeon's words. But they were no doubt even more astonished when Simeon spoke words of prophecy that warned Mary what to expect out of the life of her son: "This child will be rejected by many in Israel, and it will be their undoing. But he will be the greatest joy to many others. Thus, the deepest thoughts of many hearts will be revealed. And a sword will pierce your very soul" (Luke 2:24–35).

What Simeon was telling Mary and Joseph was that, yes, this boy was the long-awaited Messiah, the Savior of Israel, but that his life would be very different from what they and other Jewish people might have been expecting. He would suffer rejection, but he would also be a blessing to many people. Also, his life would bring Mary heartache.

Back to Bethlehem First

The gospel of Luke concludes this part of Jesus' life by telling us that Mary and Joseph took him back to their original home in Galilee, where he would spend his childhood and, most likely, his early adult years. What Luke leaves out but Matthew includes in his gospel is that the three of them first returned to Bethlehem, where they were to meet some more visitors who wanted a glimpse of the Messiah.

The Least You Need to Know

- The birth of Jesus, as well as John the Baptist, was announced by the angel Gabriel.

- John's and Jesus' births were miraculous—John's because his mother was old and infertile, Jesus' because his mother was a virgin.

- Jesus was born in humble circumstances—in a stable in a tiny village called Bethlehem.

- Jesus, like the other "firstborn" sons of Israel, was presented at the Temple in Jerusalem, where he was blessed and prophesied over by an aging priest named Simeon.

Chapter 6

When God Was a Child

In This Chapter

- ◆ The visit of the magi
- ◆ Herod's search for the Messiah
- ◆ Jesus' family's flight to Egypt
- ◆ Jesus' family's return to Nazareth

In Chapter 5, we covered the events surrounding the announcement of the coming of Jesus (and John the Baptist) as well as those surrounding his birth and infancy. Now, we want to talk about what happened to Jesus—and why it happened and what it meant—during his early childhood.

Just one episode during Jesus' childhood touched off a series of occurrences that would help shape his incredible story. That event was the visit by men called "magi." Let's start this chapter by taking a look at some of the myths and misunderstandings—some of which you might believe yourself—surrounding the magi's visit to the "newborn King of Israel."

We Weren't Kings, There Weren't Three of Us, and We Weren't There on Christmas Day (Matthew 2:1–12)

If you take a close look at most of the "Nativity scenes" on people's front yards around Christmastime, you'll probably see not only Jesus, Mary, Joseph, and the shepherds we mentioned in the last chapter, but three "kings" standing next to the cradle holding the baby Jesus. You probably also remember the old Christmas carol "We Three Kings," which tells the story of the magi like this:

> We three kings of Orient are;
>
> Bearing gifts we traverse afar,
>
> Field and fountain, moor and mountain,
>
> Following yonder star.

But there are some historical problems with this scene *and* song. Yes, the magi probably traveled from a great distance to see Jesus (more on that later), and yes, they followed a star. But that's where the similarities between this scene and song and truth of the story as it's told in the Gospel of Matthew ends.

First of all, the magi, or "wise men" as the Bible calls them, weren't kings at all. Secondly, nowhere in the Bible does it say that there were three of them, only that they brought three gifts—gold, *frankincense*, and *myrrh*. For all we know, there could have been 2 of them, or 500! Lastly, the magi weren't in Bethlehem at the time of Jesus' birth but came to visit him in the little village after his presentation at the Temple in Jerusalem (see Chapter 5).

Let's Come to Terms

Frankincense and **myrrh** are both fragrant materials that were of great value in the culture of the magi. Frankincense was made out of an amber resin and produced a sweet aroma when it was burned. It was used in perfume and used by the Jews in their sacrificial services. Myrrh was a mixture of resin, gum, and an oil called "myrrhol." It was used in perfumes for garments and furniture and to pack wrappings of bodies before they were buried.

Who Are These Wise Guys?

Outside of the fact that they traveled to Palestine—first to Jerusalem, then on to Bethlehem—to see the newborn King of the Jews, Matthew doesn't tell us a whole lot about the magi. He doesn't tell us where they were from (other than to say they were from "the East"), what kind of religion they practiced, or even what their names were (although western tradition has it that they were named Gaspar, Melchior, and Balthazar). Almost everything we know about the magi of that time comes from studies of the ancient history of that part of the world.

The only known magi who lived east of Palestine at the time of Jesus' birth were in Media, Persia, Assyria, and Babylonia, meaning that they had to travel as much as 900 miles to see the Savior. Ancient records show that the magi were a class of priests from ancient Persia who were probably followers of the teachings of the Persian teacher and prophet Zoroaster, who lived from 630 to 550 B.C.E. and founded the religion of Zoroastrianism.

Let's Come to Terms

The first mention of "wise men" in the Bible is in Genesis 41:8, which tells us that Pharaoh "called for all the magicians and wise men of Egypt" to interpret a dream he'd had. There are several words used for "wise men" in the Old Testament.

The magi were well versed when it came to politics, science (particularly astronomy, at least as it was known then), and religion. Many or most of the magi at and before the time of Jesus studied and practiced sorcery and astrology, but Matthew doesn't tell us whether or not these men were into that sort of thing.

The magi who visited Jesus apparently knew something about the Messianic prophecies of the Old Testament. This, many experts tell us, is likely the result of the fact that there were many Jews living in Persia, Babylon, and other places to the east of Palestine.

For that reason, there was a sense of expectancy in those places that a ruler or Messiah would arise out of Israel and usher in an era of peace throughout the world. It may be that the magi were especially familiar with the Old Testament Messianic prophecy found in Numbers 24:17: "I see him, but not in the present time. I perceive him, but far in the distant future. A star will rise from Jacob; a scepter will emerge from Israel."

His Name Is Jesus, a.k.a.

"Bright Morning Star" (Revelation 22:16). The apostle Peter also says that the "day star dawns in our hearts" and the new dawn will be his second coming when the dawn of a new day, a new eternal kingdom, will draw nigh.

A Star Is Born

Just as mysterious as the magi themselves was the star they followed to Bethlehem. For centuries, people have speculated what exactly the "star" the magi followed really was. Some believe that it was some natural celestial occurrence, such as a comet, an unusual alignment of planets, or even a nova.

Indeed, astronomers believe that there were several celestial events like these around the time the magi first set out to find the Jewish Messiah. Others believe that the star was an act of God specifically for the purpose of announcing the arrival of Jesus into the world. Still others believe that the "star" was really an angelic being who had been sent to guide the magi on their way.

Whatever the "star" actually was, the magi knew to follow it. And it took them first to Jerusalem, the one place in Palestine they would logically expect to find a king!

The magi knew in general who they were in Palestine to see, but what they didn't know was that their presence there would be the beginning of an amazing chain of events during Jesus' infancy and early childhood.

What News of the Newborn One? (Matthew 2:1–12)

When the magi and their traveling party first arrived in Jerusalem, they created quite a stir when they started asking, "Where is the newborn king of the Jews? We have seen his star as it arose, and we have come to worship him."

Walking into a city like Jerusalem at that time and asking about a newborn king was sure to get people's attention, and that's exactly what happened. Matthew tells us that the entire city was "disturbed" by the magi's questions. Keep in mind that at this time, no one in Jerusalem knew about the birth of Jesus, and even if they did, they had no idea that he could be their promised Messiah.

But no one in Jerusalem was more disturbed than the man who occupied the throne as King of Judea, Herod the Great.

Even a Baby Could Do Your Job

When Herod heard that a group of visitors from the east were asking questions about a king of the Jews being born in Israel, he immediately became alarmed—maybe even frightened. As you may recall from Chapter 2, Herod was as paranoid as he was vicious when it came to protecting his position from outside invaders and from internal opposition.

Herod would stop at nothing, slaughtering thousands of Jews who opposed him (or who he thought opposed him) and even executing his wife, Mariamne, and two of his favorite sons, Alexander and Aristobulus, because he believed they were plotting against him.

It has been suggested that Herod, who was so deathly afraid of an attack from the East that he erected a series of fortresses and palaces along the eastern border of his kingdom, saw the magi as an outside threat. But what seems almost certain is that he felt threatened when he heard the words "King of the Jews" in reference to the one the magi were looking for.

The Good Shepherd from Bethlehem

Obviously Herod believed that the magi knew something he needed to know. Herod wanted to find out who this King of the Jews was and where he could find him, so he summoned the Jewish religious leaders in Jerusalem (the Sanhedrin, which you read about in Chapter 3) to come and see him. When they arrived, he started asking some questions of his own. Specifically, he wanted to know where, according to the prophecies of the Old Testament, the Messiah was to be born.

Of course, the religious leaders knew all the prophecies of the coming Messiah, and they told him what the prophet Micah had written centuries before about where he would be born: "In Bethlehem in Judea," they told him, then recited that very prophecy word for word: "O Bethlehem of Judah, you are not just a lowly village in Judah, for a ruler will come from you who will be the shepherd for my people Israel" (Matthew 2:6).

> **W.W.J.K. (What Would Jesus Know?)**
>
> King Herod was very meticulous when it came to obeying the letter of the Law of Moses. For example, he wouldn't eat pork. But he obviously knew little about the "Messianic prophecies," which were a big part of the Jewish culture at the time of Jesus. When he heard that there was a "newborn King of the Jews" in this territory, he had to ask the religious authorities where he had been born.

Take the Long Way Home ... or Else!

After talking to the members of the Sanhedrin, Herod "secretly" sent for the magi and asked them to meet privately with him. It was then that Herod learned that they had first seen the star that led them to Palestine about two years prior to their arrival in Jerusalem.

Herod told the magi that the one they were looking for was probably in Bethlehem, then asked them to go and find out exactly where in Bethlehem this "newborn king" was living. When they found out, he said, they were to come back to him and tell him where Jesus (although he didn't know at the time that it was Jesus they were looking for) was so that he could go and worship him also.

However, as you'll see as you read on, Herod was not motivated by any desire to worship the newborn King of the Jews. Rather, he was intent on killing him, just as he had killed so many others he had seen as a threat to his throne.

Now the Story Gets Spicy

The magi left Herod and continued on their journey, again guided by the star that had brought them as far as they had come. When they arrived in Bethlehem, they worshipped Jesus (although their worship probably wasn't in the "worship of God" context, but more likely the kind of reverence they had probably given other worldly kings) and presented him their gifts of gold and spices.

Everything had gone fairly smoothly for the magi, but what happened next was a departure from what they—or King Herod—had planned when first began their journey to Palestine.

The magi probably planned to go back to their homeland the way they had come. But when it came time for them to leave Bethlehem and head for home, the magi were warned in a dream to take a path different from the one they used to get there. They were to avoid returning to Jerusalem and avoid talking to Herod again.

Makin' a Run for the Border (Matthew 2:12–18)

Both Matthew and Luke tell us of Joseph receiving instructions from God through dreams. If you'll recall from Chapter 5, the first of these dreams was at the time Joseph was considering—or, more accurately, had *decided*—to quietly cancel his and Mary's plans to be married.

The second time Joseph had such a dream is recorded in Matthew's gospel, which tells us that right after the magi had departed for their home an angel appeared to him in a dream telling him that someone wanted to kill Jesus and that he needed to get up and take Mary and Jesus and flee to Egypt.

This wasn't an order to leave after Joseph and Mary woke up the next morning. It was an order to leave immediately. Just wake up your family, pack up what you need for the trip, and hightail it for Egypt *right now* and stay there until receiving further instructions.

Taking No Prisoners Under Two

The reason for this directive? Herod was enraged when he found out that the magi had taken a different way home so that they could avoid talking to him and telling him who and where the newborn King of Israel was. As a result, he ordered the slaughter of every male child in Bethlehem under two years of age.

Remember, the magi had told Herod that they'd first seen the star that led them to Palestine about two years before their arrival in Jerusalem. The way Herod figured it, killing every boy in Bethlehem under the age of two would ensure that the newborn King of the Jews would be dead and no longer a threat to his throne.

A Different Kind of Pyramid Scheme

It wasn't going to be an easy trip for Joseph and his new family. The border of the land of the pyramids was a long haul from Bethlehem, between 80 and 100 miles one-way, and it was about another 200 miles to Alexandria, which was home to about a million Jews at that time and which would be the ideal place for them to lay low for a while.

A trip like that would be tough for any man alone, but the fact that Joseph would be taking a baby and his mother with him made it all the more difficult.

But Egypt was the safest place Mary and Joseph could have taken Jesus. Why? While Egypt was at that time a province of the Roman Empire, it was not under Herod's jurisdiction, meaning that he would have no authority to harm the child or his family in any way.

Without delay, Joseph obeyed the command the angel had given him. In the middle of the night, he woke up his wife and the baby and they headed to Egypt. Matthew doesn't say where in Egypt the family settled. They may have camped out in a quiet place just on the other side of the border from Palestine, or they may have traveled west along the Mediterranean coast and on to Alexandria. It's also possible that they had kinfolk in Egypt and stayed with them until they were told to go home.

Mary, Joseph, and Jesus weren't in Egypt long—probably a matter of months—when they received from an angel the news that the man who wanted to kill Jesus was dead and that it was safe to return home.

> **W.W.J.K. (What Would Jesus Know?)**
>
> Matthew tells us that Herod's order that all male children in Bethlehem under the age of two be killed was a fulfillment of a Messianic prophecy found in the book of Jeremiah: "A cry of anguish is heard in Ramah—weeping and mourning unrestrained. Rachel weeps for her children, refusing to be comforted—for they are dead" (Jeremiah 31:15).

The flight to Egypt.

(Copyright © 2001 Tyndale House Publishers)

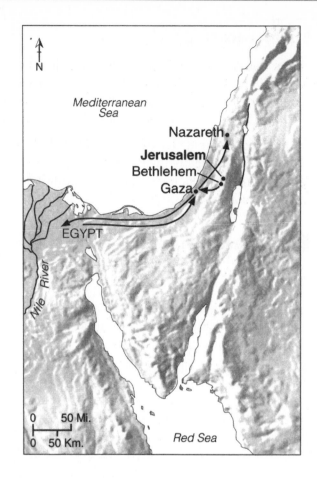

Ding Dong, the Tyrant's Dead!

In March or April of 4 B.C.E., King Herod died in his palace in Jericho, a city not far from Jerusalem, after a long and extremely painful illness. Matthew doesn't tell us what he died of, but historical accounts from Josephus and others say that it was an ugly, excruciating, and long death brought on by what sounds today very much like stomach or intestinal cancer.

Herod was so concerned with how the people in Palestine would take his death (remember, the Jews hated Herod and had wished for his death from the moment he took the throne) that as his illness progressed he issued an order to have some of the more influential and popular Jews in Palestine rounded up and executed after he died. His reasoning, if you want to call it that, was that if the people weren't going to mourn his death, then they were going to mourn something when it finally happened! Fortunately, the directive to kill these Jewish leaders wasn't carried out, as Herod's own sister, a woman named Salome, revoked the order.

Avoiding the Mourning Hours

The death of any king will bring about a time of mourning. Many dignitaries, kings, and leaders from outside Palestine came to pay their last respects at the elaborate funeral thrown in memory of Herod. But the mourning was not shared by the Jews in Palestine at that time. They, for reasons we've covered in this chapter and Chapters 2 and 3, were more than happy to see him gone. In fact, many historians say that a huge celebration broke out in the Jewish communities in Palestine.

Probably none were happier to learn of Herod's death than Joseph and Mary, who could finally return home safely.

There's No Place Like Home (Matthew 2:19–23)

Joseph didn't have to be told twice to pack up and take his wife and Jesus back to Israel. Matthew's account tells us that after the angel give him the "all clear" to head home, he took Jesus and his mother home immediately. But Matthew also tells us that on the way home, Joseph became frightened when he found out that Herod's son Archelaus had succeeded him as King of Israel. How could he know that he and his family could return to Bethlehem safely?

My Three Sons

In his waning days, Herod had written and rewritten his last will and testament, which in his case included all the "whos" and "wheres" when it came to running Palestine after his death, at least seven times. Finally, he decided that the kingdom would be divided among his three sons—Archelaus, Herod Antipas (who, as you'll see later, will play a big part in Jesus' story), and Herod Philip.

Archelaus, who was given authority over Judea, didn't take long following in his father's footsteps when it came to cruelty to the Jews in Palestine. Archelaus was every bit the tyrant his father was, and he quickly became well known for his extreme cruelty when it came to putting down uprisings or rebellions among the Jewish people.

In one instance, Archelaus stopped a revolt that took place near the Temple in Jerusalem during the Passover by sending in troops who killed some 3,000 pilgrims (meaning the Jews from outside Palestine who had left their homes and traveled to Jerusalem for the Passover feast). His tyrannical ways worried Roman emperor Caesar Augustus, who feared that his brutality would incite a major uprising among the Jews. In 6 C.E. Archelaus was deposed and banished to Gaul, the land southwest of the Rhine River, west of the Alps, and north of the Pyrenees.

Galilee? Dream On!

No doubt, Joseph had heard some of the reports of Archelaus's cruelty, and he was afraid to take his family back to Judea. But, as it turns out, he didn't have to worry about that. In yet another dream, an angel told Joseph to take his family to the province of Galilee, which was not under the rule of Archelaus but under his brother Herod Antipas, who didn't have Archelaus's reputation for brutality.

W.W.J.K. (What Would Jesus Know?)

Matthew points out in his gospel that the journey of Jesus' family from Egypt to Nazareth was the fulfillment of two Old Testament prophecies about the Messiah. The first was by the prophet Hosea, who wrote, "I called my Son out of Egypt" (Hosea 11:1).

This meant an even longer journey home for Jesus' family, but it also meant Joseph and Mary's return to their own home—the place where they had met and where the angel Gabriel had announced to them the birth of Jesus. Nazareth, the tiny Galilean town where they would settle after returning from Egypt, was located about 70 miles north of Jerusalem, making their journey home one of up to 370 miles (remember, Jews at that time would add to the length of their journeys in order to avoid traveling through Samaria, which is between Jerusalem and Nazareth).

His Name Is Jesus, a.k.a.

"The Son of Man" (Matthew 13:37). Jesus used this title in reference to himself almost 80 times in the gospels. Though he claimed to be the Son of God, he wanted to identify so much with us in our humanity that this was his preferred self-description. He is the firstborn of a new race of humans who will themselves, because of him, be like God.

When Jesus Became "Jesus of Nazareth"

Nazareth was a tiny village—probably home to less than 1,000 people in Jesus' day— that sat around 1,200 feet above sea level in the hills of southern Galilee. It was located about 15 miles east of the Mediterranean Sea and about 15 miles west of the Sea of Galilee. Nazareth was apparently an agricultural town. Recent archaeological digs in the area have uncovered items such as wine and olive presses, caves for storing grain, and man-made reservoirs for storing water and wine.

It was here that Jesus spent his boyhood years, here that he played and went to school with other children, and here that, as the Gospel of Luke puts it, he "grew up healthy and strong. He was filled with wisdom beyond his years, and God placed his special favor upon him" (Luke 2:40).

The Least You Need to Know

♦ Jesus was visited in Bethlehem by wise men, or "magi," who worshipped him and brought him gifts.

♦ The magis' stop in Jerusalem on the way to Bethlehem set off a series of important events in the life of Jesus.

♦ Joseph was instructed to take Mary and Jesus and leave Bethlehem for Egypt.

♦ After the death of Herod the Great, Jesus and his family settled in Nazareth, a tiny town in Galilee.

The Life of the Boy Jesus

In This Chapter

- ◆ Jesus' visit of the Temple in Jerusalem as a 12-year-old
- ◆ Attempts to "fill in the blanks" left by the four gospels concerning Jesus' childhood.
- ◆ The life of a Jewish boy growing up in Palestine
- ◆ Jesus' learning and development in Nazareth

It wouldn't take you long to read the gospel accounts of Jesus' childhood. That's because out of all four books, there are only two passages that tell us anything at all about Jesus' years growing up, and only one of them (Luke 2:41–52) gives us a specific story about his youth.

Luke's account tells us of a time of anxiety, maybe even panic, for his parents as well as amazement on the part of some Jewish religious leaders.

A Quick Glimpse of Jesus As a Child (Luke 2:41–51)

Several times a year, Jews from all over the known world would converge on Jerusalem, the site of the Holy Temple, for religious festivals.

The best known and most important of these festivals were Passover (or the Feast of Unleavened Bread), *Pentecost*, and *Tabernacles*. It was during these three celebrations that the Law of Moses required all adult male Jews to appeared at the place of the altar in Jerusalem. Women were not required to attend these feasts, but were allowed to and often did so.

Let's Come to Terms

Pentecost (also known as the "Feast of Weeks" was an annual festival celebrating Moses' receiving of God's laws during the time of the Exodus. Pentecost, which means "50 days," fell exactly 50 days (or a week of weeks) after the Passover. The Feast of **Tabernacles** commemorated God's provision and care for the people of Israel during their travels in the wilderness after their exodus from Egypt. Tabernacles was near the first of our October.

Pass the Mint Jelly

When Jesus was 12 years old, Mary and Joseph took him to Jerusalem to attend the Passover Feast. Luke's gospel tells us that Mary and Joseph attended the festival every year. While Luke doesn't specifically say that Jesus went with them every year, it's likely that he did make the trek with them from their home in Nazareth to Jerusalem.

The Passover feast commemorated God's deliverance, through Moses, of the Israelites (the descendants of Abraham and the people who would later settle in what would become Israel) from the bondage of slavery to the Egyptians. The Passover celebration was held on the 15th day of Nisan, the first month of the Jewish calendar (in March/April of our calendar). On the afternoon of Nisan 14, devout Jews would sacrifice lambs at the Temple. That evening (Passover began, according to Jewish law and tradition, after sunset), the lambs were roasted and eaten with unleavened bread. For the next seven days, the celebrants would eat the unleavened bread.

Passover wasn't just a time of celebration for the Jewish people as a nation, but also for the family units. At the Passover feast, families would gather together to enjoy one another's company and to reflect on and talk about God's blessings.

When the Passover celebration was over, the families living in and around Jerusalem returned to their homes and those who had made their pilgrimages from other parts of the Jewish world hit the road and headed back. That they did in large caravans, which gave them protection against wild animals and robbers.

W.W.J.K. (What Would Jesus Know?)

The Jewish Festival of Passover got its start just as the Jews were about to be released from the bondage of slavery to Egypt. God had instructed Moses to have each Jewish family slaughter a blemish-free year-old lamb, then take some of the blood and put it on the doorframes of their homes. That night, the blood on the doorframes ensured that God would "pass over" that house when it came to his judgment on the people of Egypt for Pharaoh's refusal to set the Jewish people free (Exodus 12).

Mary and Joseph had already made the journey home from Jerusalem following the Passover several times, and they no doubt expected the one they made when Jesus was a 12-year-old to be pretty much the same as all the others. At least at first!

Say, Have You Seen This Twelve-Year-Old?

With the Passover celebration over and their packs filled with food and water for their trip, Joseph and Mary headed north for the three-day journey back to Nazareth. They assumed that Jesus had gone on ahead with friends or relatives (that was a common practice in that situation) and that they would meet up with him on the road to Nazareth. But they assumed wrong!

The caravan of people stopped to camp out the first evening of the trip. It was then that Mary and Joseph expected Jesus to show up at their camp. When he didn't, they asked around among their friends and relatives to see where he might be. No one in the caravan had any idea where Jesus was. Of course Mary and Joseph were very worried, so they turned back south and into Jerusalem to look for him.

It might seem inconceivable that two devoted parents could travel that long without seeing their son before they became concerned. But we must keep in mind that this wasn't a matter of packing the wife and kids into the minivan and heading out for a weeklong party in Jerusalem. Mary and Joseph were traveling with what was probably a caravan of hundreds of people. It was very likely that many of the parents had allowed their children to travel and play with the children of friends and relatives.

Knowing that, it's fairly easy to understand how Mary and Joseph lost track of Jesus for a time.

You May Be Grounded, Young Man

Luke tells us that from the time Mary and Joseph learned that Jesus was missing from the caravan, it took them three days to find him. These parents, now gripped with dread over what had become of their son, must have looked high and low in Jerusalem.

Finally, they found him. He had never been lost at all but was sitting at the Temple with the religious teachers talking about some pretty deep spiritual issues. Of course, even though Jesus was only 12 years old, Mary couldn't believe that he would be so inconsiderate, and she scolded him: "Son! Why have you done this to us? Your father and I have been frantic, searching for you everywhere" (Luke 2:48).

Luke doesn't tell us whether Jesus had stayed behind in Jerusalem intentionally, only that he explained to his irritated but much-relieved mother, "Why did you need to search? You should have known that I would be in my Father's house."

> **W.W.J.K. (What Would Jesus Know?)**
>
> Luke goes out of his way to tell us as when Jesus sat at the feet of the teachers at the Temple, he asked them questions. This was a custom in the Jewish rabbinical schools at that time. The rabbis, or teachers, taught in question-and-answer format.

Acting His Age ... and Quite a Bit More

While Mary and Joseph were irked that Jesus caused them so much worry, the religious teachers he had been spending time with were really impressed with him.

It wasn't uncommon for outstanding young Jewish boys to come to the Temple to talk with these teachers about issues of the faith and issues of their time. But there was something really special about this particular 12-year-old. He sat at their feet asking and answering questions, just like young men in that culture would do in the presence of these rabbis. Luke tells us that Jesus amazed all of these men not just with his ability to quote the Jewish Scriptures by letter and verse but by his understanding of what they meant.

> **His Name Is Jesus, a.k.a.**
>
> "Good Teacher" (Mark 10:17). Jesus was later known in his ministry as "rabbi" or teacher because of the incredible wisdom and knowledge of the Scriptures he had with no formal training.

That must have been quite a scene. Here were all these learned men, many of whom who had spent literally decades studying and memorizing the Torah, and this 12-year-old amazed even them with his understanding, which was far beyond what most Jewish children had.

Heading Back Home with the Boy Genius (Luke 2:51–52)

Luke closes this chapter in Jesus' life by telling us that he returned with his parents to Nazareth, where he lived a life of obedience to them, just as Jewish law required him to.

The results of this obedience? Luke puts it this way: "Jesus grew both in height and in wisdom, and he was loved by God and by all who knew him" (Luke 2:52). In other words, Jesus grew up pretty much like most Jewish boys in Palestine at that time. He grew physically, intellectually, spiritually, and socially into the culture of his time.

W.W.J.K. (What Would Jesus Know?)

Obedience to one's parents was a huge deal in the Jewish culture. In fact, one of the Ten Commandments was "Honor your father and mother. Then you will live a long, full life in the land the Lord your God will give you" (Exodus 20:12). Jesus, like all good Jewish boys, knew this commandment, and, according to Luke, he obeyed it flawlessly.

So What More Do We Know About the Boy?

Outside of the account in the Gospel of Luke of Jesus going to Jerusalem to celebrate the Passover with his parents, there aren't any more specifics in the Bible when it comes to Jesus' life after he moved with his family from Egypt to Nazareth.

The one minor exception to this is found in the gospels of Matthew and Mark (Matthew 13:55 and Mark 6:3). They both tell us that Jesus was not the only child growing up in the home of Mary and Joseph. Jesus had four younger brothers— James, Joseph, Simon, Judas (no, not *that* Judas!), and some younger sisters, although the Bible doesn't tell us how many or what their names were.

This time in Jesus' life has been referred to as "the silent period" simply because the four gospels don't address it.

Nice Try, but No One's Buying This

There were *apocryphal* accounts of Jesus written in books such as the "Gospel" of Thomas, which was said to have been written by Jesus' brother Thomas and which is included in a list of extra-biblical writings called the *"Apocryphal"* or *"Spurious" Gospels.* They were deemed unreliable and, therefore, left out of the Bible.

Okay, Now for What We *Do* Know!

Outside of his visit to the Temple when he was 12 years old, we simply don't know many details about Jesus' childhood. All we really know for sure when it comes to the specifics about Jesus' boyhood is that he grew up with his family in a place called Nazareth. We also know some things about childhood in the Jewish world in Palestine at that time, and we can safely assume that Jesus' boyhood was a lot like that of other children growing up there.

Nazareth: The Place Jesus Called "Home"

When it comes to geography and scenery, Nazareth was known for being a beautiful place. Set on the northwestern slope of the mountains of Galilee, it provided a beautiful view of the nearby hills and meadows.

But Nazareth didn't have a very good reputation among a lot of the Jewish people at the time of Jesus. We know that from the words of a soon-to-be-disciple named Nathanael (also known in the gospels as Bartholomew). When Nathanael was told that a man named Jesus was the Messiah and that he had come from Nazareth, he quipped, "Nazareth! Can anything good come from there?" (John 1:46)

Nazareth was located near two larger cities called Tiberias and Sepphoris, both of which were predominately Gentile (non-Jewish) cities. Nazareth, which was a predominately Jewish town, had been in existence for nearly 2,000 years, yet it wasn't mentioned in the Old Testament and rarely mentioned in ancient historical accounts of the area.

There was poverty and overpopulation in Nazareth at Jesus' time, but it wasn't what we might think of as "destitute." The people there eked out a living by farming, ranching, and through various trades, such as carpentry.

Nazareth was built into a small ridge and had one source of water, which was located several hundred yards from the village itself. The homes themselves were built out of limestone, which was plentiful in the area. Most of the homes there were actually built into small caves or underground and had been used for generations before Jesus' arrival. Most of the homes were one-room dwellings but there were some (probably owned by the better-off Nazarenes) with several rooms.

It was in this tiny, insignificant, mostly unknown village—far away from the academics, culture, and more advanced social structure of cities like Jerusalem—that Jesus grew up and matured. It was here that he lived with his family, played with his brothers and sisters and friends, studied the Torah, and worked with his father.

It was also here that Jesus received his primary education, which was likely very much like that of other Jewish youth of that time and culture.

Quoting Chapter and Verse

By the time Jesus "went public," he was obviously well versed when it came to the Scriptures and Jewish tradition. As you will see later in this book, Jesus taught and preached extensively using not just parables and knowledge of Jewish traditions and lifestyles, but also with direct quotations from the Jewish Scriptures.

This tells us two things about Jesus: First of all, he truly was gifted when it came to understanding the meaning of Scripture. But it also tells us that he must have spent a lot of time as a youth and as a young adult studying and learning them.

Time to Hit the Books

Education on the ways of the Jewish religion was a huge deal for the people of Jesus' time. The tradition of educating children was as ancient as the Jewish nation itself. At the time of the Exodus, God had told the people this concerning teaching their children his commandments: "Repeat them again and again to your children" (Deuteronomy 6:7).

In the Jewish culture, education began at home, where the children learned, using the Old Testament as their primary "textbook." It was the responsibility of the parents, as well as the grandparents, to begin the education of the children at an early age.

When Education Goes "Formal"

Almost all children in the culture at Jesus' time received a formal education at school. At the age of six or seven—around the same age children in our culture begin elementary school—Jewish boys and girls began studying in the schools of their time and culture—the ones in the synagogues. Nearly every town and village in Palestine had its own synagogue, and every synagogue operated a school for the children in its town. Nazareth was no exception, and Jesus very probably attended school in the local *synagogue*.

Let's Come to Terms

The **synagogues** came into wide use in Palestine after the Jews returned from the Babylonian exile. A synagogue could be established in any city, town, or village with 10 or more married Jewish men. For that reason, there were synagogues in nearly every Jewish town. While the Temple in Jerusalem was more for worship of God, the synagogues were places for studying the holy Scriptures.

The teaching in the synagogue schools was centered on the Torah. They learned to read Hebrew from small scrolls that contained selected passages from Scripture. The children also had to memorize passages of the Torah (remember, the Torah was the scroll containing the Pentateuch, the first five books of the Old Testament, which were the books of the law), and they did so by reading as well as chanting and singing them, much the same way that young children today memorize the English alphabet by singing it.

The Board of Education

In just about every culture ever known, fathers taught their sons a craft, usually the craft they themselves used to earn a living. In Jewish culture, there was great respect for manual labor. In fact, they saw working with their hands as an act of religious devotion. For that reason, the passing on of a "skill" from father to son wasn't just encouraged but required.

In Jesus' case, that craft would have been carpentry, for Joseph himself was a carpenter (Matthew 13:55). It is very likely that Jesus spent a lot of time working with Joseph, using the tools of the trade, such as hammers, saws, and measuring devices. In fact, in Mark 6:3, Jesus himself is referred to as "the carpenter."

Jesus' upbringing in Nazareth was probably a happy one in which he learned a great deal from his family and through his education. Those parts of his life certainly influenced him in his earthly ministry. Sometime during this period his stepfather Joseph must have died, for he is not mentioned as being with Mary in the gospels.

Observe and Learn

Jesus never made direct reference to the things he observed as a youth and young adult living in first-century Nazareth. You never read in the gospels that Jesus said anything like, "When I was growing up ..." or "Back in Nazareth ..." But as you read on in this book (and in the gospels) and see the way he spoke and taught, you just might catch a glimpse of what he must have seen and heard living in that rural setting.

In his youth and early adulthood, Jesus must have spent a lot of time observing the beauty of nature around him as well as the work of the farmers and sheep herders who made their living in the fields and hills around Nazareth.

Jesus' teachings (his sermons, his parables, and his conversations with individuals) were filled with references to the beauty and workings of nature—"the lilies of the field," "the birds of the air," "the hen gathering her chicks under her wing," "the fox in its lair."

A Country Boy at Heart

Jesus also often made reference to agriculture, suggesting that prior to his ministry he observed those who "reap and sow" as well as those who tend sheep. Jesus spoke often of the duties of the shepherd of his time, likening their work to his own on earth. The shepherds of his time worked hard to feed and guard the flock, and he had even more work to do when one of the sheep strayed.

> ### His Name Is Jesus, a.k.a.
>
> "The Good Shepherd" (John 10:14). Shepherds roamed the fields of Nazareth and would protect their sheep from predators at the risk of their lives. Jesus leads, feeds, and protects his sheep (the church) and laid down his life for them to deliver them from eternal death.

The gospel writers obviously didn't see the need to tell us much about the years that would make up the majority of Jesus' life, probably because his ministry had not yet begun. But, like anyone else, the things he learned and observed went a long way in shaping his personality, his outlook, and the way he spoke.

The Least You Need to Know

- The only reference in the four gospels to Jesus' youth involves his visit to Jerusalem with his parents for the Passover feast.

- The four gospels don't tell us a lot about the specifics of Jesus' life growing up in Nazareth.

- Over the centuries, there have been attempts by some to "fill in the blanks" concerning Jesus' youth and early adulthood.

- Jesus' education as a Jewish youth shaped his teaching and actions during his earthly ministry.

3

Jesus' Teaching and Work

Most people in our culture know at least a little bit about the life of Jesus, but many of us don't know a lot of details about the things Jesus said and did during his earthly ministry.

As he preached and taught, Jesus also put real action behind his words. He offered compassion to those who suffered from a wide variety of illnesses and handicaps. He also offered acceptance and forgiveness to the worst "sinners" of his time. He even took the time to reach out to people from outside the Jewish world.

If you know just a little bit about Jesus and would like to know more about his character, what he said, and the things he did, the following chapters will help you to better understand him and his message.

Chapter 8

Jesus Launches His Ministry

In This Chapter

- The life and teachings of John the Baptist
- The baptism of Jesus in the Jordan River
- The temptation of Jesus
- Jesus' first miracle: turning water to wine

The four gospels finally break their silence about the life of Jesus when he was over 30 years old. A lot had happened in Palestine in those "missing" years, and there were big changes on both the political and religious scenes.

Those years were a time of great political and religious intrigue, a fact that Luke points out in his account of the beginning of Jesus'—and John the Baptist's—ministries.

It's a Whole New—But Still Ancient—World

John the Baptist began his ministry (which started just prior to Jesus') in the 15th year of the reign of the second Roman emperor, Tiberius Caesar, the stepson and successor of Augustus Caesar. Tiberius began his reign in 14 C.E., meaning that John began his ministry in the year 29.

At that time, Pontius Pilate was "procurator" or governor of Judea, and Herod Antipas was governor of Galilee. Herod the Great's son, Archelaus, had ruled as king of Judea for around 10 years after Herod's death in 4 B.C.E., but was deposed because of the brutality of his rule.

W.W.J.K. (What Would Jesus Know?)

Iturea and Traconitis were located northwest of Galilee. Abilene is also located northwest of Galilee but in Syria.

After that, Palestine was split into districts, each of which was ruled by a Roman governor. Pontius Pilate was the fifth governor to rule Judea. Luke also tells us that Tiberius's brother Philip was governor over Iturea and Traconitis, and Lysanias was ruler of Abilene.

My Son in the Law

Luke also reports that people by the name of Annas and Caiaphas were the Jewish high priests at the time John the Baptist started his ministry. Even though the Jews recognized only one high priest (who was to hold this office for life), Luke mentions two high priests. Here's why:

His Name Is Jesus, a.k.a.

"The Way, the Truth, and the Life" (John 14:6) He told his disciples that no person could come to the father in heaven except through him. These three things are not concepts but an actual person—everything ultimate is found only in him. Thomas à Kempis said he is "the way unchangeable; the truth infallible; and the life everlasting."

Annas had held the office of high priest from 6 C.E. until 15 C.E., when he was deposed by Pontius Pilate and eventually succeeded by Caiaphas, who happened to be his son-in-law and who held the office until 37 C.E. Though Annas had been deposed, he still held a lot of influence over the Jewish people, most of whom still considered him their high priest.

It was into this political and religious world that both John the Baptist and Jesus first made their appearances and began their ministries.

A Trailblazer on the Scene (John 1:6–37)

One of the most important figures in the life of Jesus was John the Baptist, who took on the life of a prophet and preacher in the sparsely populated desert wilderness of the mountainous area of Judea. The gospels tell us that John was the forerunner of Jesus, meaning he was the one the Jewish prophet Isaiah and others had said would come to prepare the people of Israel for the Messiah's arrival. He came to make a path in the wilderness of not hearing from God about the Messiah and prepare the way for his arrival.

Clothes Definitely Didn't Make *This* Man

You might think that the person who announced the coming of Jesus would be among the best-known and most powerful people in Palestine. But if you thought that, you'd be wrong.

John lived a life of extreme poverty. He wore sackcloth, which is made of camel's hair, with a leather belt around his waist. This was not camel skin with hair on it, but a very coarse fabric woven out of the shaggier hair on the camel.

Honey Makes the Locusts Go Down Smoothly

John also didn't dine in the finest establishments of the day. In fact, he didn't even eat at anyone's home. Matthew tells us that his diet consisted of locusts and wild honey. Both were plentiful in the desert and both were permitted foods according to Jewish law.

John definitely had the look and lifestyle of an Old Testament prophet. In fact, many experts on the subject point out that he probably looked very much like the Jewish prophet Elijah, who the Old Testament book of 2 Kings tells us also dressed the same way and who also spent some time on the banks of the Jordan River.

But it wasn't just John's scraggly appearance and simple diet that reminded many of the prophets of old but also his words, which were very direct and sometimes a little on the harsh side.

John's "Turn or Burn" Message

John the Baptist had a tough message for the Jews living in Palestine: "Turn from your sins and turn to God, because the Kingdom of Heaven is near!" (Matthew 3:2). In other versions of the Bible, John is recorded as using the word *repent* when it came to doing what it took to prepare the way for the Messiah.

Let's Come to Terms

Repentance, as John the Baptist and Jesus used the word, literally meant a change of attitude toward God and his law that changed the way a person lived and thought. It meant having remorse for, as well as confession and abandonment of, sin. When John the Baptist called people to repent, what he meant was that they needed to return to the reverence for God and obedience to his laws as demonstrated by Jewish heroes such as Moses, David, and Solomon.

John's message was a radical one in that culture, because it went against the very popular idea that being a descendant of Abraham made someone right in God's eyes. John taught that this kind of righteousness came not from family lineage but from a pure heart that motivated people to change their lives.

Is That Any Way to Talk to Religious Leaders?

John's harshest words were for the Pharisees and Sadducees. As you may recall, the Pharisees were the more "pious" of these two religious parties in that they meticulously observed religious rites and ceremonies. The Sadducees, on the other hand, were more "worldly" or materialistic and didn't believe in things such as a spirit world or an afterlife, and were in cahoots with the Romans for political power.

John scolded both the Pharisees and the Sadducees severely, going so far as to call them "a brood of snakes" who probably wouldn't know the Messiah if he were standing right in front of them.

Let's Come to Terms

The practice of **baptism** was continued after the ministry of John the Baptist. The gospels tell us that Jesus' disciples baptized people, as did the apostles whose stories are recorded in the Acts of the Apostles. To this day, baptism in one form or another is practiced among Christians.

Clean Inside and Out

John's *baptism* was simply an outward sign that people had turned from their sins and that God had forgiven them. In other words, the baptism itself didn't change anything. That change came from within, and it resulted in a change of heart, mind, and behavior.

The practice of baptism (at least various forms of it) was not new in the Jewish world at the time of John the Baptist. In fact, there were all kinds of "ceremonial washings" practiced in Judaism, all of which symbolized purification.

Fire and Water: Both Are Needed

One of the differences between John's baptism and those practiced by the Jews over the previous centuries was that John's was a one-time baptism that identified the person being immersed with the coming Messiah.

John was also very clear that his baptism was just a first step in preparing the people for the arrival of their Messiah. He taught that the more important baptism was the one the Messiah himself would bring. That baptism would be with "the Holy Spirit and with fire," meaning that only those who were receptive to the coming of the Messiah would receive God's eternal blessings of the Spirit to live inside of them and the fire to purge one's sins.

John taught that the others, including some of the most religious people of that time, would see eternal fire if they rejected the Messiah.

No Longer "Distant" Cousins (John 1:29–34)

The gospels don't tell us how well John the Baptist and Jesus knew one another. It's possible that they had never met in person, but since their mothers—Elizabeth and Mary—were cousins and good friends, it's likely that John and Jesus knew one another, maybe well. One thing that appears certain in the gospels is that John at least knew that there was something very special about this man Jesus. In fact, he said he was not worthy to even untie his sandals!

At first, John didn't think it was a good idea for him to baptize Jesus. After all, it was Jesus who had come to bring salvation to John and others, not the other way around. But Jesus knew what he was doing. He told John that what was about to happen was right and needed to fulfill everything Jesus had come to do. So, just as Jesus had asked him to do, John invited him into the water, where he baptized him.

The gospels all record that when Jesus came up out of the water of the Jordan River, a voice from heaven said, "This is my beloved Son, and I am fully pleased with him." And then the Spirit descended on him like a dove.

Let's Come to Terms

John 1:29–34 and other New Testament passages are the basis for the Christian teaching of the **Trinity,** which means that God has revealed himself as God the Father, God the Son (Jesus), and God the Holy Spirit. One of the objections that some of the Jews had to Jesus claiming to be the Messiah was that he claimed to be the Son of God. To them, that didn't jibe with the belief that there was only one God. The doctrine of the Trinity was finally formalized at the Council of Chalcedon in the fifth century.

John's baptism was a sign of preparation for the mission in the life of Jesus, but there was another step he had to take.

It's Tempting, but No Thanks (Luke 4:1–13)

The second part of Jesus' preparation for his ministry on earth was a 40-day *fast* and some "devilish" temptation in the wilderness of Judea. Both Matthew and Luke tell us that immediately after his baptism, Jesus was led "by the Holy Spirit" to head into the desert.

W.W.J.K. (What Would Jesus Know?)

Fasting—going without food for a certain amount of time—was a common practice among devout Jews before, during, and after the time of Jesus. It was seen as a sign of devotion to God and as a time of meditation and prayer in preparation for some great event or work. The Old Testament records that both Moses and Elijah fasted for 40 days and nights in preparation for something God had for them to do.

A Time of Vulnerability ... and of Strength

After 40 days and 40 nights of fasting and prayer in the desert, Jesus became very hungry. If there is ever a time in someone's life when they can be tempted, it's when they haven't eaten in a long time. Matthew and Luke both report that it was during this time of vulnerability that the devil showed up on the scene.

Promising Him the World

Three times the devil came at Jesus with a different kind of temptation, and all three times Jesus answered using quotations from the Old Testament book of Deuteronomy.

The devil started out by challenging Jesus to change some rocks into bread. After all, if he was hungry, there would be no reason not to use his power to whip up something to eat! But Jesus answered with a quotation from Deuteronomy: "No! The Scriptures say, 'People need more than bread for their life; they must feed on every word of God.'"

Then the devil took Jesus to Jerusalem to the highest point on the holy Temple, and challenged him to jump off. After all, the Scriptures said that if he really was the Son of God then God's angels would make sure nothing happened to him. Again, Jesus answered by quoting the book of Deuteronomy: "The Scriptures also say, 'Do not test the Lord your God.'"

Finally, the devil took Jesus to the top of what must have been a very high mountain and told him that he could have everything his eye could see and more. The condition? Bow down and worship the devil himself. For the third and final time, Jesus answered with a quotation from Deuteronomy: "Get out of here, Satan. For the Scriptures say, 'You must worship the Lord your God; serve only him.'"

The devil left Jesus and angels came and cared for him, and you can bet that part of that was a good meal!

Rollin' on the River (John 2:19–27)

When Jesus finished his time of fasting and testing in the wilderness, he returned to the Jordan River, where he again saw John the Baptist, who'd had a time of testing of his own.

John, You're Still a Mystery

From the very beginning, John the Baptist made it clear that he was not the Messiah. But by the time Jesus had finished his 40-day stay in the wilderness, John's ministry had become so popular and well known that a lot of people wondered if he was the Christ.

The Jews at that time not only believed that the Messiah would be coming, but that his coming would be preceded by that arrival on the scene of the prophet Elijah, who the Old Testament had said never died (he went to heaven in a chariot) and who was prophesied to return before the Messiah's arrival. They also expected the coming of still another prophet who would usher in the Messiah.

Apparently, word of John's ministry had gotten back to the Jewish religious authorities in Jerusalem, and they sent Temple priests and assistants to Bethany, a little village on the east bank of the Jordan River, to find out if John claimed to be either the Messiah, Elijah, or the prophet they had been expecting. But John flatly denied being any of those people.

Only a Servant to the Main Man

That wasn't enough for these representatives. They needed to tell those who had sent them who John was, so they asked him to identify himself. John identified himself, quoting the prophet Isaiah: "I am a voice shouting in the wilderness, 'Prepare a straight pathway for the Lord's coming!'"

Still, that wasn't enough. The representatives wanted to know that since John wasn't the Messiah, Elijah, or the prophet, what made him think it was okay for him to baptize people? John replied, "I baptize with water, but right here in the crowd is someone you do not know, who will soon baptize with the Holy Spirit. I am not even worthy to be his servant."

In a nutshell, John was telling these Jewish representatives two things: First, he wasn't the Messiah, and second, the Messiah, who was a man far greater than John himself, was already here.

You See a Man, He Sees a Lamb

The day after his confrontation with the representatives from Jerusalem, John was again standing on the banks of the Jordan River when he saw Jesus approaching him.

His Name Is Jesus, a.k.a.
"The Lamb of God" (John 1:19). In the Old Testament a lamb was sacrificed for the sins of the people as a symbol of innocence and purity. Jesus became the Father's sacrificial lamb for the sins of the whole world because he, too, was pure and without sin.

Immediately, he told the people around him that the man approaching him was the same one he had told the representatives about: "Look! there is the Lamb of God who takes away the sin of the world!" (John 1:29).

John said that he became convinced that Jesus was indeed the long-awaited Messiah at the moment he baptized him. The apostle John (John was a very common name in the Jewish world in those days) quotes the Baptist as saying that God had told him that when he saw the Holy Spirit resting on someone, he could know that this person was the Messiah.

On His Way to an Even Dozen (John 1:35–50)

It was during Jesus' second meeting with John as recorded in the gospels that he called five men to be part of his "inner circle" of followers, the apostles. The first two he called, Andrew and John, were disciples of John the Baptist. That day, Andrew went and found his brother Simon (later called Peter) and told him, "We have found the Messiah."

The next day, Jesus set out for Galilee, his home province in Palestine. It was on the way that he called men named Philip and Nathanael to be disciples. (More on the calling of the 12 disciples in Chapter 10.)

It was also in Galilee that Jesus would begin to establish his reputation as not only a great teacher, but also as a miracle worker.

This Man Knows How to Keep a Party Going! (John 2:1–11)

When Jesus and the five disciples arrived in Galilee, his mother informed them that there was a wedding celebration in a village called Cana, and that they were invited to come with her.

It must have been a big wedding party because, well before it was over, the hosts ran out of wine. In that culture, running out of wine at an event like a wedding party was a huge social *faux pas*. The host, the families of the bride and groom, and the guests would all be mortified if the wine ran out at a wedding party, so something had to be done to "save face" for the wedding host.

W.W.J.K. (What Would Jesus Know?)

The actual location of **Cana**, the site of the wedding party as recorded in John's gospel, isn't known for certain. The traditional site of Jesus' first miracle is *Kefr Kenna* (Arabic for "City of Cana"), which is about 4 miles northeast of Nazareth. However, modern scholars believe the actual site is *Khirbet Kana* (meaning "ruins of Cana"), which is a little over 8 miles north of Jesus' hometown of Nazareth.

I'm Not Ready Yet, Mom

With the wine supply tapped out, Mary approached Jesus and simply told him, "They have no more wine." John doesn't tell us what Mary expected Jesus to do to fix the problem, and Jesus' response, at least at a glance, seemed to be asking the same question.

In our own language, it seems that Jesus responded to Mary rather sternly: "How does that concern you and me?" he asked her. "My time has not yet come." In another version of this gospel account, Jesus' words seem to cross the line from stern over to rude: "Woman, what does your concern have to do with me?"

There must have been something in Jesus' reply that led Mary to believe that he was willing to do something to help the situation. After talking with Jesus, Mary turned to the servants of the wedding hosts and told them to do whatever Jesus asked them to do.

Jesus saw that there were six stone water pots at the site of the wedding party, which were used in Jewish culture for ceremonial washing. The

W.W.J.K. (What Would Jesus Know?)

In the Jewish culture, people were considered ceremonially unclean if they didn't wash both before and after eating. For that reason, it would make perfect sense that the wedding party at Cana had water pots for that purpose.

pots each had a capacity of between 20 and 30 gallons. Jesus instructed the servants to fill each of them to the brim with fresh water.

Once the water pots were filled, Jesus told the servants to dip some of the liquid out and give it to the wedding host. That's when some people found out that they were witnessing something very special.

Hey, This Is Good Stuff!

The wedding host took the small container of liquid from the servant, and when he tasted it, he found that it wasn't just wine, but some of the best wine he'd ever tasted! Of course, he didn't know what had just happened, although the servants knew full well that what had been water was now some very good wine.

W.W.J.K. (What Would Jesus Know?)

In the Jewish culture in Palestine, there were different beverages referred to as "wine." There was fermented wine with a low alcohol content, unfermented grape juice, and the kind of wine very much like what we're used to in our culture (wine that can intoxicate, if you drink too much).

The wedding host saw what had happened as a departure from the usual party customs in that area and culture. Usually, he told the bridegroom, the host serves the good wine first, then after everyone has had their fill, he brings out the cheap stuff. By then, nobody knows the difference between good wine and cheap wine. This, he said, was the best he'd had at that wedding party.

Now Your Followers Believe, Too

We're not told what kind of wine was being served at the wedding party at Cana. What we are told is that this miracle was the first display of Jesus' divine power. We're also told that the five disciples who were with Jesus that day believed in him, meaning that they believed that there was something very special about this man.

This wouldn't be the last miracle these disciples (as well as the others who would join later) would see Jesus perform. As you read on, you'll see that miracles were a part of what made Jesus who he was.

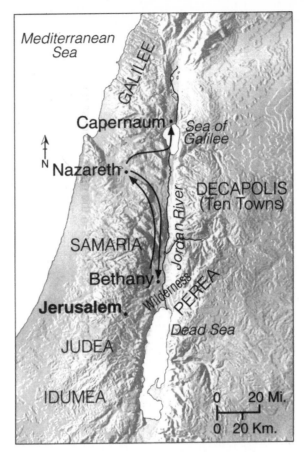

Jesus begins his ministry.

(Copyright © 2001 Tyndale House Publishers)

The Least You Need to Know

♦ The ministry of Jesus was preceded by that of John the Baptist, a preacher who worked in the desert of Judea.

♦ Though he was at first reluctant to do so, John baptized Jesus in the Jordan River.

♦ Following his baptism, Jesus headed for the desert (or wilderness) of Judea, where he was tempted by the devil.

♦ Jesus performed his first miracle—changing water to wine—at a wedding in a village called Cana.

9

The Message Makes This Man

In This Chapter

- ◆ Jesus clears the Temple in Jerusalem of merchants and money-changers
- ◆ A late-night conversation with a Pharisee named Nicodemus
- ◆ Jesus shows a Samaritan woman that he is the Messiah
- ◆ Jesus' rejection as Messiah in his own hometown
- ◆ Jesus' teaching, preaching, and miracles in Galilee

After Jesus and his disciples left Cana, they, along with Jesus' mother and brothers, headed north into Capernaum, a village in Galilee, where they stayed for a short time.

Not long after this visit to Capernaum, Jesus, who was born and raised a Jew and had been taught the ways of the Jewish religion, did what all devout Jewish men did: travel to Jerusalem for the annual Passover Feast.

It was during this time in Jerusalem that Jesus showed a side of himself no one had seen up to that point.

The Not-So-Meek-and-Mild Jesus (John 2:13–25)

The first thing Jesus did when he arrived with his disciples in Jerusalem was head for the Temple. This was his first recorded visit to the Temple since he was 12 years old.

What he saw at the holy Temple that day was merchants selling animals, as well as moneychangers. The way he responded to what he saw would be a defining moment in his life and in his personality and reputation.

What in the Name of Everything Holy Is Going On Here?

The people in town for the Passover bought these animals—sheep, kid goats, doves, and others—at the Temple for the purpose of sacrificing them, as their religious law told them to do. It wasn't practical for the Jewish pilgrims who came to Jerusalem for the Passover to bring their own animals for the sacrifice, so the priests began selling them in the Temple.

Let's Come to Terms

Shekels were the Jewish currency used in Jerusalem at the time of Jesus. A half-shekel was a piece of silver weighing about 1/5 of an ounce and was the equivalent of a day's wage for the typical Jewish worker. The practice of collecting a "Temple tax" of a half-shekel started after the Jewish exodus from Egypt, when the Jews worshipped in a portable tabernacle.

The Jews who came to the Temple for Passover each paid a half-shekel for its operation. Most of the Jews who came from abroad for the celebration carried with them money from their home countries. Since this money was not accepted at the Temple, they needed to exchange it for Jewish currency. That is where the moneychangers came in. For a hefty surcharge, they would trade the foreign money for Jewish money.

All of this would probably have been fine with Jesus if it had been done away from the Temple. But the priests had allowed these things to take place in the Temple, and that was something Jesus, being a devout Jew, couldn't tolerate. He then went about "cleansing the Temple."

Jesus made quite a scene that day. He took some ropes and made a whip, then drove the animals out of the Temple area. He turned over the moneychangers' tables, scattering the coins all over the floor. Jesus then turned to the merchants and moneychangers and told them, "Get these things out of here. Don't turn my Father's house into a marketplace!"

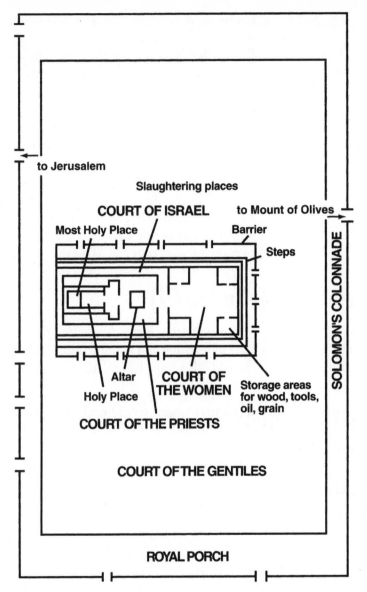

The Temple in Jesus' day.

(Copyright © 2001 Tyndale House Publishers)

Credentials, Please

The Jewish religious leaders, who had previously approved of the presence of the merchants and moneychangers in the Temple area, demanded to know what right Jesus had to create such a scene. They also told him that if he had that kind of authority, he should demonstrate it by performing a miracle.

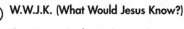

W.W.J.K. (What Would Jesus Know?)

The Gospel of Matthew also contains a "Temple cleansing" scene similar to the one described in John. Some experts believe that these were two separate but similar incidents, while others believe that they are the same episode, but not recorded in the same order.

Jesus' answer to their request for a miracle was to tell them, "All right. Destroy this temple, and in three days I will raise it up!" Neither the religious leaders nor Jesus' disciples understood what he was talking about. It was only after his death and resurrection that the disciples remembered what he had said and realized he was talking about the temple of his own body. While Jesus isn't recorded to have performed a miracle just to show the religious leaders that he had the authority to "cleanse the temple," he still stayed in Jerusalem for the rest of the Passover celebration, teaching and doing miracles. The result of this was that a lot of people began to think he was really the Messiah.

I'm on Your Wavelength (John 3:1–21)

Jesus had some amazing conversations with people from many different walks of life. As you'll see throughout this book, his style of teaching and communicating was to enter into a person's world and use that person's thoughts, beliefs, and experiences as tools to teach.

One of the best known—and most defining when it came to Jesus' identity—of these kinds of conversations was with an elderly and respected Pharisee named Nicodemus, who had obviously seen and heard some things about Jesus.

A Pharisee Who's Fair, I See

Nicodemus approached Jesus at night, maybe to avoid being seen by his fellow Sanhedrin members but maybe because it was a convenient time for him to have an uninterrupted talk with Jesus. It's very likely that Nicodemus's associates were still very upset about what had happened at the Temple. Nicodemus, on the other hand, seemed to want to know exactly who gave Jesus the authority to act as he did.

The line of questioning Nicodemus took suggests that at this point, he and the rest of the Pharisees believed that there was something special about Jesus. "Teacher, we all know that God has sent you to teach us," he told Jesus. "Your miraculous signs are proof enough that God is with you."

But Jesus didn't leave it at that. He went on to tell Nicodemus something that was at the very heart of his message, namely that in order to see God's kingdom, he had to be *"born again."*

Of course this surprised and confused Nicodemus. Like the rest of the Pharisees, he no doubt believed that people were ensured a place in God's kingdom by obeying the law that had been a part of Jewish culture for centuries.

Nicodemus, who had spent most of his life studying the Scriptures, knew there was no way he could literally be "born again." So he pressed Jesus, trying to understand what he was talking about. "How can an old man go back into his mother's womb and be born again?" he asked.

Let's Come to Terms

Jesus' words "you must be **born again**" would become foundational to the Christian faith. These words refer to a "new birth" on the part of the one who puts his or her faith in Jesus. The apostle Paul later defined being "born again" this way: "What this means is that those who become Christians become new persons. They are not the same anymore, for the old life is gone. A new life has begun!" (2 Corinthians 5:17).

Of course, Jesus wasn't speaking literally when he used the words "born again." So he didn't directly answer Nicodemus's question about being born again, but instead told him what he was really talking about. Jesus told Nicodemus that no one could see the kingdom of God without being "born of water and the Spirit. By this he meant that a person had to have an inward change in order to see the kingdom of God.

Jesus went on to tell Nicodemus that this "rebirth" wasn't something that mere humans, even one as learned as Nicodemus himself, could fully understand.

Have You Ever Welcomed a Snake on a Pole?

Jesus then put what he was saying in terms that a Jewish rabbi such as Nicodemus could understand. He told the Pharisee, "as Moses lifted up the bronze snake on a pole in the wilderness, so I, the Son of Man, must be lifted up on a pole, so that everyone who believes in me will have eternal life."

In saying this to Nicodemus, Jesus was referring to the Old Testament story found in Numbers 21:4–9. The people of Israel had rebelled against God, and as a result they were plagued with poisonous snakes. But God provided a way of "salvation" for those who had been bitten. He instructed Moses to fasten a bronze snake to a pole and hold it up so that the people could see it. Whoever looked at the bronze snake lived, even though he or she had been bitten.

This was clearly a reference on Jesus' part to what was ahead for him—a sacrificial death by crucifixion—and what it meant to the people he came to minister to.

The Gospel Message in Miniature

Jesus finished his conversation with Nicodemus by telling him very plainly why he had come: "For God so loved the world that he gave his only Son, so that everyone who believes in him will not perish but have eternal life. God did not send his Son into the world to condemn it, but to save it" (John 3:16–17).

Jesus told Nicodemus that God would not condemn those who had placed their faith in his Son but that those who didn't put their faith in him were already condemned. The reason? Because they refused to acknowledge that Jesus was the Messiah that God had promised would come, not only to rescue the people of Israel but the rest of humanity as well.

Not in a Thousand Years Would I Go There (John 3:22–4:3)

Sometime after his conversation with Nicodemus, Jesus gathered his disciples and they left Jerusalem and traveled to the Judean countryside, where they began baptizing people who came to them.

But when Jesus learned that the Pharisees had heard he was baptizing more people than John the Baptist (the truth of the matter was that Jesus wasn't baptizing anyone himself, but the disciples were baptizing) and wanted to talk to him about it, he and his disciples left Judea and headed north for Galilee.

At that time, most people traveling from Judea to Galilee would have traveled through Samaria. But the most devout Jews—and Jesus and his disciples were certainly that—would have taken a longer route from Judea to Galilee, one that would have taken them east of the Jordan River and around Samaria. That's because Jews and Samaritans feuding went way back, about 1,000 years.

Jacob's Well—A Deep Subject (John 4:4–42)

As Jesus and the disciples passed through Samaria, they stopped around noon one day near a town called Sychar, which was near the ancient city of Shechem. Jesus' plan was to wait at Jacob's Well and send the disciples into town to buy some food.

Tired and thirsty from the long walk, Jesus sat at the edge of the well and waited for someone to come and dip him out some water. It wasn't long before someone came along. That someone was a now-famous biblical character known only as "the woman at the well."

What set this story in Jesus' life apart was that this person was not only a woman, but a *Samaritan* woman. In Palestine at that time, it was almost unheard of for a Jewish man to talk to a Samaritan. But Jesus did the unheard of when he asked this Samaritan woman for a drink of water. That was the beginning of another defining conversation in Jesus' life.

W.W.J.K. (What Would Jesus Know?)

Jacob's Well, where Jesus met the Samaritan woman, is located near a Galilean town called **Sychar,** which is between Mt. Ebal to the north and Mt. Gerizim to the south in what is now known in Israel as the West Bank. The well itself is about 9 feet in diameter and, at the time of Jesus, was about 150 feet deep. The well is still in existence and now has a Greek Orthodox Church built around it.

This Water Is Heavenly

Whether it was from the way he looked, dressed, or talked—or all of the above—this unnamed woman knew immediately that Jesus was a Jew. For that reason, she was astonished that Jesus would talk to her at all, even to ask for a drink of water.

Jesus, as he so often did as he taught, used the circumstances of the moment to identify himself and to teach. When the woman voiced her surprise that Jesus, a Jew, would ask her, a Samaritan, for a drink of water, he told her, "If you only knew the gift God has for you and who I am, you would ask me, and I would give you living water."

What Jesus was really telling this woman didn't sink in right away. She saw that Jesus didn't have a rope or bucket on him and therefore had no way to bring the water up out of the well. But Jesus patiently explained to her that it wasn't actual physical water he was speaking of but a "spiritual" water that could quench the thirst of any soul. "People soon become thirsty again after drinking this water," Jesus said, referring

Let's Come to Terms

Samaritans were a mixed-race people whose roots went back to the 772 B.C.E. Assyrian conquest of what was by then the Northern Kingdom. Assyrian colonists settled into what would later become Samaria. The intermarriage between them and what was left of the Jewish population produced the Samaritans of Jesus' time. There was a lot of bitterness between the Jews and the Samaritans, so much that the two rarely, if ever, had any dealings at all with one another.

to the literal water in Jacob's Well. "But the water I give them takes away thirst altogether."

Of course, the woman was intrigued by these mysterious words. But she still didn't understand what Jesus was really saying. She told him she wanted him to give her some of that "water" so that she would never be thirsty again or ever again have to walk to this well for water.

The Samaritan Version of Celebrity Marriages

Jesus set the stage for his explanation of "living water" by asking the woman to do one simple thing: "Go and get your husband."

The woman knew this meant a moment of honesty between her and this stranger. She told him simply and honestly, "I have no husband." The truth of the matter was that she had been married five times—John doesn't tell us whether her previous husbands had died or had divorced her, or whether her situation was a combination of the two—and was now living with a man who was not her husband.

In contrast to Nicodemus, who had stated that he and his cohorts in Jerusalem believed Jesus was a great teacher who was sent from God, this woman made a parallel observation about Jesus: "Sir, you must be a prophet."

Whether she was really looking for information or whether she just wanted to "change the subject" from her rather checkered past, the woman had a question for this man she considered a prophet: "Why do the Jews believe that Jerusalem is the only place to worship, while we Samaritans claim it is here at Mount Gerizim?"

True Worship Comes from Within

Jesus responded to her question, not by taking a side over who was right—the Jews or the Samaritans—about the proper place of worship, but by in essence telling her that the actual place of worship wasn't what was important. What *was* important, he told her, was that the worship of God come from a heart devoted to him.

Jesus told the Samaritan woman that God is spirit and that those who worship him must worship "in spirit and in truth." That kind of spiritual worship, Jesus said, could be offered anywhere—in Jerusalem, in Samaria, or any place where people were willing to humble themselves before God.

It's Yours Truly!

The woman at the well had come to a point of realizing that Jesus was a prophet and a man with a lot of understanding about God. In a statement that set up Jesus' identification of himself in this scene, she said, "I know the Messiah will come—the one who is called Christ. When he comes, he will explain everything to us."

Then Jesus gave her this stunning bit of news: "I am the Messiah!" While Jesus had identified himself as the Son of God and had agreed with people that he was sent from God, this is the first instance in the gospels where he is recorded to have said that he was the Messiah.

A Bunch of Good Samaritans (John 4:39–42)

Jesus' conversation with the Samaritan woman had a huge effect not just on her, but on others in that part of Samaria. She believed that Jesus was indeed the Messiah she and the others in Samaria had been waiting for. She returned to her home village and told everyone she knew that she had met the Christ. The proof that Jesus was the Messiah, she told her friends, neighbors, and relatives, was that he knew everything about her before she said so much as one word.

The people were intrigued by the news the woman brought them, and they went out to the well where Jesus and his disciples were staying and begged him to stay in the village. Jesus stayed there two days before moving on to Galilee, teaching and preaching to the Samaritans.

The people in the village later told the woman Jesus had met at Jacob's Well that they believed in Jesus not because of what she had told them but because they had heard and seen him for themselves.

International Harvesters (John 4:31–38)

When the disciples returned to Jacob's Well with the food they had purchased, they began eating and encouraging Jesus to eat something, too. But Jesus used this as an opportunity to teach the disciples about his mission. He told them, "My nourishment comes from doing the will of God, who sent me, and from finishing his work," then explained to them their roles in this work.

Jesus likened their mission to that of those who harvest crops that someone else had planted. While the disciples weren't the ones who had gone out and "planted the seed" of Jesus' message—other people, especially the prophets of Old Testament times, had done that—the disciples would be the ones who would go out and gather in the harvest of believers throughout the world after Jesus was gone, the harvest we can read about in the Acts of the Apostles.

Local Boy Makes It out Alive ... Barely (Luke 4:16–30)

When Jesus and the disciples left Samaria, they headed back to Cana. From there, Jesus went back to his hometown of Nazareth. The gospels don't make it clear whether the disciples went with him. As it turns out, Jesus' homecoming would be one with a pretty good greeting but a really lousy farewell.

In those days, it was customary for the synagogue leaders to read and explain the books of the law (the Torah), the Old Testament prophets, and to preach to the congregations. It was also customary for the leaders to invite a visiting rabbi to speak. On this particular day, that visitor was Jesus.

As I Read, It's Fulfilled

Jesus stood up to read to the congregation, then took the scroll and read this Messianic prophecy from the prophet Isaiah: "The Spirit of the Lord is upon me, for he has appointed me to preach Good News to the poor. He has sent me to proclaim that captives will be released, that the blind will see, that the downtrodden will be freed from their oppressors, and that the time of the Lord's favor has come" (Isaiah 61:1–2).

> ### His Name Is Jesus, a.k.a.
>
> "The Carpenter" (Mark 6:3). "Where did he get all his wisdom and the power to perform such miracles? He's just the carpenter from our home town," said the people of Nazareth. The man who claimed to be the pre-existent second person of the Godhead (Trinity) who created the universe also admitted to being a real, live, small-town, poor carpenter in Palestine in 28 C.E. No wonder they had trouble believing him!

When Jesus had finished reading, he rolled up the scroll, handed it to the attendant, then sat down. The eyes of everyone in the synagogue were on Jesus when he finished reading, waiting to hear what he had to say. Jesus began his message for the day by saying, "This Scripture has come true today before your very eyes!"

The Carpenter Moonlighting As a King?

At first, the people at the synagogue seemed impressed with Jesus' teaching. After all, he was the son of a simple carpenter they all knew. He grew up in their little village, studied in their schools, and played in their fields. He had little formal education, yet here he was powerfully teaching them. "How can this be?" they wondered. "Isn't this Joseph's son, the carpenter?"

But Jesus wasn't finished. He took his teaching a step further when he compared the people in the synagogue to unfaithful Jews at the time of the prophet Elijah. When they heard this, they went from being a peaceful, quiet congregation in a small Galilean synagogue to something of a lynch mob.

The End Is a Real Cliffhanger

Jesus went on to talk about the Old Testament prophets Elijah and Elisha, who were sent to live with Gentiles because of the Jews' lack of faith. When he said, "no prophet is accepted in his own hometown," they knew he was talking about them and were enraged at him.

They took Jesus to the edge of a cliff near town and were going to throw him off. Somehow (and we're not told how), Jesus escaped this scene and traveled to Capernaum, which would be the scene of some more amazing teaching and miracle-working by Jesus.

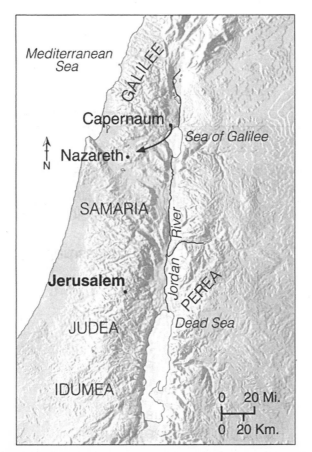

Nazareth rejects Jesus.

(Copyright © 2001 Tyndale House Publishers)

Time to Raze the Roof (Mark 2:1–12)

The news of Jesus' trip to Capernaum spread quickly, and it wasn't long before people were again crowded around him, seeking teaching and healing.

Let's Come to Terms

Capernaum, where Jesus lived during a large portion of his earthly ministry, was located at the northwestern shore of the Sea of Galilee, about 2 miles west of the upper Jordan River. Archaeologists have estimated that between 1,000 and 1,500 people lived in Capernaum at the time of Jesus. They also have found evidence that Capernaum's economy was based on fishing, agriculture, manufacturing of tools and glass goods, and trade. The Sea of Galilee in the area of Capernaum was a very good location for fishing.

But there were people there with other motives, namely the Scribes, who had come from Judea, Jerusalem, and other parts of Galilee to investigate Jesus' teaching and work. The house where Jesus was staying was so crowded with people wanting to be healed and wanting to hear his teaching that it was impossible to enter through the front door. So four very industrious men figured out that there was still a way to bring their friend, who was crippled and lying on a mat, to Jesus for healing: through the roof!

W.W.J.K. (What Would Jesus Know?)

Houses in Capernaum, which were mostly modest multi-room dwellings, were built in such a way that they could not support very heavy roofs. Usually, the houses had flat, sloping roofs supported by wooden cross beams and made of reeds, palm branches, and dried mud. These roofs had to be rebuilt every fall, before the winter rains set in. This helps explain how the men in this story could so easily dig through the roof (as well as why they didn't incur the wrath of the house's owner!) to lower their friend down to Jesus.

The four men fastened ropes to their friend's mat, then punched a hole in the clay tiles on the roof and lowered their friend down, right in front of Jesus. To Jesus, this was a great demonstration of faith, and he honored it by telling the man something neither he nor his friends probably expected: "My son, your sins are forgiven."

His Name Is Jesus, a.k.a.

"I Am" (John 8:58). Jesus not only claimed to forgive sins but he called himself by the unutterable Jewish name of God, Jehovah or "I am who I am" in response to the challenge regarding his relationship to Abraham. This was the most serious type of blasphemy, unless of course it were true. Jesus said Abraham rejoiced to see Jesus' day. The religious leaders replied that Jesus was not yet 50 years old and couldn't have seen Abraham—to which Jesus replied that before Abraham was born, "I am" meaning that he is self-existent and eternal.

A Deeper Kind of Healing

Of course, the religious authorities in attendance that night couldn't believe what they were hearing. It was one thing to heal people but quite another to tell someone their sins were forgiven. To them, this was *blasphemy!*

Jesus knew what these men were thinking, and his response to their complaints was the very definition of his ministry on Earth: "Why do you think this is blasphemy? Is it easier to say to the paralyzed man, 'Your sins are forgiven' or 'Get up, pick up your mat, and walk'? I will prove that I, the Son of Man, have the authority on earth to forgive sins!"

Let's Come to Terms

Blasphemy was a huge sin in the eyes of the Jewish people at Jesus' time and one that was punishable by death. Blasphemy included misusing or cursing the name of God, misrepresenting God or his character, falsely claiming to have heard from God, or (in Jesus' case) claiming authority to do that which only God himself can do, such as forgiving sins.

Going to the Mat with His Opponents

Jesus then focused his attention back on the paralyzed man and told him, "Stand up, take your mat, and go on home, because you are healed!" and the man did just that.

In this scene, Jesus took a stand in front of those who would oppose him in his ministry from the beginning to the end: the religious establishment of his time.

Indeed, Jesus would prove to be a troublemaker for those in the "old guard." But as he did so, he ministered with both zeal and compassion—zeal for his message and compassion for those who most needed what he was offering.

The Least You Need to Know

- ◆ Jesus drove out merchants and moneychangers from the Temple.

- ◆ Jesus told a Pharisee named Nicodemus that he must be spiritually reborn in order to enter heaven.

- ◆ Jesus told a Samaritan woman that worship of God comes from within, not from a sacred place.

- ◆ When Jesus presented himself as Messiah to the people of his hometown of Nazareth, he was rejected.

- ◆ Jesus could forgive sins as well as heal the sick.

Chapter 10

Some Really Radical—and Practical—Teaching

In This Chapter

- ◆ Jesus and the Sabbath
- ◆ The commissioning of the 12 apostles
- ◆ The "Sermon on the Mount"

From the moment Jesus burst on the public scene in Palestine, his ways and teachings were a radical departure from what the people in Palestine were used to in their leaders.

While most of the religious authorities of that time and place stressed a very "black and white" interpretation and application of the Jewish law, Jesus stressed life lived with a heart of faith and love for God and humankind.

Jesus demonstrated that very clearly when it came to the issue of the Sabbath.

What a Difference a Day Can Make (Matthew 12:1–21)

As Jesus got his earthly ministry rolling, the Pharisees and other religious leaders began following him and his disciples, watching them closely to see if they were the kind of people who followed the law as meticulously as they did.

W.W.J.K. (What Would Jesus Know?)

The Law of Moses (in Deuteronomy 23:25) stated that it was permissible for people to eat from another person's vineyard or field, but not permissible to take any more than what one could eat on the spot.

Let's Come to Terms

The **Sabbath** was a vital part of Jewish law and tradition. In Jewish language, the word Sabbath meant stopping any and all forms of work and resting, just as God had rested on the "seventh day," after the creation of the world was complete. The Torah had these very direct words about the Sabbath: "Six days are set aside for work, but on the Sabbath day you must rest, even during the seasons of plowing and harvest" (Exodus 34:21).

One day close to harvest time (probably around the first of our May), Jesus and his disciples were walking through a wheat field on the Sabbath. As the disciples strolled along, they began plucking heads of wheat and rubbing them between their hands to remove the husks so they could eat them.

The Pharisees knew that the law allowed people to take a few heads of wheat from another person's field to eat them. What they found unacceptable, however, was the "work" the disciples did in picking the wheat and husking it with their hands on the Sabbath.

The Pharisees wasted no time in confronting Jesus about this violation of Jewish law. "You shouldn't be doing that!" they protested. "It's against the law to work by harvesting grain on the Sabbath."

Jesus responded by pointing out that in Old Testament times, King David—a man all Jews, including the Pharisees, respected greatly—had technically (at least by the Pharisees' standards) violated the law when he and his traveling companions ate the only food made available to them: holy bread reserved for the priests (1 Samuel 21:1–6). Jesus also told the Pharisees that the priests who worked in the Temple had technically "worked" on the Sabbath. Besides, he said, God was more interested in people showing compassion than he was in them meticulously following the letter of the law.

Jesus further rocked the Pharisees' world, telling them, "The Sabbath was made to benefit people, and not people to benefit the Sabbath. And I, the Son of Man, am master even of the Sabbath" (Mark 2:27).

Jesus wasn't done making his point about doing good for people on the Sabbath. On a later Sabbath day, he and his disciples—followed by this group of religious leaders—headed to a synagogue (probably in Capernaum), where he would demonstrate not only his compassion but his power as a healer.

> **W.W.J.K. (What Would Jesus Know?)**
>
> When Jesus told the Pharisees that it was good to show "works" of compassion on the Sabbath, he was referring to the words of God as recorded by the Old Testament prophet Hosea: "I want you to be merciful; I don't want your sacrifices. I want you to know God; that's more important than burnt offerings" (Hosea 6:6).

I *Told* You, Now I'm Going to *Show* You

When Jesus walked into the synagogue, the first thing he saw was a man whose right hand was badly deformed. Evidently, the Pharisees knew what he was thinking, and they wanted to see if he planned on violating the law again. The Pharisees believed that doing any kind of work on the Sabbath was a clear violation of that law. That included giving people medical attention. What *was* allowed, however, was doing tasks such as rescuing a sheep or other animal that had gotten lost or fallen into some kind of danger.

Jesus pointed out that the Pharisees' approach to the law of the Sabbath was out of balance. If it's okay to rescue an animal on the Sabbath, he asked them, then why shouldn't it be okay to do good for a human being, who was much more valuable to God than any animal? In short, he said, it's not only permissible to help people on the Sabbath but the *right thing to do*.

He's My Right Hand Man

Jesus then turned his attention from these religious leaders back to the man with the deformed hand. "Reach out your hand," he told him, and the man obeyed. In an instant his right hand was healed.

This was a perfect example of, as the old saying goes, not being able to see the forest for the trees. The Pharisees had witnessed up close and personal a demonstration of Jesus' power and compassion. But rather than focusing on the good he had done in the name of God, they called a meeting to discuss plans to have Jesus killed for his violations of the law.

Give Me a Dozen, Please (Matthew 10:2–4)

After his confrontation with the Pharisees about doing good on the Sabbath, Jesus got away from everything for a night of prayer. After that night, Jesus called all of his disciples together (We aren't told exactly how many disciples followed him by that time. There could have been literally hundreds) and chose 12 of them to be his apostles.

These were the men who would travel with Jesus everywhere he went for the remainder of his earthly ministry. They were also the men who would begin taking Jesus' message to the known world after his death and resurrection.

Let's Come to Terms

The word **apostle** literally means "one sent by another" or a messenger or ambassador. The word disciple, as the gospel writers use it, means followers of Jesus who listened to his teachings. All the apostles were disciples, but only 12 of the disciples were apostles. They had special spiritual authority beyond that of other followers, and Jesus even told them that they would help him judge the tribes of Israel at the end of time. He entrusted them to take his message to the world once he was no longer with them.

Reeling Them In

As you may recall from Chapter 8, shortly after Jesus' baptism and temptation, he called Andrew, John, Peter, Philip, and Nathanael to be his disciples. As Jesus' ministry progressed, more and more disciples joined him, and it was from that crowd of people that he called the 12 apostles.

The gospels record different accounts of the apostles' call to follow Jesus. For example, one story tells us that Jesus called Andrew and Peter while they were casting their nets from the shore of the Sea of Galilee. Jesus called out to them, "Come, follow me and I will make you fishers of men," and they both left their nets and followed him. Farther down shore from where Jesus called Andrew and Peter, he saw James and John, who were working on their fishing boat with their father Zebedee. When Jesus called them to be disciples, they literally dropped their fishing gear and followed him.

Here are the rest of the 12 apostles: Thomas, Matthew the tax collector (also known as Levi), James the son of Alphaeus, Thaddaeus (also known as Judas, the son of James), Simon the Zealot, and Judas Iscariot.

Resumés That Will Knock 'Em Dead

If most of us were to pick 12 men to take Jesus' message to the ends of the earth, we probably wouldn't pick these guys. They came from a variety of professional backgrounds (at least four of them were fishermen) and, as far as we know, none of them had extraordinary educational backgrounds. In short, they were ordinary, everyday people.

Jesus' calling of one of those apostles in particular caused quite a stir among the religious leaders. That apostle was Matthew, who had spent his life working in the far-less-than-respectable profession of tax collection.

You're *All* in a High Tax Bracket

In the eyes of the Jews—the religious leaders and the common folks alike—tax collectors were the lowest form of human life that existed. While tax collectors in any culture aren't going to be your most popular citizens, the Jews in Palestine had a special hatred for the tax collectors.

In reality, tax collectors were representatives of the Roman Empire, and therefore seen in the Jewish population as being in cahoots with the enemy. Also, tax collectors at that time were allowed by their superiors to take a "surcharge" on all taxes they collected. Some of them abused this system terribly, soaking the citizens for every penny they could get.

On the night Jesus called Matthew to be an apostle, Matthew invited Jesus and the rest of the 12 to come to his home for dinner. It wasn't going to be a small gathering, though. Also coming to the party that night would be a collection of the most notorious scoundrels in Galilee (in other words, Matthew's buddies).

Hangin' Out in the 'Hood

Of course, the Pharisees were indignant that Jesus would associate himself with such lowlifes as the ones who he dined with that night. But when Jesus found out what they were saying to one another, he told them, "Healthy people don't need a doctor—sick people do. ... I have come to call sinners, not those who think they are already good enough" (Matthew 9:12, 13).

His Name Is Jesus, a.k.a.

"The Great Physician" (Luke 4:23). Just as we seek an oncologist to help us rid our bodies of cancer, Jesus is the specialist capable of dealing with the consequences of sin. The outcasts in his day were more willing to acknowledge their need for a spiritual doctor, and thus he hung out with them over the Pharisees, who claimed to have it all together.

This was in perfect keeping with Jesus' life. While the religious leaders wanted to associate themselves with people they considered "righteous," Jesus hung out with the sinners, the sick, and the outcasts—the prostitutes and thieves.

It was this very kind of people who sought him out and followed him, and the very kind who heard the greatest teaching he ever gave.

A Foolproof Way to Inherit Both Earth and Heaven (Matthew 5–7)

Sitting on a small hill on the shore of the Sea of Galilee, in front of his apostles and who-knows-how-many of his followers, Jesus delivered the world's most famous teaching, which has come to be known as the "Sermon on the Mount."

Jesus' teaching in this "sermon" was different from anything the people had ever heard. It was radical teaching that turned their view of the world upside down, but it was filled with simplicity and practicality. It was—and still is—the kind of teaching that people who followed Jesus could hear and use in their everyday lives.

Beatitudes Begin with Good Attitudes (Matthew 5:3–11)

Jesus started the Sermon on the Mount by speaking what is now known as the *beatitudes*. The word *beatitude* literally means "declaration of blessing." Each of Jesus' beatitudes—there are eight of them—starts out with the phrase "God blesses" (or "Blessed are ..." in other versions of the Bible), then gives the heart attitude it takes in order to receive that blessing and finishes with the blessing itself.

The Beatitudes

- God blesses those who realize their need for him, for the Kingdom of Heaven is given to them.

- God blesses those who mourn, for they will be comforted.

- God blesses those who are gentle and lowly, for the whole earth will belong to them.

- God blesses those who are hungry and thirsty for justice, for they will receive it in full.

> ◆ God blesses those who are merciful, for they will be shown mercy.
>
> ◆ God blesses those whose hearts are pure, for they will see God.
>
> ◆ God blesses those who work for peace, for they will be called the children of God.
>
> ◆ God blesses those who are persecuted because they live for God, for the Kingdom of Heaven is theirs.

Blessed When You're Trashed? (Matthew 5:11–16)

Jesus closed out the beatitudes with these words: "God blesses you when you are mocked and persecuted and lied about because you are my followers." That only makes sense, as the teachings Jesus is about to give would set his followers apart in the world around them—not an easy thing to do in that culture.

Living Out the Law—Perfectly (Matthew 5:17–48)

Jesus told the people at his sermon that it was important for them to understand why he had come in the first place. He told them that he didn't come to abolish the law or the writings of the Old Testament prophets but to fulfill them. Jesus told those in the crowd that day that God's law would remain in place until it had fulfilled its purpose. He also encouraged the people to obey the law, telling them that those who kept the law would be rewarded in the afterlife.

But Jesus' approach to obeying the law was radically different from that of the religious authorities. His approach was not just to obey the *letter* of the law, but to obey the *spirit* of the law. He even went so far as to tell the people that if they didn't obey the spirit of the law, they would never make it to heaven.

Jesus also addressed some specific Jewish laws, giving his own spin on them:

Murder Begins in the Mind

Jesus taught that sin takes place in the heart first and that people who speak and act hatefully toward others are as guilty of murder as if they'd pulled the trigger. He told his followers that they should do all they could to make sure they were at peace with others and that they should seek to be reconciled with those they have offended and those who have offended them.

Adultery: Not Just a Deed

As with murder, Jesus taught that adultery was more than just "the act." He said that looking at a woman who is not your wife in a lustful way is just as bad as actually committing adultery with her. He also taught that divorce for any reason but marital infidelity is just as bad as adultery.

Promises, Promises

Jesus taught that making promises you don't intend to fulfill is wrong, so it's better just to say "yes I will" or "no I won't" when someone asks you for something. If you have to make a vow or promise, then it means your intentions aren't right. In short, don't make promises you don't intend to keep!

Revenge: It's So Old School!

The Law of Moses held that someone who had been injured by another had a legal right to vengeance. But Jesus taught that while you have that right, it is better not to seek revenge on those who have done you wrong. Instead, show God's kind of love by giving more of yourself, even to those who hurt you or try to take advantage of you.

Loving the Guy Who Wants to Help ... and Hurt

By the time Jesus arrived, the meaning of the Old Testament law "Love your neighbor" had undergone a lot of change. The authorities on the law taught that God wanted the Jews to love their neighbors (meaning other Jews) but hate their enemies (meaning those outside their cultural and religious worlds). But Jesus presented them with the radical idea of loving even those who hated them and persecuted them. Jesus pointed out that even the worst of sinners love those who love them in return, but that when those who followed him loved those who didn't love them back, they demonstrated the kind of love Jesus came to bring the world.

Can It Be Both Right *and* Wrong? (Matthew 6:1–18)

Jesus taught that being one of his followers meant living in a way different from the rest of the world. But he also taught that doing and saying all the right things didn't do one a bit of good in God's eyes if those things were done with the wrong motives.

Jesus called people who did even the best things but for the wrong reasons *"hypocrites."* In saying that, he was referring in the immediate case to the Pharisees, who obeyed the Law of Moses to the very letter. The Pharisees' problem as Jesus saw it? They did these things out of a sense of duty and personal gain, not out of love for God and for their fellow man.

A Secret Among the Three of Us

Jesus told his followers that when they give or help others, they should never do it for the applause or approval of others. Instead, "acts of kindness" should be done quietly, if possible, so that only the giver, the receiver, and God know what has been done.

Let's Come to Terms

When Jesus used the word **hypocrite,** he used a word that, in its original language, referred to a theatrical actor who plays a part. What he was referring to was people who tried to look "religious" by following laws and traditions but who didn't love God and their fellow man from the heart, the way they were commanded to in Old Testament law.

Keeping Prayer in the Closet

When it came to prayer, Jesus taught that it should be done in private (or as one translation says, "in the closet") without making a "show" out of it. Those prayers, he went on, should be from the heart and not through the repetition of "mantras," like the ones the hypocrites recited.

You Really *Can't* Take It with You (Matthew 6:19–34)

Jesus had some very direct words to say when it came to how those who followed him were approaching money and possessions. While he never condemned the acquisition of wealth, he did condemn making that a life focus.

Jesus told his listeners not to spend their lives pursuing earthly riches but rather to store everlasting treasures in heaven. He understood human nature, and he knew that part of that nature is the desire to accumulate "stuff" and to worry about how we are to pay our way here on earth. People can't focus on earthly wealth and on God at the same time, Jesus taught.

Some Really Relaxed Birds and Flowers

Jesus illustrated his point by using illustrations from the natural world. He told his followers that birds didn't worry about planting or harvesting, yet God feeds them every day. He also told them to look at the flowers in the nearby field, and remember that the lilies were far more beautiful than King Solomon in his finest royal robes.

If God took care of the birds and the flowers the people saw around them, Jesus taught, then they could rest assured that God would take care of them, who were much more important to him than any other thing of magnificent beauty that he created.

Jesus finished this point by speaking some of his better-remembered words: "Your Father already knows all your needs, and he will give you all you need from day to day if you live for him and make the Kingdom of God your primary concern" (Matthew 6:32–33).

> **His Name Is Jesus, a.k.a.**
>
> "The Rose of Sharon" (Song of Solomon 2:1). Jesus talks about the wildflowers and King Solomon in this illustration and is traditionally compared to the speaker in the sensuous love song of Solomon as the one who is both the rose of Sharon (a beautiful spot in Palestine) and the lily-of-the-valley, another lovely wildflower in his area.

> **W.W.J.K. (What Would Jesus Know?)**
>
> Jesus wasn't the first leader to give people the "Golden Rule." Socrates (Greek), Confucius (Chinese), and Hillel (Jewish) all had their own versions of this teaching. The difference between their teaching and Jesus', however, was that theirs came at it from a more negative standpoint. They all taught their followers *not* to do to others what they would *not* want done to them, and none of these men taught others to not resist their enemies.

You're Golden If You Keep the Rule (Matthew 7:1–12)

Jesus underscored all his teachings by telling the people, "Do for others what you would like them to do for you. This is a summary of all that is taught in the law and the prophets." This is what has come to be known as *the "Golden Rule"* for living.

Jesus warned his followers, "Stop judging others, and you won't be judged. For others will treat you as you treat them." He told the people to take care of their own problems and their own sins before they tried to "help" others see the error in their ways.

Jesus illustrated this rule by reminding the people that God was more than willing to meet their needs if they would just ask him. If they liked the fact that God treated them that way, then they should do the same for others.

Lose Weight to Get Through the Gate (Matthew 7:13-27)

As Jesus prepared to close out the Sermon on the Mount, he spoke some very direct words about who would enter heaven and who would not. He described the way to heaven, using the phrase "narrow gate," suggesting that there was only one way to heaven and that not very many people would be able to find it.

Jesus' words concerning the narrowness of the gates to get into the kingdom of God were a warning to those at the Sermon on the Mount first to shed the weight of their sins in order to squeeze through, and second to be wary of those who would try to lead them astray.

W.W.J.K. (What Would Jesus Know?)

When Jesus talked of entering heaven through "narrow gates," he was using language that the people of Palestine could easily understand. Nearly every town in Palestine was surrounded by walls and could be entered into only through gates, some of which were barred and could only be entered if someone were to first knock.

Time for Some Fruit Inspection (Matthew 7:15-23)

Jesus warned his followers to be careful of *"false prophets,"* those who appeared to be speaking and acting in the name of God but who were really wolves in sheep's clothing.

But how were the people to know the difference? Jesus explained that all it took was to look at the results of their words and deeds. Jesus used two of the most important food crops in Palestine at that time—grapes and figs—to make this point.

Jesus brought into his teaching that day some commonly known laws of nature and agriculture. He pointed out that good grapevines don't produce thistles and good fig trees don't yield thorns.

Go Ahead, Rock My World

Jesus finished the Sermon by making this very bold statement: "Anyone who listens to my teaching and obeys me is wise, like a person who builds a house on solid rock." That house,

His Name Is Jesus, a.k.a.

"Rock of My Salvation" (2 Samuel 22:47). This title demonstrates his strength and steadfastness. We don't trust in what we've done to get to heaven, but in what he has done, which is his death and resurrection—a work that is eternal and secure. If we build our life on his commands, the storms of life will not blow us away.

Jesus said, could withstand even the worst of storms, unlike the house built by the kind of person who wouldn't listen to his words and obey. That house, he said, would collapse and be washed away just as soon as a storm came.

Saying It with Style

When Jesus had finished teaching that day, the people in attendance were amazed not only at *what* he had said but at *how* he had said it. Matthew contrasts their response to his teaching to that of the Pharisees and Scribes, saying that the people recognized that Jesus spoke with authority like none they'd ever heard or seen in any religious leader.

The Least You Need to Know

- ◆ Jesus angered the religious authorities of his time when he gave them a "new" look at the Old Testament law.

- ◆ Jesus challenged the religious leaders' view of the Sabbath and what it was permissible to do on that day.

- ◆ When Jesus picked his 12 apostles, he didn't pick the most "religious" people but instead chose very ordinary men.

- ◆ Jesus gave what is considered the greatest "sermon" ever preached—the Sermon on the Mount.

Deep Compassion and Mysterious Stories

In This Chapter

- ◆ The healing of a Roman military leader's servant
- ◆ Raising a widow's son from the dead
- ◆ Jesus begins teaching in parables

Everywhere Jesus went, his reputation for doing miracles on behalf of those in need preceded him. There was never a shortage of people wanting him to perform a miracle, either for themselves or for someone who was close to them.

With the Sermon on the Mount behind him, Jesus returned to his "home away from home" in Capernaum, where a rather unexpected group of people—some Jewish religious leaders—asked him to do something. What made this story even more amazing is *who* needed the miracle.

A Gentile Who's a Gentleman (Matthew 8:5–13)

As Jesus walked into the city of Capernaum, he was met immediately by a group of some very respected Jewish leaders who begged him to come to the aid of a Roman *centurion*—a military officer—whose servant was very sick, in a lot of pain, and near death.

Most of the time, the Jews hated the Romans and especially their military. But this particular centurion was obviously well liked in Capernaum. He had shown great respect for the Jews and for their religion. "If anyone deserves your help, it is he," the Jewish leaders told Jesus. "He loves the Jews and even built a synagogue for us."

Gentiles who showed this kind of kindness and respect for the Jews and for their religion were highly regarded and well liked in Palestine, and because of this the Jewish leaders of Capernaum were willing to approach Jesus and ask him to help the man.

Whether it was through the stories that were making their way around Galilee or through the accounts of the religious leaders themselves, the Roman centurion knew that Jesus could help him.

> **Let's Come to Terms**
>
> **Centurions** were Roman military officers whose rank was roughly the same as captain in our modern military. Palestine was under Roman military rule at the time of Jesus, and there were soldiers in all the larger towns. The centurions led groups of about 100 men each.

> **His Name Is Jesus, a.k.a.**
>
> "Commander" (Joshua 5:14). The Roman centurion recognized Jesus as a leader and in fact he is given a similar military title in the book of Joshua. "The Commander of the Lord's Army" who was Jesus, the Son of God, before coming in the flesh, met Joshua in the appearance of an angel to strengthen him on his way to leading the Israelites in battle. Both the names Joshua and Jesus are the Hebrew for this very title.

I Don't Schmooze with the Jews

Either way, the centurion showed an understanding of Jewish laws and customs when he told Jesus, "Lord, don't trouble yourself by coming to my house, for I am not worthy of such an offer."

The centurion understood that since he was not a Jew, it would have gone against Jewish tradition for Jesus to enter his home. To do that would have rendered any Jew "ceremonially unclean." The most devout Jews of that time did not socialize with Gentiles, and the centurion probably didn't expect Jesus to come into his home.

But this particular military leader was more than willing to "meet Jesus halfway" if that's what it took to see his servant healed.

You Say "Jump," I Say "How High?"

The centurion told Jesus that if he would just "say the word," his servant would be healed, then acknowledged that Jesus' authority to heal was a lot like his authority over his soldiers and servants, only on a far greater scale.

"I have authority over my soldiers," he told Jesus. "I only need to say, 'Go,' and they go, or 'Come,' and they come. And if I say to my slaves, 'Do this or that,' they do it.'"

Heaven: Land of Equal Opportunity

Jesus understood what the man was saying and was amazed at his faith. He turned to the crowd following him and said, "I tell you, I haven't seen faith like this in all the land of Israel!"

Then Jesus told the people something many of them probably didn't understand, namely that there would be many non-Jewish people welcomed into the kingdom of heaven, simply because they showed the kind of faith in him the centurion had. On the other hand, he told them that there would be many from the nation of Israel who would never see the kingdom, because they had rejected the Messiah.

With the teaching surrounding this miracle complete, Jesus told the centurion that his faith would be rewarded. Within an hour, his young servant was healed.

Not long after Jesus healed the centurion's servant, he and his disciples, with the big crowd of followers in tow, visited a town called Nain. It was here that he would perform a miracle that would surpass that of any of the healings he had done to that point.

> **Let's Come to Terms**
>
> The village of **Nain** is believed to be a gated town at the site of the modern town of Nain, which is around six miles southeast of Nazareth.

You Can't Keep This Young Man Down (Luke 7:11–16)

As Jesus and his followers approached Nain, they were met by a large funeral procession. The one who had died was a young boy who was the only child of a widow in that town.

When Jesus saw this grieving woman, he felt deep compassion for her. He knew the sorrow she felt over the loss of her loved one, but he also understood that she would face a very difficult life with her son gone. But Jesus, like he always did for those who were in need, put action behind his feelings of compassion.

W.W.J.K. (What Would Jesus Know?)

In Jewish culture, widows were seen as being the most vulnerable and needy of all people, making them the objects of acts of compassion. That was especially true of a widow who had lost her only son, because there would be no one in the family left to support her.

Jesus went to the widow and comforted her. "Don't cry," he told her, as the funeral procession stopped. Jesus then walked over to her son's lifeless body.

In Jewish culture, when the dead were being taken to be buried, their bodies were anointed with spices, wrapped in cloth, and placed on a bier, or plank, so that they could be carried to the place of burial.

Jesus reached out and touched the bier, and spoke to the boy: "Young man," he said, "get up," and in an instant, the boy sat up and began talking. Jesus took him down from the bier and took him back to the arms of his waiting mother.

Naturally, the crowd of people from Nain, who up to that point had been mourning with the widow over her loss, was in a state of awe over what had happened. They had seen the hand of God at work before their very eyes, and it was the work of this Jesus from Nazareth.

A Baptist Behind Bars (Luke 7:18–35)

Stories of Jesus' miracles and teachings made their way not only around Galilee, but to Judea to the south. These reports apparently made their way to John the Baptist, who at the time was languishing in a prison for having offended Herod Antipas and his wife.

W.W.J.K. (What Would Jesus Know?)

John the Baptist had been thrown in prison by Herod Antipas, the Tetrarch of Galilee, who was enraged when John confronted him about his marriage to Herodius, the wife of his brother Philip. Herod was reluctant to execute John because he feared an uprising among the Jews but was later persuaded, through the actions of his wife, to have him beheaded.

The Messiah: Complex

John was having some doubts about whether Jesus was really the Messiah sent from God. So John sent two of his disciples to ask Jesus if he really was the Messiah.

When John's disciples arrived in Galilee, they witnessed up close and personal Jesus' miracles—healings of all kinds of diseases, restoring sight to the blind, and the casting out of demons.

After allowing them to see his work for themselves, Jesus sent the two back to John and asked them to tell him what they'd seen and heard. When they had gone, Jesus talked to his followers about John, explaining to them that he was the prophet sent to announce that Jesus was the long-awaited Messiah.

Everyone who heard Jesus talking about John agreed with what he had to say about him. Everyone, that is, except the Pharisees and Scribes.

Darned If We Do, Darned If We Don't

At this point, Jesus seemed genuinely irked with some of the people he had come to serve, comparing them to children playing games. After all, John the Baptist didn't drink wine and fasted often, and the religious leaders called him "demon possessed." Jesus, on the other hand, came into the world eating and drinking and they called him a glutton, a drunk, and a friend of the worst kinds of sinners.

What Do Weeds, Seeds, Pearls, and Nets Have in Common? (Matthew 13:1–52)

One day, Jesus left the house he was staying at in Capernaum and headed down to the shore of the Sea of Galilee. In no time at all, a huge crowd had gathered around him, so large that Jesus had to get into a boat, sit down, and begin teaching the people.

At the Sermon on the Mount, Jesus had given easy-to-understand principles for those who followed him to live by. But the teaching he gave that day from the boat was radically different from what the people were used to hearing from him.

Instead of using the direct-but-tough approach he had used before, Jesus began teaching through parables, stories that each had a different spiritual application for the people.

W.W.J.K. (What Would Jesus Know?)

Matthew points out in his gospel that Jesus' teaching in parables was the fulfillment of a Messianic prophecy, paraphrasing the psalmist Asaph: "I will speak to you in parables. I will explain mysteries hidden since the creation of the world" (Matthew 13:35).

What's the Story ... and *Why?*

When Jesus began making parables the foundation of his teaching, many of the people who followed him were confused. That included the disciples, who at first were really befuddled at what they were hearing.

Jesus explained to the disciples that his message was a spiritual one and that he had started using parables as a way to separate out those of his followers who weren't "in tune" with that message.

At that time, there were many people following Jesus who expected that he would be not only a healer and miracle worker, but a military leader much like Judah Maccabeas, who had brilliantly led the Jewish people in revolt against the rule of Antiochus Epiphanes.

However, Jesus hadn't come as a military leader but as peacemaker, miracle worker, teacher, prophet, and forgiver of sins, and he wanted only those who understood his message to follow him. This, he said, was in keeping with the prophecy of Isaiah:

> You will hear my words, but you will not understand; you will see what I do, but you will not perceive its meaning. For the hearts of these people are hardened, and their ears cannot hear, and they have closed their eyes—so their eyes cannot see, and their ears cannot hear, and their hearts cannot understand, and they cannot turn to me and let me heal them.
>
> —Matthew 13:14–15 (Isaiah 6:9–10)

More to This Than Meets the Eye

Although Jesus' parables weren't easy for everyone to understand, they were always based on things that Jesus and others who lived in that area had seen for themselves in everyday life.

For example, the first parable Matthew lists had to do with sowing seeds, something everyone in that area of the world had seen and something nearly everyone had probably taken part in for themselves.

It All Depends on Where You Sprout

Jesus' description of the process of sowing seeds was a very realistic one. The farmers of that time planted their fields by walking through them and scattering the seed by hand. Of course, not all of the seeds would land in the most favorable spots to take root and grow.

W.W.J.K. (What Would Jesus Know?)

Planting time in Palestine is around October, which was also about the time of year Jesus spoke his parable about the sower. Planting was always done by hand, with the farmer walking the field and scattering seeds in every direction.

Some of those seeds, Jesus pointed out, fell on the hardened soil of the paths that ran through the fields, and more often than not birds came and ate them. Others would land where there was just enough soil for them to sprout, but not enough for them to take root and grow. Still others landed among the weeds, which would later choke out the plants the farmer wanted to grow.

But some of the seeds would land in the good soil, where they could grow strong and healthy, giving the farmer a bumper crop, which of course he saw as a great blessing from God.

A Good Crop of Followers

Jesus always patiently explained his teaching to those who sincerely wanted to know what he was saying to them. When his disciples approached him and asked him what in the world he was talking about, he told them what his parable was really saying ... at least to those who listened closely.

Jesus explained that the "seed" in his parable represented his message. The hard ground that some of the seeds landed on represented those who refused to hear his message, and the shallow, rocky soil represented those who gladly heard the message but abandoned it when opposition or persecution came. The thorny areas where some of the seeds landed represented those who heard the message but were too concerned with making a living or getting rich to produce anything for the kingdom of God.

Finally, the good soil—where the seeds landed, grew, and produced such a good crop—represented those who heard, understood, and applied Jesus' message in such a way that they produced a good harvest for God's kingdom.

> ### His Name Is Jesus, a.k.a.
>
> "The Word of God" (John 1:1). Not only is the "seed" his message in this parable, but Jesus himself is the message or very word of God. Jesus told the Pharisees that they search the Scriptures for truth but the entire Scriptures point to him, because he himself is God's message to us. Or as John 1:1 says, "In the beginning the Word [Jesus] already existed ... and the Word was God."

To Kingdom Come

Jesus then continued his teaching through parables, but this time there was a different twist. He began his next parable using the words, "The Kingdom of Heaven is like..."

When Jesus spoke these parables, he wanted his followers to understand different principles and aspects of the kingdom he had come to bring them.

The first of these "kingdom parables" was similar to the Parable of the Sower, but with a different emphasis.

Infiltrated by the Enemy (Matthew 24–30, 36–43)

Jesus likened the kingdom of heaven to a farmer who had planted good wheat seeds in good soil, but whose efforts had been undermined by an enemy who snuck into his field late at night when the farmer was asleep and scattered weed seeds everywhere.

Of course, as the wheat seeds germinated and began to grow, the farmer's servants could see the problem. "Sir," they told him, "the field where you planted that good seed is full of weeds!"

Immediately, the farmer knew that this was the work of an enemy. He also knew what to tell his servants to do. Rather than have them go out and pull up the weeds, which would also hurt the wheat itself, he told them to leave the wheat alone and wait until the harvest to deal with the weeds.

When it was time to harvest the wheat, the farmer would order the harvesters to sort out the worthless weeds and burn them, then put the valuable wheat in storage.

When Jesus had finished these two parables, he left the boat and went to the house where he had been staying. But he wouldn't be there alone—at least not for long.

Jesus' disciples, again looking for some understanding of Jesus and his ministry, came to the house and asked him to explain what the parable of the wheat and weeds meant.

Look Out, You May Be in Deep Weeds

Jesus explained that in the parable of the wheat and weeds, the farmer represented him, the seed represented his message, and the field represented the people in the world around them.

The wheat that grew out of the good seeds were the people who had listened to Jesus' message and lived according to it, and the weeds were those who continued to live sinful lives. The "enemy" who had planted the weed seeds? That was the devil himself.

Jesus explained that all of the characters represented in his parable—the good people, the sinners, and the devil himself—would live in the same world, but that this would all change at the time of judgment. That is when the wheat and the weeds would be separated. The wheat would be "saved" while the weeds would be thrown into the fire.

This parable was one of several of Jesus' teachings that told his followers of eternal reward for the righteous and eternal punishment for the wicked.

More Symbols of the Kingdom

That day, Jesus taught the disciples using several other parables, all of which compared the kingdom of God with something the people who heard him could easily understand, even if they didn't get the message itself:

- ◆ **The Parable of the Mustard Seed** (Matthew 13:31–32), which compared the kingdom of heaven to the tiny mustard seed, which can grow so large that it can provide roosting and shelter for birds.

- ◆ **The Parable of** *Leaven* **(Yeast)** (Matthew 13:33), which compared the kingdom of heaven to yeast, which when it is used in the baking of bread affects the whole loaf and causes it to expand.

- ◆ **The Parable of the Hidden Treasure** (Matthew 13:44), in which Jesus tells his audience that his message was not only of great value but priceless, and that it was worth going to great effort to find it.

- ◆ **The Parable of the Pearl of Great Price** (Matthew 13:45–46), which compared the kingdom of heaven to a fine pearl, for which a pearl merchant will sell everything so he can acquire it.

> **Let's Come to Terms**
>
> Yeast—or **leaven** as some versions of the Bible call it—was almost always referred to negatively in the Bible. For example, God commanded that the bread eaten at the Passover Feast was to be unleavened (Exodus 12:8). Jesus himself used the word in the negative when he said, "Beware of the yeast of the Pharisees—beware of their hypocrisy."

- ◆ **The Parable of the Net** (Matthew 13:47–51), which compares Jesus' message to a fishing net, which will trap every kind of fish—useful and worthless alike. The edible fish would be kept, but the ones that were of no use would be tossed away.

Something Old, Something New

Jesus finished his parable teaching by telling the disciples, "Every teacher of religious law who has become a disciple in the Kingdom of Heaven is like a person who brings out of the storehouse the new teachings as well as the old" (Matthew 13:52).

Jesus never condemned anyone, including the most conservative religious leaders of his time, for their love of the Torah and the Old Testament prophets. In fact, he pointed out to his disciples that those who knew the law and prophetic writings of the Old Testament would be of great benefit to the kingdom of God.

When Jesus had finished this time of teaching through parables, he left the part of Galilee where he first used that kind of teaching. But Jesus continued to teach using parables, some of which you'll read about in the coming chapters of this book.

The Least You Need to Know

- ◆ Jesus demonstrated that his message was for Gentiles, too, when he healed the servant of a Roman centurion.

- ◆ Jesus showed both his compassion and his power by raising a young man from the dead.

- ◆ As his ministry progressed, Jesus changed his "teaching style" and used parables.

Showing the Disciples How It's Done

In This Chapter

- ◆ Jesus deals with violent storms
- ◆ Casting out demons, raising the dead, healing the sick
- ◆ Instructing and sending out the 12 apostles
- ◆ Jesus walks on the water

Jesus had already put in a long day of teaching in parables, but he had other things to tend to, so that afternoon he got in the boat and told his disciples, "Let's cross to the other side of the lake."

The 12 of them hopped into the boat, and they headed out away from the crowd. As they set sail, Jesus, by now exhausted, found a spot in the back of the boat, laid his head on a seat cushion, and took a nap.

This Guy Can Sleep Through *Anything* (Matthew 8:18–27)

The start of their journey across the lake started out peacefully enough, but it wasn't long before that routine trip across the lake—one the fishermen in the group had likely taken many times—became a struggle for survival.

As was common on the Sea of Galilee, a violent storm appeared almost out of nowhere, pounding the disciples' boat mercilessly.

The wind-driven waves nearly swamped the boat. We can picture the disciples doing everything they could to get through this trip alive—some of them on the oars trying desperately to keep the boat straight, and others bailing water out of the boat in what must have seemed like a futile attempt to keep it from sinking to the bottom of the lake.

The disciples were terrified. Many of them were fishermen and experienced sailors, and they had no doubt encountered storms, but this one had them at a point where they were sure they would die that day. With all of this going on, Jesus was still in the back of the boat, fast asleep.

Let's Come to Terms

The Sea of Galilee (also called Lake Kinneret, Lake Gennesaret, and the Sea of Tiberias in the Bible) is a body of water 27 miles inland (east) from the Mediterranean Sea and more than 680 feet below sea level. It is about 12½ miles long and 7½ miles wide at its widest point. It is surrounded by high mountains, and is notorious for sudden violent storms, which are caused when the subtropical winds from the Mediterranean Sea blow inland over the mountains and through the valleys into the area.

Complain About the Weather? He *Did* Something About It!

The disciples knew they were out of options, so they woke Jesus up by telling him (make that *screaming* to him) what was happening.

"Lord, save us! We're going to drown!" the disciple cried.

The disciples probably had no idea what Jesus could do to help their situation. All they knew was that he was their leader and that they had seen him do many other miracles.

With the wind howling, the waves pounding the boat, and the disciples panicking, Jesus simply got up from his nap, calmly surveyed the situation, and said "Quiet down!" Even more suddenly than it had arrived, the storm ended and everything was calm.

W.W.J.K. (What Would Jesus Know?)

The Bible doesn't tell us anything about the boat that Jesus and his disciples sailed in, not even who it belonged to. But recently, a fishing boat from around that time and place was discovered buried in the silt of the Sea of Galilee. It measured a little over 25 feet long and 7 feet wide. It could easily have accommodated four or five crew members as well as up to 10 passengers.

With the storm taken care of, Jesus turned to the disciples, who were probably soaked and shivering as they sat in the water-filled boat, and said, "Why are you so afraid? Do you still not have faith in me?"

Another Miracle That Rocked the Boat

The disciples had already seen Jesus perform miracle after miracle. Some of these miracles brought on great rejoicing and some brought controversy. They'd seen him cure diseases, cast out demons, and even raise people from the dead.

But stopping a storm in its tracks? That was almost too much for them to comprehend. "Who is this man, that even the wind and waves obey him?" they asked one another as they finished their trip to the other side of the lake.

A Man You Wouldn't Want to Meet in a Dark Alley (Luke 8:26–40)

When Jesus and his disciples reached the shoreline in a region called Gerasenes, they had no sooner stepped off the boat when they were confronted by a demon-possessed man.

This was not just an evil spirit, but a violent one, too. The people who lived in the area had tried to shackle the man with chains, but he broke them every time. The man was so deranged and so violent that people were afraid to go near him. The man was homeless and naked and had been living in the graveyard.

Let's Come to Terms

The word **legion**, as it appears in the gospel accounts of the demon-possessed man living among the tombs, refers to a Roman regiment of approximately 6,000 men.

W.W.J.K. (What Would Jesus Know?)

Many people today, including some theologians, have come to believe that the gospel accounts of demon possession were actually instances of people suffering from medical or psychological disease. However, the gospel accounts make a clear distinction between those things and demon possession.

When the demon-possessed man saw Jesus, he ran to him and fell at his feet and screamed, "Why are you bothering me, Jesus, Son of the Most High God? For God's sake, don't torture me!"

Jesus looked at the man and asked, "What is your name?" But he wasn't talking to the man himself, but to the evil spirits inside him. *"Legion,"* came the reply, "because there are many of us here inside this man."

This Exorcism Is Not Kosher!

The demons knew they were history as far as this man was concerned, so they begged Jesus not to send them to the bottomless pit (or hell) but to allow them to enter a herd of 2,000 pigs feeding on a nearby hillside. Jesus gave the demons permission to enter the pigs, showing that he had compassion even for those who were evil. But when they entered the pigs, the whole herd ran squealing down the steep hillside and plunged into the Sea of Galilee, where they drowned.

A Mixed Review for a Miracle

When the men tending to the herd of pigs saw what had happened, they were terrified and ran away from the scene, telling everyone what they had seen. The result of their commotion was that a crowd of people gathered around Jesus, wanting to know what had really happened.

But Jesus didn't have to say anything. All the people had to do was look at the man who before had been an object of terror for them. There he was, sitting at Jesus' feet—clothed and in his right mind.

You would expect these people to be amazed at what had happened, and that they were. But they were also afraid, so afraid that they asked Jesus to leave the area. Jesus did just that, and he never returned.

Say, Do You Have Room for a Thirteenth? (Mark 5:29–30)

When Jesus and his disciples returned to the boat, the newly healed man begged Jesus to allow him to come with them. But Jesus had another mission in mind for the man: "No, go home to your friends and tell them what wonderful things the Lord has done for you and how merciful he has been" (Mark 5:29).

Jesus and his disciples got in the boat and headed back across the sea to Capernaum, while the formerly demon-possessed man went to the Decapolis, where he told everyone he saw what had happened.

His Name Is Jesus, a.k.a.

"The Holy One of God" (Luke 4:34). To be "holy" means in the original language to be set apart from ordinary things for sacred use. In the Old Testament, vessels used in sacrificial ritual were washed to symbolize purification. Jesus was set apart as the only completely pure vessel (without any sin) that God could use to accomplish his purpose of providing salvation for those who were in themselves impure and not able to attain heaven on their own.

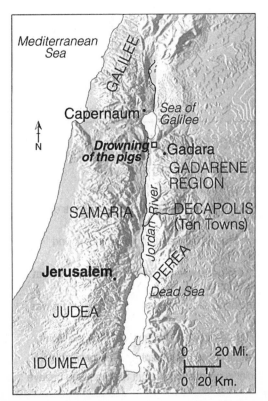

Jesus' miraculous power displayed.

(Copyright © 2001 Tyndale House Publishers)

When Desperation Turned into Faith (Luke 8:40–56)

Having given the formerly demon-possessed man his mission, Jesus and his disciples set sail back to Capernaum, where the people had been waiting for him.

They gave Jesus an enthusiastic greeting upon their return. One of those greeters was a man named Jairus, a leader of the local synagogue who had a very special need: His 12-year-old daughter was very sick and near death.

By this time in Jesus' ministry, many of the religious leaders had rejected his claims to be the Messiah. But Jairus knew about Jesus' reputation as a miracle worker, and he was ready to do whatever it took to see his daughter healed.

Jairus ran to Jesus, fell at his feet, and begged him to come to his home and see his little girl. Jesus was never one to turn down a request for healing, not from someone who was in need and who believed that he could do it. He agreed to go to Jairus's home and help his daughter.

Jairus got to his feet, then led Jesus and his disciples to home, where his daughter lay sick in bed.

His Name Is Jesus, a.k.a.

"Master of the Sabbath" (Matthew 12:8). Jesus who, claiming to be God, had invented the Sabbath, claimed the right to challenge the Pharisees interpretation of it as well as their added rules. By his miracles on the Sabbath, he showed that people can honor that day by doing good on the day set apart by God, rather than simply by doing nothing on that day.

Faith Overcomes Fear (Mark 5:37–43)

Jesus was on his way to Jairus's home when he and his disciples received the news that Jairus's daughter had died. Now, the messenger told him, there was no reason for Jesus to trouble himself with going to see her.

But Jesus wasn't about to allow a little thing like death to keep him from meeting the needs of a man with faith. "Don't be afraid," he told Jairus. "Just trust me."

Jesus stopped the crowd. Only he, Jairus, and his closest disciples—Peter, James, and John—would be seeing what was about to happen.

Who's Laughing Now?

When Jesus arrived at Jairus's home, he heard the dirges and the crying and grieving over the death of Jairus's little girl. But when Jesus told the people that Jairus's daughter wasn't dead but only sleeping, the crying was turned, at least for a moment, to incredulous laughter.

Jesus told everyone to leave, then took his disciples and the girl's parents into the room where her body lay. He took her by the hand and said "Get up, little girl!"

Immediately, she stood up and walked around. Her parents, of course, were overwhelmed with joy. The people outside? They were amazed—and probably a little red-faced—over having laughed at Jesus.

The Disciples' Marching Orders (Matthew 9:37–10:42)

After raising Jairus's daughter, Jesus continued his traveling ministry, with his disciples at his side. He preached, he taught, he healed, he cast out demons. During that time, the 12 men who were closest to Jesus saw him say and do some amazing things. But it was soon to be time for them to do some pretty amazing things themselves.

Jesus' ministry was based on compassion for lost people. He came to heal the lost, teach the lost, and to save the lost. One day he told his disciples, "The harvest is so great, but the workers are so few. So pray to the Lord who is in charge of the harvest; ask him to send out more workers for his fields."

A short time later, Jesus called his apostles together again to give them some very important instructions concerning their going out for "the harvest."

Jesus wasn't going to just send them out to fend for themselves. He not only gave them specific instructions but also gave them the power and authority of the Holy Spirit to do the kinds of things he himself had been doing.

First Class Mission, Economy Class Travel

Jesus was very specific in instructing his apostles that theirs would be a ministry of outreach to the Jews only. They were not to go to the Gentiles or the Samaritans. The outreach to those people groups would take place later.

They were to go out and preach the same message that Jesus—and John the Baptist before him—had preached: "The Kingdom of Heaven is near." They were to heal the sick, raise the dead, and cast out demons, just like Jesus had been doing all along.

Jesus told the disciples not to take any money, luggage, or even extra clothes or sandals. Instead, they were to rely on the hospitality of those they preached to.

Jesus told the disciples that if the people in a certain village or city refused to hear their message, they were to simply "shake off the dust of that place from their feet" and move on.

Persecution and Prosecution

Jesus made sure the disciples knew that theirs would be a difficult mission. They would be taking their message to people who didn't want to hear what they had to say and who might respond negatively, even violently, to the message.

Jesus wanted his disciples to prepare themselves for persecution and prosecution by local Jewish courts and by the government authorities.

Jesus told his disciples that the message they would be taking with them as they traveled throughout the Jewish world that would cause some pretty serious division among the Jewish brothers and sisters.

He went on to tell them that they would be hated because of their association with him, but that they were to endure that persecution, knowing that they were no greater than their teacher, who had to endure the same things.

The Pay's Not Great, but the Benefits Are Heavenly

The disciples weren't to be afraid of those who could do no more than kill them physically. The only one they had to fear, Jesus said, was God himself, who had the authority to both kill the body and to condemn the soul but who also was so lovingly involved in their lives that he knew how many hairs each of them had on their heads.

He told them that if they endured the opposition that was ahead of them, they would be welcomed with open arms into the kingdom of heaven.

You Deserve a Break Today ... but You Won't Get It (Mark 6:30–44)

When the disciples returned from their tours of ministry, they excitedly told Jesus what they had done and taught. (Don't bother looking up what they did and said or how long they were gone. The gospels don't say.)

Jesus must have seen that the disciples needed a break, because he said, "Let's get away from the crowds for a while and rest." But try as they might, Jesus and the disciples couldn't get away from the crowds of people even long enough to grab a bite to eat.

We Gotta Make Some Bread, Man (John 6:1–13)

Finally, around dinnertime one evening, the disciples and the crowd were all hungry. The problem as the disciples saw it? They were out in the wilderness, and there

wasn't any food available to feed everyone. And even if there were enough food,
they didn't have the money to pay for it.
They were looking at feeding 5,000 men,
plus women and children. It's hard to say,
but there might have been as many as
20,000 people in the crowd.

The disciples had a pretty simple solution
to the problem: Just send the people into
town to get their own dinner. But Jesus had
another plan. He simply told the disciples,
"You feed them." The disciples might have
responded, "Yeah, right!"

Jesus sent the disciples out into the crowd to
see if anyone had any food they could spare.
Only one of them, a young boy, had anything.
Even at that, it wasn't even close to being
enough to feed this many people—just five
loaves of barley bread and a couple of sardines.

W.W.J.K. (What Would Jesus Know?)

The miracle of the feeding of
the 5,000 was the only miracle Jesus did that is recorded in
all four gospels. It is recorded
in Matthew 14:15–21, Mark
6:30–44, Luke 9:12–17, and
John 6:5–14.

Let's Come to Terms

Loaves of bread in
the culture in which Jesus lived
weren't "loaves" in the sense that
we think of them: big slabs of
bread you keep in the cupboard
for up to a week. The loaves
Jesus used in this miracle were
actually about the size of large
biscuits, making them easy to
carry in a pack.

The Miracle That Keeps on Giving

It wasn't much—in fact, it might as well have been nothing—but it was all Jesus
needed. He took the bread and the fish, blessed it, and started giving … and giving …
and giving. And when he was done doing that, he gave some more. When dinnertime
was finished, everyone in the crowd had eaten his or her fill. Not only that, when the
disciples went around picking up the leftovers, they collected 12 baskets of bread and
fish.

A Draft-Dodger of a Different Kind (John 6:14–15)

Of course the people Jesus had just fed were amazed at what had just happened, and
they were sure that he was the Prophet-Messiah they had been waiting for. They
wanted to draft him as their king.

In their minds, it was time for them to follow Jesus' lead and get rid of the rule of the
Romans. But to them, it wasn't just a matter of following Jesus; they were going to
take him by force and make him their king.

That, however, was not a part of Jesus' plan—at least not in the way these people saw it happening. Jesus knew he and his disciples needed to get away from this scene, so he told the 12 to get in the boat and head for Capernaum while he went into the hills for some time alone with the Father.

Taking the Red-Eye to Capernaum (Matthew 14:22–36)

The disciples hung around the shoreline, waiting for Jesus to come down from the hills. But when nightfall had come and he still hadn't shown up, they decided to head for Capernaum by boat and meet up with him later.

W.W.J.K. (What Would Jesus Know?)

Some versions of the Bible say that Jesus appeared to the disciples on the Sea of Galilee "about the fourth watch." The Roman military divided the 12 hours of the night into four three-hour "watches," the last of which was from 3 to 6 A.M.

As the disciples made their way across the sea, another one of those sudden Sea of Galilee windstorms hit the lake. The disciples were rowing hard, trying to make progress, but they were barely moving against what must have been a very strong headwind. The disciples were in trouble. Around three in the morning, they had only made it to the middle of the lake. By this time, they must have wondered once again if they were going to make it through the night alive.

A New Kind of Late-Night Stroll

These 12 men had been in the same kind of situation before. This time, however, Jesus was nowhere to be seen. Then, suddenly, the disciples spotted something on the water. It looked like a man, but they knew that men don't walk *on* the water. The disciples screamed in fear, thinking what they were seeing was a ghost, something the sailors in the group knew meant trouble for them.

But then they heard a voice telling them, "It's all right. I am here! Don't be afraid." They all knew that voice. It was Jesus, and he was walking toward them … *on the water.*

If God Is My Co-Pilot, Maybe I'll Take the Train This Time (Matthew 14:28–33)

The disciples were all relieved—and no doubt amazed—that Jesus had come to them. But one of them wanted more out of the experience. Peter, the most impetuous one of the bunch, called out, "Lord, if it's really you, tell me to come to you by walking on the water."

Jesus called back and told Peter to come to him, so Peter left the other 11 disciples behind and stepped over the side of the boat and onto the water. At first, he stood on the water like a baby taking its first steps. But when he looked around him and saw the wind-whipped waves, he was terrified.

Peter was sinking like a rock when he cried out, "Lord, save me!" Instantly, Jesus reached out his hand and pulled him to safety. "You don't have much faith," Jesus told Peter as they got back in the boat. "Why did you doubt me?"

The moment Jesus and Peter stepped back into the boat, the wind and the waves stopped, and the disciples exclaimed, "You really are the Son of God!"

Jesus walks on the water.

(Copyright © 2001 Tyndale House Publishers)

The Least You Need to Know

- ◆ Jesus performed many miracles around the Sea of Galilee, including calming a storm, walking on the water, and feeding thousands with next to no food.

- ◆ Jesus performed miracles for a wide range of people, including Jewish religious leaders and even Romans.

- ◆ Jesus gave his apostles the very difficult mission of taking his message to the Jewish world around them.

Chapter 13

Setting the Stage for the Main Event

In This Chapter

- ◆ Jesus calls himself the "bread of life"
- ◆ Peter's confession then scolding of Jesus and Jesus' response
- ◆ Jesus is transfigured on a high mountain in Galilee
- ◆ Jesus comes to make the blind see, and vice-versa

After Jesus had fed the 5,000 on the shoreline of the Sea of Galilee, many people continued following him. Not long after he had performed that miracle, a large crowd met him at the synagogue in Capernaum. Sadly, they weren't there because they wanted to hear his teaching, but because they were hoping to be fed again.

Jesus indeed gave them bread that day, but it wasn't the kind he had given them earlier. This bread had much more of an eternal flavor.

Some Food for Thought (John 6:26–59)

Jesus very honestly told the people in the crowd that they had followed him only because he had fed them, and not because they had seen the miracle it took to feed them. He went on to say that they should stop worrying about temporary things like food and start focusing on what was eternal. The people heard what Jesus had said, then asked him what God wanted them to do. So he very plainly told them that they were to believe in the one God had sent for them—Jesus himself.

Let's Come to Terms

Manna refers to the bread from heaven that God gave the people of Israel during their journey to the Promised Land, as recorded in Exodus 16:4. God told Moses that the people could go out daily and pick up as much of the bread as they needed for the day. The people who were at the scene when Jesus called himself the "bread of life" were well aware of that Old Testament story.

Jesus told his followers that the "bread" he had come to give them was the kind of bread that gave them eternal life. He even contrasted his kind of bread with the *manna* God had given the people of Israel as they wandered in the wilderness centuries before. The people who ate that manna, he said, still died, but the bread he was giving them gave them eternal life.

Isn't This Getting Too Personal?

Of course, not everyone in the crowd was tracking with Jesus on this point. Many of them were from Nazareth and had known Jesus since he was a boy. They just couldn't believe that he had been sent from God, let alone that he could give them bread that led to eternal life.

But Jesus took his point even further by telling them that the bread of life he had been talking about was his actual flesh, which had been given to them so that they could live eternally. The people still didn't understand what he was telling them, so he went on to say, speaking very figuratively, that unless they ate his flesh and drank his blood, they would never go to heaven.

Don't Take Me *Too* Literally

After Jesus finished talking to the crowd, he met with his disciples (we're talking about the 12, as well as the others who had followed Jesus and listened to his teaching up to that point), who asked him what he had meant.

Jesus told them, "The very words I have spoken to you are spirit and life," meaning that they weren't to be taken literally but on a spiritual level. He explained that the things he said were meant for those who had spiritual understanding, which God himself would give to those who believed in him.

Jesus' words that day were simple but hard. He wanted the people following him to understand that he had come to give people a way to come to God, a way to eternal life. In the end, however, many of his disciples were offended at what he said about his body and blood—or just couldn't understand it—and deserted him.

However, many of Jesus' disciples had minds that could grasp what he was saying, including the Big Twelve. They were the ones who would stay with him for the long haul.

The Greatest Question Ever Asked (Matthew 16:13–19)

Jesus got into a boat with the disciples and crossed the Sea of Galilee to an area that included the villages of Magadan and Dalmanutha, which were near the westernmost point of the lake.

From there, Jesus continued his traveling ministry around Galilee. Later on, they headed to a place called *Caesarea Philippi*, where Jesus would reveal to the disciples things about him they hadn't yet realized.

One day when they were in the area of Caesarea Philippi, Jesus asked the disciples, "Who do people say that the Son of Man is?"

God, Prophet, or Megalomaniac?

By this time, there were many opinions about who Jesus really was. Many people believed he really was the Messiah, but others thought he was just another impostor who claimed to be the Messiah and they wouldn't listen to him any more. Still others believed he was a prophet of Israel's past, returned to lead them.

Let's Come to Terms

Caesarea Philippi was located in the extreme northern part of Palestine, to the north/northeast of the Sea of Galilee. It was near the headwaters of the Jordan River and near the base of Mt. Hermon. Caesarea Philippi was governed by Herod Philip, one of Herod the Great's three sons. Philip had rebuilt the city in honor of Tiberius Caesar and named it Caesarea Philippi, after his own name, to distinguish it from a Mediterranean coast town also called Caesarea.

The disciples told Jesus that they'd been hearing word that some thought he was John the Baptist, who had been executed by Herod Antipas just a few months before, come back to life. Others had been saying that Jesus was a "second coming" of the prophet Elijah, who the Jews believed would reappear prior to the arrival of their Messiah. Still others were saying that Jesus was Jeremiah or one of the other Old Testament prophets.

Oh Lord, I Just Figured It Out!

Now that the disciples had told Jesus who others had said they believed he was, he asked them very directly who *they* believed he was. Peter, who was never one to keep what he was thinking to himself, spoke up and said, "You are the Messiah, the Son of the living God."

Jesus praised Peter for having the insight to know who he was and told him that he didn't know these things because he was smarter than other people. Rather, Jesus told Peter that God himself had revealed Jesus' identity to him. He went on to tell Peter that his confession of Jesus as Lord or Messiah would be the way of entry into the Kingdom of God, which would be established after Jesus' death and resurrection.

Let's Come to Terms

Peter, whose name in Aramaic (*Cephas*) means "Rock," would be the leading figure in the establishment of the church, first in Jerusalem then in the rest of the Jewish world. Legend has it that he died a martyr's death in Rome by being crucified upside down, claiming he wasn't worthy to die in the same way as his Lord.

Key places in Jesus' ministry.

Copyright © 2001 Tyndale House Publishers

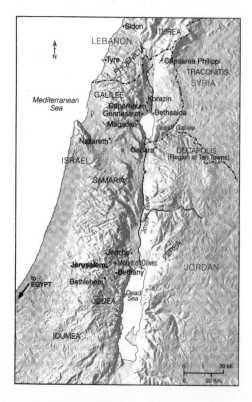

But Peter was soon to find out that the Jesus who called him "blessed" was also more than willing to call him out on the carpet when he refused to hear Jesus telling them how he would establish his spiritual kingdom.

The Good Times Won't Roll Forever

From the time Peter identified Jesus as the Messiah, Jesus began filling the apostles in on what would become of him. He explained to them that one day he would enter Jerusalem, where he would suffer at the hands of the religious leaders. He told them that he would die but that he would be raised from the dead three days later.

But Peter didn't like what he was hearing. There was no way Jesus was going to die, not if Peter had anything to say about it. He took Jesus aside and privately told him that something like that would never happen to him.

But Jesus knew his mission on earth, and he knew it was time to put Peter in his place as a follower: "Get away from me, Satan!" he said. "You are a dangerous trap to me. You are seeing things merely from a human point of view and not God's."

> **His Name Is Jesus, a.k.a.**
>
> "Savior" (1 John 4:14). John Newton, the former slave-trader turned pastor who wrote the famous hymn "Amazing Grace," said, "I remember two things: that I am a great sinner and that Christ is a great Savior." The world is full of converted people like Newton whose lives have been turned upside down for good by the saving power of Christ.

This Is Not a Rose-Strewn Path

Jesus then gave his disciples the following stern and direct words about what part they would play in the establishment of his kingdom, and also what it means for anyone to follow him:

- ◆ "If any of you wants to be my follower, you must put aside your selfish ambition, shoulder your cross, and follow me" (Matthew 16:24).

- ◆ "If you try to keep your life for yourself, you will lose it. But if you give up your life for me, you will find true life" (Matthew 16:25).

- ◆ "How do you benefit if you gain the whole world but lose your own soul in the process? Is anything worth more than your soul?" (Matthew 16:26).

- ◆ "I, the Son of Man, will come in the glory of my Father with his angels and will judge all people according to their deeds" (Matthew 16:27).

Jesus finished this time of teaching by telling the disciples that some of them would not die before they saw him coming in his kingdom. Some scholars believe that this meant the coming of the Holy Spirit into the apostles after Jesus' death, when he would be reigning in glory at the right hand of the father in heaven. Then, he took three of them to the top of a mountain, where he would show them a glimpse of that heavenly kingdom.

You Look Positively Glowing (Matthew 17:1–9)

Six days after Peter's confession of Jesus as the Messiah and the conversation that followed, Jesus took Peter, James, and John to the top of a high mountain in Galilee, where he was about to demonstrate to them who he really was.

W.W.J.K. (What Would Jesus Know?)

The gospels don't tell us what mountain in Galilee was the site of Jesus' Transfiguration. Tradition held it that the Transfiguration took place on Mt. Tabor, but that is not likely, as there was a town on the top of Mt. Tabor. It is more likely that this scene took place on Mt. Hermon, by far the highest (almost 10,000 feet) peak in Palestine. That would make sense, since Caesarea Philippi, the scene of Peter's confession, was near the southern slope of Mt. Hermon.

Once the four of them reached the top of the mountain, probably the better part of a day's climb, Jesus began praying. At that moment, Jesus' appearance changed.

Peter, James, and John, all exhausted from the long climb up the mountain, had dozed off while Jesus was praying. But when they awoke, they saw a glorified Jesus—the way he will look as we see him in heaven. His face glowed as bright as the sun, and his clothes were a brilliant white.

Peter Thinks He's Got a Bright Idea

At that moment, Moses and the prophet Elijah appeared, and they began talking to Jesus about how he would fulfill God's plan of salvation for humankind by dying in Jerusalem. As the three apostles watched Jesus, Moses, and Elijah talking in the absolutely blinding light they were terrified. Peter, trying to hide his fear, suggested to Jesus that they build three shrines—one for Jesus, one for Moses, and one for Elijah.

Just as Peter was talking, a bright cloud appeared overhead, and a voice came out of the cloud saying, "This is my beloved Son, and I am fully pleased with him. Listen to him." The sound of that voice scared Peter, James, and John so bad that they cowered face down on the ground.

Jesus walked over to the trembling apostles, touched them, and told them to get up and not to be afraid. When they looked up, all they saw was Jesus standing there looking at them. Moses and Elijah were gone.

> **Let's Come to Terms**
>
> The apostle Peter made reference to this **Transfiguration** experience in 2 Peter 1:18: "We ourselves heard the voice when we were there with him on the holy mountain."

What's Elijah Got to Do with This?

As Jesus and the three disciples headed back down the mountain to rejoin the other nine apostles, Jesus told them not to tell anyone—not even the other apostles—what they had seen that day but to keep it to themselves until after his resurrection. He didn't want to draw attention to himself prematurely. In his humility, Jesus never focused on himself but only on what the Father wanted, but he did want these disciples to get a glimpse of his glory so they would better understand who he is.

As they made their way down the mountain, the disciples had some questions for Jesus concerning what they had just seen. They asked Jesus about the prophecies of Elijah's return to prepare the people for the coming of the Messiah. Jesus told them that Elijah would be coming. In fact, he had already come but was mistreated and killed because people didn't recognize him as God's messenger. Jesus also told them that he himself would soon suffer in the same way and at the hands of the same people.

John, the Mystery Man, Revealed

At that moment, the disciples realized that Jesus was talking about John the Baptist, who had fulfilled the prophecies of the second coming of Elijah when he came and ministered and taught in very much the same way as Elijah had.

Once Jesus, Peter, James, and John joined the others at the foot of the mountain, Jesus continued teaching them and clarifying to them what was going to be happening to him.

Jesus' ministry in Galilee was about to come to a close. For the next several months, Jesus taught, performed miracles, had some conflicts with religious leaders, and prepared his disciples to go to Judea.

Jesus travels toward Jerusalem.

(Copyright © 2001 Tyndale House Publishers)

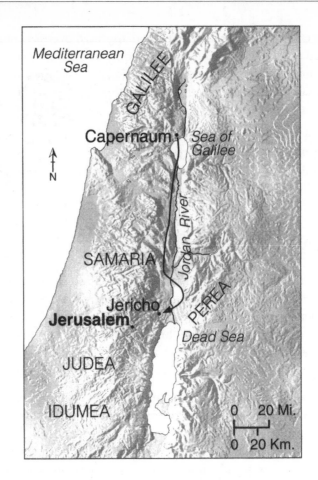

To the Bad Hat Brothers: You Go on Ahead (John 7:1–52)

Jesus had stayed out of Judea because he knew that there were Jewish religious leaders in Jerusalem who were plotting to have him killed because of the claims he had been making about himself.

When it was time for the Feast of Tabernacles, which was held around September of our calendar, Jesus' brothers encouraged him to go to Jerusalem for the celebration so that his followers could see him perform miracles. But they said this sarcastically, because they didn't believe Jesus was the Messiah.

Jesus told his brothers to go on ahead to the feast without him. When they left, Jesus remained in Galilee for a short time. It wasn't long before he headed to Jerusalem himself, but he did it apart from the caravans of Jews who would be heading south from Galilee to Jerusalem. He did that so he could escape notice—at least for the time being.

A Wanted Man, Though We're Not Sure Why

Around the time of the Feast of Tabernacles, the Jewish authorities looked for Jesus but couldn't find him. Finally, Jesus made his presence known to them. That he did about halfway through the festival, when he showed up at the holy Temple and began teaching.

When Jesus spoke to the people at the Temple, he told them very plainly that God had sent him and that they needed to turn to God. His teaching was met with a wide array of responses. Some people saw the miracles he performed and believed that he was the Messiah. Others believed he was a prophet, and still others wanted him arrested.

The Pharisees and leading priests of the Temple heard the things people were saying about Jesus and sent Temple guards to arrest him. But even the guards were amazed at Jesus' teaching and couldn't arrest him. Basically, everyone wondered how he could have such learning and wisdom when he had never been taught in an advanced or formal way.

Bread, Water, and Light—Life's Essentials

Jesus tried to convey during this period of his ministry that without him (as God) sustaining them, they would have no spiritual life and would be in darkness. He said he was the bread of life to feed them, the light of the world to guide them, and he also spoke of rivers of living water to slake their thirst for God. This living water was actually the Holy Spirit, or third person of the trinity, that would dwell within them after Jesus left this world. (More on that later.)

Caught in the Act (John 8:1–11)

When the Feast of Tabernacles was over, Jesus went to a place the Gospel of John called the Mount of Olives for the night. The next day, he was back at the Temple, teaching a crowd of people who had come to hear him.

As Jesus was teaching the people, a group of Scribes and Pharisees brought to Jesus a woman caught in the very act of adultery. It does take two to tango, but they didn't bring the man who had committed adultery with her.

With a crowd of people looking on, the Scribes and Pharisees pointed out to Jesus that the Law of Moses said that anyone caught in the act of adultery was to be stoned to death. Then they asked him what he would have them do with the woman.

W.W.J.K. (What Would Jesus Know?)

The Mount of Olives is a 2-mile-long flat-topped ridge of a hill east of the city of Jerusalem. It rises above 200 feet over the city and was one of Jesus' favorite places to go when he was in Judea. In the Old Testament book of Zechariah, the prophet identified the Mount of Olives as the place where God would begin to redeem those who had died come Judgment Day. It is also the site of many events of Jesus' life.

The Stones That Backfired

By this time, stonings for offenses like adultery were very rare in the Jewish world of Palestine. But the Pharisees probably had no intention of killing the woman. They just wanted to trap Jesus by getting him to say something they could use against him.

Jesus didn't say anything right away. He just stooped down and began writing something in the dirt with his finger. For centuries, people have tried to figure out what he wrote, but the gospels don't tell us. Perhaps it was the names of some of their mistresses, as some conjecture.

W.W.J.K. (What Would Jesus Know?)

The Scribes and Pharisees who brought the woman caught in the act of adultery were right in saying that the Law of Moses required that adulterers be put to death (Leviticus 20:10). But what they forgot, or conveniently overlooked, was that the law also required that those who witnessed the act were to be the ones to cast the first stone (Deuteronomy 17:5–7).

Finally, Jesus stood up, looked at the Pharisees, and told them, "All right, stone her. But let those who have never sinned throw the first stone." Then he went back to writing in the dirt.

The plan of the Pharisees and Scribes to trap Jesus had backfired in a big way. In fact, they felt embarrassed at what they had tried to do. So instead of pressing the issue any further, they left the scene one by one until only Jesus and the woman remained.

This Woman Gets a Complete Makeover

Jesus wasn't done with this woman, either. He stood up again and looked at her and asked her where her accusers were and if anyone had condemned her to die. When she acknowledged that they were all gone and that no one was there to condemn her, Jesus told her that he didn't condemn her either but that she was to go and leave her sinful lifestyle. She needed to become a completely new woman by repenting and trusting in God to change her.

In this one incident, Jesus demonstrated wisdom, compassion, and the willingness to forgive even the worst of sins. But he also showed that by this time in his ministry, he was willing to offend and even embarrass the Jewish religious leaders who tried to trap him.

Another "On Site" Healing (John 9:1–41)

One day not long after Jesus' encounter with the religious leaders and the adulterous woman, he and his disciples were walking around Jerusalem when they saw a man near the Temple who had been born blind. He had never seen anything, not even his own mother's face. In fact, he didn't even know what sight was! Like so many people in those kinds of circumstances, this man made his living by begging.

Rather than let the poor man remain sightless and dependent on the good will of the people around him, Jesus stopped to heal him. In the process, he had a chance to teach his disciples some things about himself. In the process, he also created another storm of controversy between himself and the Pharisees.

Here's Mud in Your Eye

In the Jewish culture of Jesus' time, people believed that when something bad happened to people, it was often because they had sinned and brought God's judgment on themselves. The disciples assumed that this man's blindness was a form of judgment from God. To them, the only question was whose sin it was—mom's or dad's—that caused the man to be born blind.

But Jesus told these men that the man's blindness had nothing at all to do with sin—his or his parents'. He didn't tell them that the man's parents had never sinned. Rather, he told them that the man was born blind so that Jesus' power and identity could be demonstrated in front of the disciples and the rest of the population of Jerusalem.

When Jesus had finished explaining those things to his disciples, he did something that seems very strange to us. He stooped down, spat on the ground, made mud out of the dirt and spit, then smeared it in the man's eyes.

W.W.J.K. (What Would Jesus Know?)

The Pool of Siloam (Siloam means "Sent") was a 53-foot-long rock basin that was fed by an underground spring. The pool can be seen in Jerusalem to this day.

Jesus then told the blind man to go the Pool of Siloam, which was not far from the Temple, and wash the mud out of his eyes. The man did just that, and when he came back to Jesus, he could see.

That must have been an incredible day for the man who had been born blind. But his healing was just the beginning of what would be a very busy day for him.

A Seeing Man in Blind Man's Clothing

The appearance of this former beggar confused some of the people in Jerusalem. Some of them wondered out loud if that was the same man they had so many times seen begging near the Temple. Others thought it wasn't him, just someone who looked a lot like him.

The man kept insisting that he was the same one who used to be blind, and he even explained that a man named Jesus had put mud in his eyes then told him to go wash at the pool. When he did that, he could see.

But the people still didn't know quite what to make of this man's story, so they took him to the synagogue, where the Pharisees questioned the man about who had healed him and how.

Jesus, Take a Sabbatical!

When the man who could now see first appeared before the Pharisees, he told them the same story he had told the people on the streets of Jerusalem.

The Pharisees had a huge issue with his story. It just so happened that Jesus had healed the blind man on the Sabbath, which in the Pharisees' eyes meant that Jesus couldn't have been from God. After all, if he had been sent from God, he would have known better than to "work" on the Sabbath by healing this man.

The Pharisees continued questioning the man again and asked him who he thought the one who had healed him was. The man told them that he must be a prophet.

Parental Guidance Suggested

The Pharisees were in a state of confusion as a group over what had happened that day. Obviously, a man who could give sight to a man born blind had to be from God. But on the other hand, if he healed the man on the Sabbath, he couldn't have been from God because a man God had sent would know better than to work on the Sabbath.

To them, the obvious conclusion had to be that this man hadn't been born blind at all. So they called the man's parents to the synagogue to further check out the story.

The formerly blind man's parents, who were afraid of what the Pharisees might do to them if they said anything positive about Jesus, were willing to concede that he was their son and that he had been born blind. Beyond that, they said, the Pharisees would need to ask him about what happened for themselves.

Can't You Guys See the Point?

The Pharisees' questioning of the man's parents got them nowhere, so they called the man himself back to the synagogue. This time, they tried to get him to say that Jesus was a sinner because he had healed on the Sabbath.

That, too, got the Pharisees nowhere. Instead of saying that Jesus was a sinner because he had healed on the Sabbath, he pointed out that if Jesus hadn't been from God, there is no way he could have given him his sight. Nobody had ever opened the eyes of a man born blind.

Frustrated that they couldn't get the man to answer their questions the way they wanted him to, the Pharisees threw him out of the synagogue.

> **His Name Is Jesus, a.k.a.**
>
> "The Light of the World" (John 9:5). As Jesus was about to heal this blind man, he declared that he was the light of the world. He claimed that only he could restore our spiritual sight and dispel the darkness that comes from rebellion to God. Later, in one of his letters, this same apostle John says that only he who truly loves his neighbor walks in the light of God—otherwise, he stumbles around in spiritual darkness.

Double Vision: Physical *and* Spiritual

When Jesus got word that the man he had healed of blindness had been thrown out of the synagogue, he went out to look for him. When he found the man, he asked him if he believed in the Son of Man. "Who is he, sir, because I would like to," came the reply.

Jesus told him that the one he saw standing in front of him was the Son of Man, and the formerly blind man told Jesus that he believed he was the Messiah and worshipped him.

Then Jesus said something that both identified himself to the man and that also was a bit of a verbal dig at the Pharisees, who were standing there listening to the exchange: "I have come to give sight to the blind and to show those who think they see that they are blind."

Of course, the Pharisees were offended at what Jesus had said. He was basically telling them that they were spiritually blind because they couldn't see that God had sent him to be the Messiah and that he was the Son of God.

The Proof Is Before Your Eyes

Jesus held fast to his message. Later on, during the Feast of Dedication (held in our December) he spelled it out in very direct words for the Pharisees. He told them that the things he had been doing were proof enough that his Father God had sent him to be the people's Messiah. For that reason, some of the Jewish leaders were ready to kill him on the spot on the charge of blasphemy against God.

Jesus left the city of Jerusalem, but it was only a matter of time before the Jewish leaders would find a reason to arrest him, charge him with blasphemy, and try him. That, however, would happen at a time of Jesus' own choosing.

The Least You Need to Know

- When Jesus asked the disciples who they believed he was, Peter said that he was the Messiah and the Son of God.

- Jesus showed three of the disciples his "divine side" at the Transfiguration.

- Jesus continued to divide opinion in Jerusalem, where he taught, forgave sins, and healed people.

- Jesus came to make the spiritually blind see, and those who thought they already could see spiritual truth to be made blind.

Chapter 14

Love, Prayer, and Getting a New Lease on Life

In This Chapter

- Jesus teaches what love really means in the parable of the Good Samaritan
- The disciples learn what prayer should look like as Jesus gives them The Lord's Prayer
- Jesus befriends two sisters, Mary and Martha, and their brother Lazarus
- Jesus raises his friend Lazarus, who had died four days earlier, from the dead

After Jesus left Jerusalem—following the Jewish religious leaders' plans to kill him or have him arrested for claiming to be the Messiah—he continued his ministry in other parts of the region, continuing his teaching and miracle working.

The exact sequence of events during this time in Jesus' life have been debated for centuries. With four gospel accounts—some of which treat parts of Jesus' life in more of a topical rather than sequential way—it's difficult to tell for certain exactly what order many of these events took place.

What we do know, however, is that they *did* take place and that they tell us a lot about who Jesus was, what he did, and how he taught.

One of the better known and more important of these events was when he taught a very well-educated man about the true meaning of God's kind of love, using the Parable of the Good Samaritan.

You Can't Choose Your Neighbors (Luke 10:25–37)

One day, Jesus was teaching a crowd of people when a scholar in Jewish religious law approached him with a test. He knew of Jesus' reputation as a teacher, so he asked Jesus what he had to do to receive eternal life. Jesus turned the man's question around and asked him what the Old Testament law said he must do to gain eternal life. The man answered by quoting from the Torah: "You must love the Lord your God with all your heart, all your soul, all your strength and all your mind" and "Love your neighbor as yourself" (Deuteronomy 6:4–5).

Jesus told the man that he was right on target, but the man had another agenda that day. He wanted to justify his own actions toward others, especially those he considered his "enemies," so he asked Jesus just who his neighbor really was.

Jesus didn't just answer the question, but showed this man who the neighbor he was to love really was by telling him a parable.

W.W.J.K. (What Would Jesus Know?)

Jericho is located about 18 miles northwest of Jerusalem, in an oasis in the desert of Judea. During Jesus' lifetime, there were actually two Jerichos. One was the Jericho of the Old Testament, which was by then uninhabited. The other was a newer Jericho, which was just a mile south of the old one. Herod the Great had a palace in Jericho, which is where he died.

Hitting the Road ... Literally

Jesus told the man the story of a very unfortunate Jewish man who was taking a trip from Jerusalem to Jericho. As he traveled along, he was jumped by bandits who robbed him of everything from his money down to his clothes, beat him up badly, and left him for dead at the roadside.

Later, a Jewish priest and then a Temple assistant passed the section on the road where the man lay, but neither did anything to help him but instead went to the other side of the road as they passed. They may have thought he was dead, and because touching a dead body rendered a Jew "unclean" according to Jewish law, they didn't put their hands on him. However, they didn't even stop to see if the man was still alive or ask for help.

The Original Good Samaritan

Fortunately for the man who had been robbed, a third man—a Samaritan—came along and stopped to see if he could help him. The Samaritan saw that the man was alive—albeit very groggy—then went to great lengths to help him out.

Keep in mind that the Samaritans and Jews had an unhealthy case of hatred for one another at that time and that it would have been unheard of for a Samaritan to do anything for even the most needy Jew—and vice versa.

But this particular Samaritan showed incredible love and compassion for a man he should have seen as his enemy. He tended to his wounds, putting oil and wine on them, which had medicinal qualities, and bandaging them. Then he put him in his own donkey and took him to the nearest inn so that he could rest and recuperate. Not only that, the Samaritan paid for his lodging and asked the innkeeper to keep an eye on this unfortunate man. He also promised the innkeeper that if the injured man's stay ran into more money than he had already paid, he would be back later to square things up.

That Samaritan, Jesus pointed out, was the only one of the three men who passed the badly injured man who had loved his neighbor as himself. In telling the legal expert this, Jesus was pointing out that loving his neighbor as himself meant showing compassion, even to his worst enemies.

W.W.J.K. (What Would Jesus Know?)

By this time Samaritans and Jews had been at odds for over 950 years, when the kingdom of Israel split after King Solomon's death. The tribes of Benjamin and Judah became the southern kingdom of Judah with the capital in Jerusalem. The other ten tribes became the northern kingdom of Israel with the capital in Samaria. Each was headed by two different lines of kings who at times fought each other.

A Primer on Prayer (Luke 11:1–13)

One day not long after talking to the Jewish legal scholar about what it meant to love his neighbor, Jesus went to a private place so he could pray. As he finished, one of his disciples approached him and asked him to teach him and the others to pray, just as John the Baptist had taught his disciples.

Jesus would never have passed up a request like that one, so he gave the disciples sort of a template for prayer, which has come to be known as "The Lord's Prayer":

Let's Come to Terms

The Lord's Prayer is actually a model for what elements should be contained in prayer for his disciples, rather than the prayer of Jesus to his Father. The Lord's personal prayer to his Father is found in John, chapter 17, where he prays before his death on the cross that his disciples and all his followers will be unified in the love coming from himself and his Father.

"Father, may your name be honored.
May your Kingdom come soon.
Give us our food day by day.
And forgive us our sins—
just as we forgive those who have sinned against us.
And don't let us yield to temptation."

Other ancient manuscripts add a few more supportive lines you may be familiar with, but this is the original in a nutshell. Basically, it tells us to put God's interests first, our needs next, then the need to be in a right relationship with him and others, and finally, to protect us from evil.

But Jesus didn't stop there. He went on to teach the disciples something more about prayer using yet another parable.

A Midnight Supper? Don't Knock It Too Much!

Jesus told the disciples to imagine one of them going to a friend's house late at night, waking that neighbor up out of a sound sleep, and asking to borrow three loaves of bread so that he could feed a guest in his own home.

He then asked them to imagine what he would do if that particular friend told him to get lost because he was in bed and didn't want to get up. Jesus then told the disciples that the man persists because no Jew wanted the reputation of being inhospitable. So the friend gives in and groggily gives him the bread.

The Scorpion Trick Won't Work

Jesus' point wasn't that God was reluctant to answer their prayers. His point was that when they prayed, they needed to be persistent as they knocked, asked, and sought him out for an answer. People who do that, he told them, receive what they ask for.

Jesus took his point a step further when he taught that God was their heavenly Father and was more than willing to provide them just what they needed and asked for. Would a good father give his child a snake or a scorpion when what they asked for was a fish or an egg? "Of course not!" Jesus told them, then said that if mere people, being the sinful creatures they are, give good things to their children who ask for them, then God is even more willing to give his people what they need and ask for.

Home Cooking and Home Teaching (Luke 10:38–42)

One day as Jesus and his disciples were traveling around Judea, they came to a village called Bethany, which was not far from Jerusalem. There they were welcomed into the home of two sisters named Mary and Martha and their brother Lazarus.

While he was in their home, Jesus started a very close friendship with the three of them. Both Mary and Martha showed Jesus incredible hospitality, but in different ways. At one point in Jesus' visit, Mary sat at Jesus' feet, listening to his teaching, while Martha kept herself busy cooking a big dinner for Jesus and his disciples.

Finally, Martha had had enough. She was doing all the work while her sister just sat with that night's guest of honor. She went to Jesus and asked him if it didn't seem a little unfair that she was scurrying around the house doing all the work preparing their evening meal.

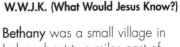

W.W.J.K. (What Would Jesus Know?)

Bethany was a small village in Judea about two miles east of Jerusalem, on the eastern slope of the Mount of Olives. Presently, a village called *el-'Azareyeh* sits where Bethany used to be.

Just Chill ... and Listen!

Jesus told Martha that she was getting herself agitated over something that just wasn't that important. Yes, serving him through her hospitality was a nice thing for her to do, but Mary had found what was really important when she just sat and listened to his words.

The friendship that Jesus struck up with Mary, Martha, and Lazarus would lead to a later incident in all of their lives, one that would play a key part in Jesus' ultimate earthly destiny.

I'm Not Dying to Get There (John 11)

One day as Jesus was ministering in an area called Perea, he received a message that Lazarus, the brother of Mary and Martha, had become very sick. When Jesus heard this, he said that Lazarus's illness would not end in death but that it would glorify God the Father and himself.

W.W.J.K. (What Would Jesus Know?)

Perea was the region east of the Jordan River, opposite Judea and Samaria. The Bible refers to this area as "the land beyond the Jordan." It is where John the Baptist baptized people and where Jesus spent some of his time ministering. Today, Perea is the Arab kingdom of Jordan.

The message Jesus received was an urgent one, and Lazarus's family no doubt expected him to come immediately. But rather than head for Bethany right away, Jesus waited two days, then told his disciples that they were going to leave Perea and head for Judea.

Of course, the disciples remembered that the Jewish leaders in Judea wanted to kill Jesus. In fact, they had tried to take his life only a short time earlier. They asked Jesus if he really thought it was a good idea to go to a place where there was a price on his head.

Asleep ... or Just Dead Tired?

Jesus then explained the situation to the disciples in a mysterious way when he said, "Our friend Lazarus has fallen asleep, but now I will go and wake him up." The disciples, probably still trying to talk their way out of going back to Judea, said that if Lazarus was sleeping, then that must mean he was getting healthy again.

Jesus then put things a little more literally. He told the disciples very plainly that Lazarus had died but that his death would give Jesus another chance to demonstrate his power in front of them. He then told the disciples that they were going to Bethany to see him.

Thomas said what the others were probably thinking, namely that following Jesus to Judea at this time was a suicide mission. But he and the others were more than willing to follow him wherever he went, even if it put his life and their lives in danger.

In Bethany with Mary, Martha, and Lazarus.

Copyright © 2001 Tyndale House Publishers

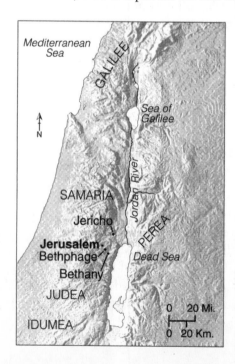

Rise and Shine

When Jesus and his disciples arrived at the outskirts of Bethany, he was told that Lazarus had been dead for four days and that he had already been buried. He also saw that there were many Jewish people from Jerusalem, many of them influential and powerful people, there to pay their respects and to console Mary and Martha.

When Mary and Martha received word that Jesus was in town, Martha hurried off to see him while Mary stayed at home. In what sounds like a mixture of bitter disappointment and unshakable faith, Martha told Jesus that if he had only been in Bethany when her brother fell ill, he would not have died. She knew that Jesus had the power to heal, but she wasn't quite ready for what Jesus had to say next: "Your brother will rise again."

Of course, Martha already knew that. As a Jew, she believed that there would come a day when all the dead who had served God faithfully—which Lazarus had—would be resurrected. Jesus wasn't talking about *that* resurrection but the one she was about to see that very day.

> **Let's Come to Terms**
>
> The name **Mary** was very common among the Jewish people of Jesus' time, and there were several who played big roles in his life story. One was his mother, another was Mary of Magdala, and the third was Mary of Bethany, the sister of Martha and Lazarus.

Believe and Live Forever

Jesus went on to tell Martha that he had absolute power over death: "I am the resurrection and the life. Those who believe in me, even though they die like everyone else, will live again. They are given eternal life for believing in me and will never perish" (John 11:25–26).

When Jesus asked Martha if she believed what he had just told her, she said that she did and that she had known from the time she first met Jesus that he was the Messiah and the Son of God.

When Jesus was finished talking with Martha, she went home and told Mary that he wanted to talk to her. Mary darted out of their home, followed by a big crowd who assumed she was going to Lazarus's grave, and found Jesus at the edge of the town, where Martha had told her he would be.

When Mary saw Jesus, she fell at his feet crying, and told him, just as her sister had, that if Jesus had only been there, Lazarus would still be alive. Jesus, very much moved with compassion, asked where Lazarus had been buried.

Two Words That Say It All: "Jesus Wept"

Everybody was crying on the way to the tomb of Lazarus, and that included Jesus. At first glance, it doesn't seem like he should have been crying. After all, he knew what was going to happen. He knew that he would see and talk to his dear friend Lazarus that very day.

His Name Is Jesus, a.k.a.

"Creator" (Colossians 1:16,17). Most people think of God the Father as the creator, because all things were made by him. But all things were made in and through Jesus. Colossians says, "Christ is the one through whom God created everything in heaven and earth. He made the things we can see and the things we can't see—kings, kingdoms, rulers, and authorities. Everything has been created through him and for him. He existed before everything else began, and he holds all creation together."

While this scene is in a lot of ways similar to earlier ones in which Jesus raised people from the dead, it is different in that Jesus himself, and not just the mourners around him, was crying. Earlier, he had comforted the widow whose son had died and told her not to cry. He had also told Jairus "don't be afraid" when he learned that his son had died.

There are many possible reasons why Jesus wept. It may have been because he saw the sadness and crying of the others, including Mary and Martha, both of whom he loved dearly. Perhaps it was because the scene that was about to take place was very similar to his own resurrection, which was not far off.

One of the most common interpretations is that Jesus hated what death did to his creation. He hated its ugliness, its pain, and for some, its eternal negative consequences. He knew the excruciating pain he would undergo in order to remove its effects due to sin. Regardless, when Jesus wept he identified at a deep level with our vulnerability and weakness as humans.

Some of the people who made their way to the tomb assumed that Jesus was crying because he had lost a very dear friend. They also wondered aloud why Jesus, who had healed a man born blind, couldn't have kept Lazarus from dying.

This Could Be a Stinky Situation

When Jesus and the crowd arrived at the grave, which was actually a cave—either man-made or natural—with a big rock at its entrance, Jesus directed some men there to move the rock out of the way. Martha told Jesus that moving the rock wouldn't be a good idea. After all, Lazarus had already been dead four days, and by now the odor would have been unbearable.

But Jesus wasn't going to be stopped. When Martha allowed the men there to roll the stone away from the opening of the grave, Jesus prayed and thanked God for what was about to happen, then shouted "Lazarus, come out!"

With that whole crowd of mourners looking on, Lazarus stepped to the mouth of the cave, still wrapped head to toe in the grave clothes in which he was buried. Then Jesus gave the people their part in the miracle when he told them to unwrap Lazarus and let him go free.

Everyone there was stunned and amazed at what they had just seen, and many of them became convinced that Jesus was everything he had said he was, that he was indeed the Messiah they had been waiting for. However, others in the group ran to the high priests and Pharisees to tell them what they had seen.

> **His Name Is Jesus, a.k.a.**
>
> "The First Born of the Dead" (Revelation 1:5). Though Jesus raised Lazarus before he himself was raised, Lazarus would die again. But Jesus was the first to rise from the dead and never die again. Since he is the first born, all who believe in Jesus as the Resurrection and the Life will be born into eternal life after we die.

We can't know for sure why they went to the Pharisees, but we know that their doing that only intensified the resolve of the religious establishment to do something about Jesus before this movement got out of hand.

The Least You Need to Know

- Jesus taught the meaning of "loving one's neighbor" using the well-known Parable of the Good Samaritan.

- Jesus gave the disciples a "template" for prayer, which has become known as "The Lord's Prayer."

- Jesus performed the ultimate miracle when he raised Lazarus from the dead.

Chapter 15

Seeking the Lost to Find Them an Eternal Home

In This Chapter

- A plot by Jewish religious leaders to kill Jesus
- Jesus' ministry in the time leading up to his final entrance into Jerusalem
- Some more parable teaching
- Jesus anointed in Bethany just prior to going into Jerusalem

It didn't take long for news of Jesus raising Lazarus from the dead to make it all over Judea, including Jerusalem, where the chief priests and the Pharisees called together a meeting of the Sanhedrin to figure out what to do about him.

The members of the Sanhedrin were alarmed at what they had heard, especially accounts of many people in Bethany believing in Jesus. The way these religious leaders saw it, this was a crisis situation. They feared that if they didn't do something about this rabble-rouser, then the people would rebel against Roman authority, which just might cause the Romans to invade and destroy Jerusalem in an effort to put down a rebellion.

We're Divided, and So We're ... Sad You See (John 11:45–57)

The Sanhedrin, led by the Sadducees, debated back and forth over what they should do about the mounting threat they believed Jesus represented. Some of the council members actually believed in Jesus, or at least were sympathetic with him. Others probably wanted to leave the situation well enough alone, while still others wanted him arrested so that he couldn't incite the crowds any further.

The Jewish high priest at that time was Caiaphas, a Sadducee who had held the position for about 15 years. Caiaphas knew what he believed had to be done, and when he told his associates on the Sanhedrin about it he unwittingly spoke a prophecy concerning Jesus' main mission on earth: "How can you be so stupid?" he said. "Why should the whole nation be destroyed? Let this one man die for the people."

From that meeting forward, it was the official policy of the Sanhedrin that Jesus must be arrested, tried, then executed. When Jesus found out about the plan, he stopped his public ministry in the area around Jerusalem and went to a place called Ephraim, a village 16 miles northeast of Jerusalem, near the wilderness of Judea.

Cleaning Ten Leper-Skin Coats (Luke 17:11–19)

After Jesus left Ephraim, he and the disciples traveled to a little village near the border of Galilee and Samaria, where he healed 10 lepers.

As Jesus reached the edge of this unnamed village, the 10 lepers—9 of them Jews and one of them a Samaritan—stood at a distance from him, as was required by Jewish law and tradition, and shouted, "Jesus, Master, have mercy on us!"

Jesus healed the men, but at a distance. He didn't approach them, but called back to them and told them to go show themselves to the local priests. When the lepers went to the priests, they did it so that the priests could examine them and pronounce them "clean."

All 10 of the lepers did as Jesus had told them, and all 10 were healed. But only one of them, the Samaritan, came back to thank Jesus for healing him. He ran to Jesus, praising God every step, then fell at Jesus' feet and thanked him. Jesus told him that his faith had made him well.

The fact that the one man who came back to him to give thanks for the healing was a Samaritan didn't escape Jesus' notice. From the beginning of his ministry, Jesus had taught that simply being born a Jew wasn't what made people right with God. Rather, he taught that it was those who approached him with a heart of faith and seeking forgiveness who would be saved.

The Lost-and-Found Department

At this time in Jesus' ministry, he spoke several parables concerning the kingdom of God and what it took to be welcomed into it. In speaking those parables, he taught that he had come to bring "lost" people into the kingdom of God.

Several of these parables he spoke to Pharisees who obviously didn't understand that faith in God was a matter of the heart and not a matter of strictly obeying Jewish law and tradition.

Ninety-nine Down, One to Go (Luke 15:1–32)

One of the hallmarks of Jesus' ministry is that he allowed the most sinful of sinners to come to him to hear his teaching. As we pointed out before, He spent a lot of time with tax collectors, adulterers, and other "outcasts"—in other words, those who most needed to hear what he had to say.

The religious leaders at that time didn't think Jesus should be associating himself with those kinds of people but that he should do as they did and avoid any kind of contact with sinners.

These ultrareligious guys just weren't getting it, so Jesus spelled it out for them by teaching through a series of parables. He pointed out that if one of them owned 100 sheep and 1 of the sheep had wandered off and became lost in the wilderness, he would gladly leave the other 99 to go look for it. Furthermore, when he found that lost sheep, he would call together his friends to celebrate bringing that one lost sheep back into the flock.

It's Not Just Pocket Change

The same thing would be true of a woman who had 10 valuable silver coins but lost one of them, Jesus told them. She would light a lantern and look high and low in her home until she found it. When she found it, she would celebrate with her friends and neighbors.

Jesus told them that there would be more rejoicing in heaven over one lost sinner who repented than over many others who didn't need to be rescued. (In the case of most of the Pharisees, they wrongly thought they didn't need to be rescued.)

This Place Has Gone to the Pigs (Luke 15:1–32)

Jesus moved his teaching about seeking and finding the lost from the "material" to the "human" realm when he spoke what is now called the Parable of the *Prodigal Son*.

The Prodigal Son was the younger of two who lived with and worked for their father. One day, he approached his father and told him that he was tired of living with the family and working on the farm and wanted his share of the estate right now instead of waiting until his father died.

Let's Come to Terms

The word **prodigal**, which Jesus never used when he was telling the story about the young man who took his share of the family fortune and wasted it, literally means "wastefully or recklessly extravagant."

The father divided up his wealth and gave his younger son his share. A few days later, the son packed his bags and moved far away from home, where he spent all the money on wine, women, and song.

With all his money spent, the young man faced another crisis: a famine where he was living at the time. He was in deep financial trouble, so deep that he had to take a job feeding a farmer's pigs. Even then, he wasn't making enough to eat well and became so hungry that the empty pods he was feeding the pigs started looking pretty good.

An Opportunity for Rapid Advancement

The boy was starving, and to make matters worse, he realized that his father's servants back home had plenty to eat. Soon, he came up with a plan. He was going to go home, confess to his father that he had sinned and wasn't worthy to be called his son anymore, and beg him to take him on as a hired hand.

When the father saw his wayward son approaching home, he ran to him and gave him a big hug and a kiss. The first thing out of the boy's mouth was the suggestion that his father hire him to work for him. The father, however, wouldn't hear of such a thing. Rather than hiring his son as a servant—or worse yet, turning him away completely—he ordered his servants to fetch the best robe in his house and a ring, and put them on his son. When they were done doing that, they were to go out to the stable and kill the calf they had been fattening.

The way the father in this story saw it, it was time to celebrate! He had been promoted back to the rank of full son.

Dad Always Did Like You Better

By now the Pharisees had to be scratching their heads over the story Jesus was telling them. But Jesus wasn't finished. He finished the story by telling them about a character in the story whose attitude was a lot like theirs.

Jesus gave the Pharisees the "payoff" in this story by telling them about the rebellious son's brother, who was none too pleased with how his father was making such a fuss about his return. He was so miffed that he wouldn't even go in the house and join in the welcome-home party.

What the father's eldest son said to him about what was going on sounds pretty reasonable. He pointed out that he had faithfully served and obeyed him for years, while his younger brother had wasted half of the family fortune with wild living.

The eldest son in the story was a lot like the Pharisees. He had his facts right, but he had come to some really wrong conclusions. While both the eldest son and the Pharisees held the attitude that the Prodigal Son and other sinners should "get what's coming to them," the father in the story and Jesus himself wanted to celebrate when someone who has gone astray returns home. Jesus' bottom-line message in this story is that God prefers to show mercy and forgiveness rather than judgment.

That, Jesus wanted the Pharisees to understand, was why he spent so much of his time in the presence of sinners and not around people like them.

Rags to Riches ... and the Reverse

Jesus taught that the love of money, not money itself, was the source of evil in the hearts of people. He also taught that those who had been greatly blessed in the material sense were responsible to use their resources for the benefit of others.

One of his parables was aimed directly at those Pharisees, who loved money more than they loved God and their fellow man. That particular parable was the story of a rich man and a beggar. The rich man lived a luxurious and extravagant lifestyle. When it came to material goods, there was nothing he lacked. On this rich man's doorstep was a sickly beggar who had nothing and who just wanted the scraps from the rich man's table that were going to the dogs.

Eventually, both of these men died, and a host of angels carried the beggar into heaven, where he joined Abraham. The rich man? He was condemned to eternal damnation, from where he could see the poor beggar living the eternal high life. The rich man was in torment, and he asked that the beggar—a man he had no doubt stepped over many times as he ventured outside his home—be allowed to dip his finger in water and come and just wet his tongue.

But that wasn't going to happen. The rich man was told that when he was alive, he had everything he wanted while Lazarus lacked even the basic necessities of life. They had both received what they deserved in the afterlife and there was no way they could reverse justice now.

Jesus never taught that there was anything wrong with being rich. In fact, he associated himself with rich people who were in tune with his message of compassion.

The rich man in Jesus' parable wasn't where he was because he had lived a rich life, but because he lacked the kind of compassion that Jewish law not only made room for, but required from people.

Hell? ... Yes

The parable of the rich man and Lazarus wasn't the only time Jesus had talked about eternal punishment, also known as "hell." At least 11 times in the gospels, Jesus is recorded to have spoken of a place where the unrighteous would be punished forever.

The Old Testament made reference to a place in the afterlife called "Sheol," an unpleasant place where all people would go after they died but from which the godly would one day be delivered (Psalm 16:10). In its original language, the New Testament refers to both *Hades* and *Gehenna*, both very unpleasant places in the afterlife.

Let's Come to Terms

The words **Hades** and **Gehenna**, as they were used in the gospels, both had very interesting origins. Hades was a word more or less borrowed from Greek mythology and referred generally to death and the grave. Gehenna, on the other hand, literally meant "the valley of Hinnom" in Hebrew, referring to a garbage pit where the filth of Jerusalem and the bodies of executed criminals were taken to be disposed of and where a fire was kept constantly burning to dispose of the remains of animal sacrifices. It was, at the time, about the most unpleasant place people could think of, making it a fitting word picture of a place of eternal torment.

A Look at the "Other Place"

Here are a few of Jesus' teachings concerning the subject of hell:

◆ "You have heard that the law of Moses says, 'Do not murder. If you commit murder, you are subject to judgment.' But I say, if you are angry with someone, you are subject to judgment. If you call someone an idiot, you are in danger of being brought before the high council. And if you curse someone, you are in danger of the fires of hell" (Matthew 5:21–22).

◆ "But many Israelites—those for whom the Kingdom was prepared—will be cast into outer darkness, where there will be weeping and gnashing of teeth." (Matthew 8:12).

◆ "If your hand causes you to sin, cut it off. It is better to enter heaven with only one hand than to go into the unquenchable fires of hell with two hands. If your foot causes you to sin, cut it off. It is better to enter heaven with only one foot than to be thrown into hell with two feet. And if your eye causes you to sin, gouge it out. It is better to enter the Kingdom of God half blind than to have two eyes and be thrown into hell." (Mark 9:43–37).

> **W.W.J.K. (What Would Jesus Know?)**
>
> Did Jesus literally mean that people should begin cutting off and pulling out body parts in order to avoid going to hell? Obviously not! Most people agree that Jesus was speaking figuratively and making the point that hell was a terrible place to be and that people should do what was necessary to avoid going there.

It's hard for some people to reconcile the compassionate Jesus who came to bring people life with the Jesus who spoke so often of eternal hell. However, part of Jesus' ministry of compassion was to show people the way to heaven and to announce that he was the only way to avoid the place of judgment in the afterlife.

Don't Be Childish, Be Childlike (Mark 10:13–16)

One day, some parents brought their babies to Jesus so he could touch them and bless them. However, this really irked the disciples, who didn't think Jesus had the time to deal with something so trivial as blessing children.

> **W.W.J.K. (What Would Jesus Know?)**
>
> It was customary for Jewish people in Jesus' day to bring their babies to their local synagogues so that their rabbi could lay his hands on them and bless them. This was especially important to the people during Jesus' time, as infant mortality was as high as 60 percent.

But Jesus took the children into his arms and told the disciples, "Let the children come to me. Don't stop them! for the Kingdom of God belongs to such as these. I assure you, anyone who doesn't have their kind of faith will never get into the Kingdom of God."

In this incident, Jesus demonstrated to his disciples that he wasn't necessarily looking for the most "sophisticated" or "educated" to be his followers. On the contrary, he wanted those who had simple faith and trust in him and a kind of innocent humility, just as those children—not to mention their parents—had.

You're Okay, but Give It All Away (Luke 18:18–34)

One day, a very young, influential, and wealthy ruler—probably of the local synagogue—came to Jesus and asked him, "Good teacher, what should I do to get eternal life?"

Jesus told him that he knew the Ten Commandments: Do not commit adultery, do not murder, do not steal, do not testify falsely, honor your mother and father, and so on.

At that point, the young ruler must have thought he was doing all right. He eagerly told Jesus that he had obeyed all those commandments since he was just a boy. But Jesus answered him back again and told him that he lacked one thing: "Sell all you have and give the money to the poor, and you will have treasure in heaven. Then come, follow me."

His Name Is Jesus, a.k.a.
"Wonderful Counselor" (Isaiah 9:6). Jesus gave this rich young man the best advice possible because he knew his heart. He promises to give his followers wisdom about their own lives as they seek him in prayer.

When the young man heard this, he was crushed. He was really wealthy, and he wasn't willing to give up what he had so that he could follow Jesus. Instead of doing as Jesus had instructed him, he went away with a very long face. No doubt Jesus was sad to see him go. But Jesus never coerced or manipulated anyone—he respects our free will and ability to choose. In his gospel account of this scene, Mark says that Jesus loved this young man very much.

Start a Long-Term (Heavenly) Trust

Some have taken this passage and others very literally in applying it to their own lives. For example, St. Francis of Assisi, a thirteenth-century Christian who lived in Italy, left a life of riches so that he could live a life of poverty as he traveled and reached people for Jesus, just as the disciples had.

But after the young man had turned away from him, Jesus explained to those who saw this encounter that it was possible for rich folks to go to heaven, but not possible for those rich folks who put their trust in their money and not in God.

The Rich Deserve Some Needling

Jesus told the people that it was easier for a camel to go through the eye of a needle than it was for a rich man to enter the kingdom of God. This really shook up the people who heard it—some of whom were probably rich themselves—and they asked Jesus just who in the world *could* have eternal life. Jesus told them, very simply, "What is impossible from a human perspective is possible with God."

His Name Is Jesus, a.k.a.
"The Vine" (John 15:1). Jesus alludes to vineyards in his parables because they played an important role in the life of Israel. He claimed to be the vine and we are the branches. Without his spiritual life flowing through us, we'll wither and die.

Mysterious Tax Increases (Luke 19:1–9)

As Jesus and the disciples made their way to Jerusalem, they passed through the city of Jericho, where Jesus met a man named Zacchaeus, a tax collector who wanted very desperately to see him.

Remember, tax collectors were seen in the Jewish world as the worst of sinners. But Zacchaeus was the worst of the worst of those sinners. He was what the Gospel of Luke called a "chief tax collector," probably meaning that he wasn't just a tax collector but a tax collector who was boss over many other tax collectors.

A Tree-Mendous Opportunity

Zacchaeus probably knew there was something wrong with the life he was leading. He really wanted to see Jesus and maybe even talk to him. There was a big crowd following Jesus that day, and that included Zacchaeus himself. There was only one problem. Zacchaeus was what we in our politically correct culture might call "vertically challenged." (Okay, we'll just say it: He was short!)

Let's Come to Terms

Some version of the Bible refer to the tree Zacchaeus climbed as a **sycamore-fig** tree. This is a tree that grows in that area of the world that has a short trunk and wide branches, which made it easy to climb, even for a short man like Zacchaeus.

This chief tax collector showed just how much he wanted to see Jesus when he climbed a sycamore tree near where Jesus was passing by, just so he could get a glimpse of this man he had heard so much about. Jesus must have been impressed with his persistence—not to mention his industriousness—so he called Zacchaeus down out of the tree and told him he wanted to be a guest in his house that day.

A Little Man but Not Small-Minded

Of course, Zacchaeus was overjoyed that Jesus wanted to spend some time with him. Zacchaeus was out of the tree in a flash. But the citizens of Jericho didn't share that joy. They were upset that Jesus would spend time with such a rogue as Zacchaeus, who had kept back a portion of their taxes for himself.

But Jesus wasn't concerned with doing what was popular. He told the crowd that he had come to find and save the worst of sinners, people just like Zacchaeus. Meanwhile, Zacchaeus showed genuine remorse for doing people wrong. He told Jesus that he would give half of his considerable fortune to the poor and repay anyone he had overcharged on their taxes to the tune of four times what he rightly owed them.

Jesus knew that Zacchaeus was truly sorry for any wrongs he had done to the people, and right there in front of all those witnesses, many of whom Zacchaeus would later be giving restitution, told him that salvation had come to him and his home. He had shown himself to be a true Jew—in faith and in practice.

A Dinner in Preparation for a Funeral (John 12:1–9)

Six days before the Passover, and one day before Jesus would make his final entrance into the city of Jerusalem, he and the disciples stopped off in Bethany, the site of Jesus' raising his friend Lazarus from the dead.

A dinner in Jesus' honor was held that evening at the home of a man called Simon, a leper Jesus may very well have healed when he was in Bethany before (remember, lepers at that time were not allowed to mingle with "healthy" people). Mary and Martha, Lazarus, Jesus' disciples, and probably a host of other guests were also there.

It Has a Heavenly Scent, but Is It Heaven Sent?

As she had during Jesus' first visit, Martha kept herself busy preparing the meal and serving the guests, but Mary was again at the feet of Jesus. She had brought a very expensive bottle of perfume to the dinner and put some on Jesus' head and on his feet. After she had covered his feet with the stuff, she dried them with her hair. The whole house was filled with the fragrance of the perfume.

One of the disciples, Judas Iscariot, objected to Mary's pouring such expensive perfume on Jesus, telling him that this was wasteful; they could have sold the perfume for a lot of money, which they could have used to help the poor. Judas had ulterior motives, however. He was a thief who used to steal from the poor box. Jesus told Judas to leave her alone, for the anointing she was giving him was in preparation for his own soon-to-come burial.

It was almost time for Jesus to return to Jerusalem, where he would continue teaching, healing, and debating with the Jewish religious leaders. It was also where he would face what he had come to earth to do, namely be arrested, stand trial, and die at the hands of his accusers.

The Least You Need to Know

- ◆ Jesus' raising of Lazarus from the dead led to a plot on the part of the Sanhedrin to have him arrested.

- ◆ During the latter part of Jesus' ministry, he continued teaching on subjects such as money, hypocrisy, and faith.

- ◆ People responded differently to Jesus—the rich ruler walked away, but the tax collector restored what he had stolen.

- ◆ Once Jesus had been anointed at Bethany, he was prepared for what would be his last trip to Jerusalem.

Part 4

Jesus' Final Week of Ministry

Other than traveling to Jerusalem for religious celebrations, Jesus had spent most of his "earthly ministry" in Galilee. Both his words and deeds—and especially the claims of who he was—had given him a huge following, and the opposition of the religious establishment.

Word of Jesus' teachings, work, and claims about himself had made their way south to Jerusalem. Now he was about to head into Jerusalem and into the teeth of the opposition he'd faced for three years, where he knew that he would be watched closely and "tested" by the Jewish religious leadership. Still, he continued his ministry, while at the same time taking to task the religious leaders who opposed him.

Chapter 16

Taking the Message to the Holy City

In This Chapter

- Jesus' "Triumphal Entry" into Jerusalem
- Jesus' popularity among the Jewish people of Jerusalem during the first part of "Holy Week"
- Jesus curses a fig tree, which promptly wilts
- Another Temple cleansing and the teaching that followed

Jesus had spent three years of his life traveling around Palestine—especially Galilee—teaching, preaching, and doing all kinds of miracles. His teachings and deeds not only fulfilled Old Testament prophecies about the coming of the Messiah, but they changed the lives of a lot of people from many areas and many walks of life.

But there was more yet to come. Jesus had told his disciples repeatedly that what they saw in front of them—the teaching, preaching, and miracles—wasn't all his ministry would be about. He told them quite plainly that he was going to Jerusalem, where he would be arrested, handed over to the Romans, beaten, and killed. But he told them that his death wasn't going to be the end of his ministry. Three days after his death, he would rise from the grave. All of these things, Jesus told them, would be the fulfillment of everything the Old Testament prophets had said about the Messiah.

A Date with Destiny

Jesus was about to come face-to-face with his earthly destiny and with the purpose for which he had come in the first place. Jesus' earthly ministry was coming to a close, and what would be taking place in the coming week would change history—from then on into eternity. Jesus and his disciples were about to travel to Jerusalem, the very heart of the Jewish religious world—and the heart of the religious opposition to everything he had been doing and saying about himself.

Jesus had planned all along to attend the Passover celebration in Jerusalem. It was there where everything he had said would happen to him would come to pass. First, however, Jesus would be welcomed with open arms by the common people, those who had waited for so long for the arrival of their Messiah.

A Cosmopolitan Celebration

During Jesus' day, Jerusalem was home to about 100,000 people. While the city was mostly Jewish in its population, there were also Greeks, Romans, and others from different parts of the then-known world. But with many thousands of Jewish pilgrims arriving in the city for the upcoming Passover celebration, there were probably several times that many in the city when Jesus arrived there for the final time. Some historians and scholars believe there may have been up to a million people in the Jewish capital for that year's Passover celebration.

Many of those who had traveled from around the region of Judea for the Passover were Galileans who had heard and seen the words and work of Jesus during the past three years. And if they hadn't heard and seen these things for themselves, they at least had heard about them. In addition to the Jewish pilgrims who had traveled to Jerusalem, there were the locals. Some of them had been eyewitnesses to Jesus' work from his earlier visits to Jerusalem, and others had heard stories of the things that had been going on in Galilee.

What had before been a longing and anticipation for the coming of the Messiah grew to a fever pitch as the people eagerly looked forward to the arrival of Jesus.

No Stretch Limos, Just a King on a Colt (Luke 19:28–44)

The day after Mary, Martha's sister, had anointed Jesus at the dinner at Simon the leper's home in Bethany, Jesus and the disciples—in addition to the throngs of people who had been following him—began their short journey to Jerusalem by way of a village called Bethpage, which was close to Bethany on the slopes of the Mount of Olives.

After this crowd of people had passed through the city of Bethpage, he stopped and sent two of the apostles to a nearby small town. He told them that as they entered that village they would find a donkey tied there with its colt beside it. He told them not to say anything to anyone but to untie the animals and bring them to him. If anyone were to ask them what they were doing, Jesus said, they were to tell them that the Lord needed to use the donkeys that day.

> **Let's Come to Terms**
>
> **Bethpage,** the name of which literally means "house of the unripe young figs," was located on the southeast slope of the Mount of Olives, less than a mile from the city of Jerusalem.

The two disciples (the Bible doesn't say which two) did as Jesus had told them, and sure enough, they found the donkey tied up, just as he had said they would. When they went to untie them, someone—maybe the animals' owner—asked them why they were doing it. They did as Jesus had said and told the people that the Lord needed to use the donkeys that day, and they were allowed to take them.

Life in the Slow Lane

When the disciples returned to Jesus, with the donkeys in tow, they threw some of their garments on the colt's back. Jesus climbed aboard and they headed for the city of Jerusalem.

In their gospel accounts of this scene, both Matthew and John point out that this was the fulfillment of an Old Testament prophecy about the Messiah. Both of these accounts actually paraphrase the prophecy, which is found in

> **His Name Is Jesus, a.k.a.**
>
> "Ruler of Kings" (Revelation 1:5). The prophet Zechariah told Jerusalem to shout out loud because her king was coming on a donkey. Yet this same Jesus is described as "ruler of kings" in the book of Revelation. When we think of the pomp and majesty of other kings, we can marvel that Jesus would act in this humble way.

Zechariah 9:9. Matthew wrote, "Tell the people of Israel, 'Look, your King is coming to you. He is humble, riding on a donkey—even on a donkey's colt,'"

A Grand but Humble Entrance

The entire city of Jerusalem had been buzzing over the arrival of Jesus. Many of the people knew about him and the things he had done—especially his raising of Lazarus from the dead, which, as you may remember, had been reported in Jerusalem.

Jesus rode down the hill leading into the city of Jerusalem, surrounded by his 12 apostles as well as a large crowd of people who had been following him. All of them were shouting and singing and praising God over the things they had heard and seen Jesus say and do.

The closer Jesus got to downtown Jerusalem, the bigger the crowd got. The people who had accompanied him out of Bethany and Bethpage were met at the edge of town by what was probably a bigger crowd of locals who had been waiting for his arrival.

At a glance, we might find it a little odd that the man so many Jewish people in Palestine saw as their king would ride into town on a donkey's colt. After all, shouldn't a king ride in on a big, strapping steed, like most kings would? But in the Jewish population of Palestine at that time, donkeys were associated with peace and humility. That was due to some writings by some of the Old Testament prophets.

In riding the donkey into town, Jesus was sending the clear message that he had come in peace and not as a conqueror in human strength, which many people, particularly the Zealots in the crowd, had been expecting their Messiah to do.

W.W.J.K. (What Would Jesus Know?)

In other versions of the Bible, the translators use "Hosanna" in place of "Praise God!" The word *Hosanna* literally means "O Save" but had come to be an exclamation of praise and adoration by the time Jesus made his triumphal entry into Jerusalem.

Hallelujahs Heard in the Highest Heavens

As the massive crowd welcomed Jesus into Jerusalem, they covered the roads before him with some of their garments and palm branches and called out words of adoration for Jesus.

"Praise God for the Son of David! Bless the one who comes in the name of the Lord! Praise God in the highest heaven!" some of them called out.

Some Wet Blankets in the Crowd

The people threw their garments in front of Jesus and his contingent to "pave the way" of his coming. These were people who not only had eagerly and longingly awaited the coming of the Messiah—most Jews in those days did just that—but those who believed they were witnessing his arrival with their own eyes and on that very day.

Others saw the commotion and asked who was this man at the center of all the excitement. The people in the crowd welcoming him told them that it was Jesus, the prophet from Nazareth in Galilee.

But not everyone was so pleased that Jesus was entering Jerusalem, at least not with so much fanfare. For some time prior to his arrival into the Holy City, there had developed a growing and seething hatred among the Jewish religious establishment over Jesus' teachings and claims. Some Pharisees, who no doubt knew of the Sanhedrin's plan to arrest, try, and execute Jesus, weren't happy about what they were seeing and hearing.

Let's Come to Terms

To this day, Jesus' triumphal entry into Jerusalem is celebrated in the Christian world every Sunday before Easter. It is called "Palm Sunday," referring to the people spreading palm leaves on the road into Jerusalem. Even now, a Palm Sunday processional makes its way down a street in Jerusalem every year.

Let's Have Some Crowd Control

With thousands of people standing at the roadside as Jesus passed, waving, cheering, and singing his praises, the Pharisees approached Jesus and told him, probably very sternly, to get the crowd under control and to make his followers stop saying such things about him. Jesus, however, refused to stop them, but instead told the Pharisees, "If they kept quiet, the stones along the road would burst into cheers!"

At that point, the Pharisees knew they had a real problem on their hands. They still planned to arrest Jesus, but they knew that it would be a very tricky proposition, simply because so many people were so overjoyed to see him arrive in Jerusalem.

Your Ratings Are About to Drop

Jesus was at the height of his popularity as he entered Jerusalem, but he knew it wouldn't last. As he and his followers entered the city, he began to cry. He knew what was coming for the Holy City. He knew that one day its enemies would come and destroy the city, simply because the people had rejected their Messiah.

Once Jesus was in the city, he went to the Temple and looked around at what was going on there. It was late in the afternoon by then, so Jesus called his 12 apostles together and they all headed back to Bethany, where they stayed the night, very likely at the home of Lazarus, Martha, and Mary.

The Tree That Couldn't Give a Fig (Mark 11:12–14, 18–25)

Bright and early the next morning, Jesus and the disciples got up and headed back for Jerusalem, where Jesus would have a very busy day.

On the way from Bethany back to Jerusalem, Jesus was ready for some breakfast. He spotted a fig tree up ahead. Although it wasn't yet fig season, this particular tree was covered with leaves. (Some species of fig trees in that area of the world often produce fruit before they have leaves.) As Jesus and the disciples got closer to the tree, he saw that it had no figs on it, so he cursed the tree out loud so that the disciples could hear him: "May no one ever eat your fruit again!"

W.W.J.K. (What Would Jesus Know?)

The cursing of the fig tree and its resulting death are believed to be what some have called a "parable in action" that demonstrated what happened to people who didn't "bear fruit" for God. In short, Jesus didn't curse the tree in a fit of anger but in order to teach the disciples something about prayer and about the kingdom of God.

The very next morning they passed that same fig tree and noticed that it not only had no figs on it, but that its leaves had dried up and its branches had withered. It was no longer just an unproductive fig tree but a *dead* fig tree.

Peter was amazed that the tree had died and stated the all-too-obvious when he said, "Look, Teacher! The fig tree you cursed has withered!" Jesus then reminded the disciples of the power of prayer to change things drastically: "I assure you that you can say to this mountain, 'May God lift you up and throw you into the sea,' and your command will be obeyed. All that's required is that you really believe and do not doubt in your heart."

From where Jesus and the disciples stood, it's very likely that when he spoke the words "this mountain," he was referring to the Mount of Olives, which lay right before them, or to the Temple mount, which was just across the Kidron Valley and visible from that spot.

Another Religious Scam (Matthew 21:12–17)

On the same day that Jesus had cursed the fig tree—the day after his triumphal entry into Jerusalem, he once again entered the holy Temple and did another cleaning. As you may recall from Chapter 8, a very similar scene took place early in Jesus' earthly ministry.

Once again, Jesus made quite a scene that day, knocking over tables and driving merchants, moneychangers, and their customers out of the Temple area. This time, however, Jesus used some stronger language than he had at the first Temple cleaning: "The Scriptures declare, 'My Temple will be called a place of prayer for all nations,'" he said, "but you have turned it into a den of thieves."

Out of the Mouths of Babes (Matthew 21:14–17)

As Jesus spent time in the Temple (this could have been before or after he "cleansed" it), blind and lame people came to him and he healed them right there at the Temple. Children at the Temple saw Jesus there and shouted out, "Praise God for the Son of David."

The chief priests and Scribes who heard what the children were saying were incensed and asked Jesus if he had been listening. Jesus told them that he had heard it and had approved. "Haven't you ever read the Scriptures?" he asked them. "For they say, 'You have taught children and infants to give you praise.'"

There can be little doubt that the priests and Scribes knew what Jesus was implying. He had quoted the first half of Psalm 8:2, which ends "They silence your enemies who were seeking revenge." He was telling these religious authorities that the children were singing praise to him and that they were justified in doing so, because he had been sent from God.

No Murder Among the Masses

These incidents only strengthened the resolve of the religious authorities in Jerusalem to kill Jesus. The only reason they didn't try to do it right then and there was that they were afraid of the reaction of the common people, who loved Jesus' teaching, benefited from his healings, and hung on his every word.

As long as the common people continued following him and listening to him, Jesus was relatively safe in Jerusalem—at least for the time being. He continued teaching and doing miracles, but he also gave the religious establishment some very pointed words about where they were headed.

What Business Is This of Yours? (Matthew 21:23–27)

The day after Jesus had driven the businesspeople out of the Temple, as he was walking through the Temple area, several Jewish religious leaders (priests and other leaders, such as Scribes, Pharisees, and Sadducees) stopped him and asked him what gave him the right to drive the merchants out of the Temple the way he had.

After all, what went on at the Temple was business of the religious establishment in Jerusalem, and they themselves had permitted the merchants to operate within the Temple. Jesus wasn't a priest and he wasn't an authority in the law, at least not in any "official" capacity, and as far as the priests, teachers, and others associated with them were concerned, he had no business kicking people out.

Jesus, as he had done so many times with those who had asked him such hostile questions, didn't answer but asked a "counter-question" of his own. "I'll tell who gave me authority to do these things if you answer one question," he challenged them. He then brought up the baptisms John the Baptist performed and asked whether they were from God or if they were just a human endeavor on the part of John.

Now these religious leaders were caught by their own trap. They huddled together and came to the conclusion that if they said that John's baptism was from God, then Jesus would ask them in return why they didn't believe his message. But they knew better than to say that John's baptism was just his own idea, because saying something like that would start a riot among the people of Jerusalem who believed John was a prophet of God.

Either answer would have been the wrong one in this situation, so the leaders didn't answer the question at all but told Jesus that they didn't know where John's baptism had come from. Jesus had made these men a deal, but they couldn't come through on their part of it. So he defiantly told them, "Then I won't answer your question either."

If You Go to the Vineyard You'll Start "Wining" (Matthew 21:28–32)

Although he refused to answer their question concerning where he got the authority to clear the Temple a second time, Jesus wasn't finished with these religious leaders. He went on to tell them their own fate through a parable.

Jesus told them the story of a man who told his two sons to go out and work in his vineyard. When the eldest son heard his father's order, he rebelled at first and flatly said he wasn't going to do it. Later, however, he had a change of heart and went out to the fields to work, just as his father had asked him to. The youngest son, on the other hand, gladly told his father he would go work in the vineyard. But later he had a change of heart of his own, and decided not to go to work.

When Jesus asked the leaders which of those two sons had really been obedient to his father, they acknowledged that it had been the eldest son. Even though he had at first rebelled against his father's orders, he later changed his mind and went and did as he was told.

Jesus then told the religious leaders that the youngest son represented them and that sinners who had believed in him—including tax collectors and prostitutes, the ones the religious establishment saw as the very worst people they knew of—would see the Kingdom of God before they did, simply because the sinners believed his message but the religious leaders did not.

But Jesus still wasn't finished with these religious-but-rebellious men. He went on to tell them a parable that painted a very stark picture of what was going to happen to him, through whom, and what it would mean to them and the city of Jerusalem.

These Guys Are a Bunch of Sour Grapes (Mark 12:1–12)

Jesus knew full well that most of the religious leaders in Jerusalem wanted him out of the way. And if these leaders had any question as to whether he knew what they wanted to do to him, he answered it by telling a parable about the owner of a vineyard.

This man had gone all-out in getting his plot of land ready to produce grapes. He planted his grapevines, built a wall around them for protection against thieves and animals, dug a pit for the pressing of the grapes, and built a lookout tower so that the vineyard could be guarded.

The owner of the vineyard then leased his vineyard to tenant farmers—men who would care for the grapevines until the grapes were ready for harvest, then pay the owner of the vineyard a share of the profits—and moved to another country.

W.W.J.K. (What Would Jesus Know?)

Tenant farming was a very common practice in the Jewish world at the time of Jesus. Wealthy Jews or foreigners who owned large plots of farming land would rent it out to poor Jewish farmers, who would care for and guard the farms as if they were their own, then give the farm owners a predetermined percentage of the crop once harvest time came. Naturally, this arrangement was a source of frustration among the farmers, who resented having to do all the work but then share the crop with the actual landowners.

We May Need a Change in Management

When it came time for harvest, the owner of the vineyard sent one of his servants to collect his share of the crop. But when the servant arrived at the vineyard, the farmers, obviously feeling as if they had been "used," beat him up and sent him back to the vineyard owner … *without* his rightful share of the harvest.

The vineyard owner then sent another one of his servants to the vineyard, but he was treated the same way as the first servant who had gone before him. But that wasn't the worst the farmers were going to do. When the vineyard owner sent yet another servant, the farmers beat him to death.

The vineyard owner didn't give up, however. He kept sending servants, but each time they were either beaten to within an inch of their lives or killed outright. It wasn't long before all of the vineyard owner's servants had either been beaten or killed, except one: his son, who he loved and who was heir to his estate.

I Would Kill for This Job

The vineyard owner assumed that when the farmers saw his son, they would treat him with respect and pay what they owed. But when the farmers saw the son, they hatched a dastardly plan. They would kill the son and take possession of the vineyard for themselves. They did just that. When Jesus had finished telling the leaders what has come to be known as "the Parable of the tenants," he asked them what they thought the vineyard owner would do. Again, they didn't answer him, so Jesus told them that the vineyard owner would come and kill all the farmers and rent the vineyard to others.

There's a Violent Streak Underneath (Luke 20:17–19)

The meaning of Jesus' parable wasn't lost on these leaders. They knew the Scriptures and they knew of the claims Jesus was making about himself—as well as what other people were saying about him. They understood all too well that in this story, Jesus had likened them to the violent, murderous farmers.

They understood that Jesus was talking about how the religious establishment had treated God's prophets, most recently John the Baptist, and about how they would treat Jesus himself, who had told them very plainly that he was the Son of God.

They'd heard Jesus' story and knew what it meant, but they weren't buying it. "God forbid that such a thing should ever happen," they protested. But that's exactly what Jesus was saying would happen to them.

A Stone That *Will* Break Your Bones

Then, as if to drive home his point, Jesus challenged these religious leaders—all of whom knew the Old Testament Scriptures very well—by asking them, "Didn't you ever read this in the Scriptures? 'The stone rejected by the builders has now become the cornerstone. This is the Lord's doing, and it's marvelous to see.'"

That stone rejected by the builders was Jesus himself. And he told his listeners, "All who stumble over that stone will be broken to pieces, and it will crush anyone on whom it falls."

His Name Is Jesus, a.k.a.
"The Chief Cornerstone" (Ephesians 2:20). Many of the religious leaders rejected Jesus, and yet he told these people that he was the foundation stone on which the entire building of their religion was based. This applies to the Christian church that was established later.

This Same Stone Hit Them in the Temple

The religious leaders wanted to arrest Jesus right then and there, but they thought better of it. They were well aware that if they tried to do anything to Jesus, they would most certainly bring the wrath of thousands of people on themselves.

From the day Jesus entered Jerusalem, he began teaching daily at the Temple. He taught about the kingdom of God, about who he was, and about what would happen in Jerusalem after he was gone.

This Message Is Anti-Establishment

Jesus' teachings in Jerusalem were getting him in deeper and deeper trouble with the religious establishment. But Jesus knew his message and his mission, and he wasn't going to back down from either of them, not even for a moment. He knew why he was in Jerusalem, and a part of his plan was telling the religious leaders where they really stood with God.

That, it would turn out, was part of how Jesus would fulfill the Old Testament prophecies, as well as his own, about what would happen to him later that week.

The Least You Need to Know

◆ Jesus began his final week on Earth in the "triumphal entry" when he rode into Jerusalem on a donkey.

◆ Many people in Jerusalem welcomed Jesus into the Holy City as their Messiah-King.

◆ Jesus quickly ran into opposition from the Jewish religious establishment in Jerusalem after the triumphal entry.

◆ Jesus didn't back away from conflict with the religious leaders but told them through parables that he knew what they had planned for him.

Chapter 17

Getting to the Heart of True Religion

In This Chapter

- ◆ Attempts by the Jewish leadership to trap Jesus
- ◆ Jesus' own "tribute" to Tiberius Caesar
- ◆ A question about the greatest commandment in the Law of Moses

After Jesus had arrived with great fanfare in Jerusalem, the religious leadership redoubled their efforts to have him arrested. Part of their plan was to send people to "trap" Jesus by getting him to say something they could use against him.

Trap Doors That Fell Through (Matthew 22:15–22)

When the Scribes and priests in Jerusalem realized they hadn't made so much as a tiny dent in Jesus' popularity, they went at their plan to arrest him from a different angle. Rather than try to trap Jesus themselves, they sent representatives of the Pharisees to trick Jesus into saying something they could report to the Roman authorities.

The representatives the Pharisees sent were themselves Pharisees-in-training, young men they believed Jesus would be more likely to trust since they were not well known in Jerusalem. In addition, they sent some Herodians, members of the Jewish political party that favored the Roman rule of Palestine under Herod.

The irony of the account of the representatives of the Pharisees and the Herodians approaching Jesus together was that the Pharisees and Herodians were at odds with each other over many issues, most importantly the Roman rule over the Jewish people. The Pharisees were Jewish "separatists" and therefore wanted the Romans out of their homeland, while the Herodians were in favor of Roman rule.

The first thing these men did was attempt to flatter Jesus and make him comfortable answering their very loaded questions openly. "Teacher," they said. "We know that you speak and teach what is right and are not influenced by what others think. You sincerely teach the ways of God."

Trick Questions? Go Ahead, Make My Day!

When the representatives believed they had Jesus good and "buttered up," they posed this question: "Is it right to pay taxes to the Roman government or not?" But Jesus knew what they were up to. He knew that they wanted to put him in a "no-win" situation by taking sides either with the Romans or with the very people who had been following him.

W.W.J.K. (What Would Jesus Know?)

The Jewish people in Judea at the time of Jesus suffered under an incredible tax burden. Historians have estimated that the average Jewish citizen paid almost half of his wages in taxes. The Roman government took around 32 percent, with another 12 percent going toward the payment of various Jewish taxes. An additional 5 percent went to the corrupt and greedy tax gatherers and other officials.

Jesus knew that if he said that it wasn't right to pay taxes to the Roman government, he would be in danger of being accused of encouraging rebellion against the Romans. However, if he said that it was right to pay taxes to the Romans, he would hurt his standing in the eyes of the people, who hated the Romans and their oppressive system of taxation. This was a huge issue at that time, as many of the Jewish people in Palestine knew people who had been sold into slavery, forced off their land, or executed outright because they couldn't pay their taxes.

Jesus knew all these things, and he didn't answer the question about Roman taxation directly but instead attacked these representatives' motives for asking it in the first place: "You hypocrites!" he said. "Whom are you trying to fool with your trick questions?"

The Flip Side of the Coin

Jesus then asked them to show him a *denarius*, one of the many coins in circulation in Judea at the time. When they handed him the coin, he asked them, "Whose picture and title are stamped on it?" They could plainly see that coin contained the image of Tiberius Caesar, and they acknowledged as much to Jesus.

Then Jesus stumped the representatives when he said, "Well then, give to Caesar what belongs to him. But everything that belongs to God must be given to God."

Let's Come to Terms

The Roman **denarius,** which was the equivalent of about a day's wages at the time of Jesus, was a silver coin. The "heads" side of the coin included a picture of Tiberius Caesar in profile with the inscription "Tiberius Caesar, son of divine Augustus." The "tails" side was a picture of a woman seated on a throne and facing right with a scepter in her right hand and a palm or olive branch in her left, with the inscription "High Priest." The coins were minted in Tiberius, Herod Antipas's capital, which was named in honor of Tiberius Caesar. The images and inscriptions on the coin were considered by most of the Jews to be blasphemous, as they attribute divinity to the Caesar family.

The Pharisees' plan to trap Jesus by handing him a religious and political hot potato had not only failed but left them a little red-faced. But they weren't about to give up. Sooner or later, they believed, they would give him a question he couldn't handle, at least not to his followers' satisfaction. When that happened, they would have him right where they wanted him.

Seven Grooms for One Widow? (Luke 20:27–39)

The Pharisees and Herodians weren't alone in their attempts to trap Jesus or at least to attack the credibility of his teaching. The Sadducees also took their best shot, asking him about something they themselves didn't even believe in.

On the same day that representatives from the Pharisees and Herodians challenged Jesus concerning the lawfulness of paying taxes to Rome, the Sadducees approached him with a loaded question of their own.

Jesus and his followers—as well as most of the Jewish people of that time—believed in a final resurrection of the dead. That led the Sadducees to challenge him concerning a Jewish law that required the brother of a married man who had died to take the widow as his own wife. The scenario they gave Jesus was made all the more sticky because the husband who had died had six brothers, and each of them had died, leaving the same woman a seven-time widow.

The Sadducees then asked Jesus whose wife the widow would be at the resurrection. Obviously, this too was a trick question, because the Sadducees didn't even believe in a resurrection or an afterlife.

Married Now, Single for Eternity

The Sadducees really believed they had Jesus cornered. They believed that their scenario would prove to Jesus and his followers just how ridiculous the idea of a resurrection really was.

Jesus, however, was unfazed by the question. He boldly told the Sadducees something no one had ever had the nerve to tell them before: They didn't know the Scriptures and they didn't know about the power of God. He then told them that the very premise of their question was wrong, that there would be no marriage in heaven.

Jesus then went on to tell these Sadducees that the very writings they held to—the Pentateuch, which they saw as their only source when it came to the things of God—pointed to a resurrection of the dead: "Long after Abraham, Isaac, and Jacob had died, God said, 'I am the God of Abraham, the God of Isaac, and the God of Jacob.' So he is the God of the living, not the dead," he told them, quoting from the book of Exodus.

So far, every attempt by the Jewish religious establishment to trick Jesus had blown up in their faces. Instead of turning the people against him, his answers made them even more impressed with his wisdom and more willing to follow him and hear his teaching.

Give It All You Got! (Mark 12:28–34)

When the Pharisees heard what Jesus had told the Sadducees about the resurrection (something the Pharisees themselves believed in), they came up with some new questions they believed could trip him up.

One of these Pharisees—who also happened to be a scribe or, as the Bible calls them, "an expert in religious law"—tried to trap Jesus by asking him a question that had long been debated within the Jewish religious leadership: "Teacher, which is the most important commandment in the law of Moses?"

W.W.J.K. (What Would Jesus Know?)

The Jews at the time of Jesus divided up their commandments into greater and lesser, but there was a lot of debate among the leadership over which were more important to keep than the others. There are 613 total laws in the Talmud, 365 of them negative (you shall *not*) and 248 of them positive (you *shall*). The Jews realized that it would be impossible to keep all those commandments perfectly, so they debated which were the "greatest," or most important, so that they could keep the greatest of them instead of keeping the whole law.

Jesus had a very simple and very profound answer for this Scribe. He told him, quoting Deuteronomy 6:5, "You must love the Lord your God with all your heart, all your soul, and all your mind." That, Jesus said, was the first and foremost commandment in all the law. But there was one that was just as important. Quoting from Leviticus 19:18, Jesus told him that he was to love his neighbor as he loves himself.

Jesus explained that all the laws and commands of the Old Testament prophets were based on those two simple commandments. By that he meant that when someone approaches God with a heart of love and does the same for other humans, that person will be motivated to obey all the other commands in Scripture.

This particular Scribe was impressed with what Jesus had to say: "Well said, Teacher," he said. "You have spoken the truth by saying that there is only one God and no other." He went on to tell Jesus that he understood that it was far more important for him to love God and other people than it was to present the offerings and sacrifices required in the Law of Moses.

Jesus could see that this man had an understanding of the law and what it meant. "You are not far from the Kingdom of God," he told him.

His Name Is Jesus, a.k.a.

"Son of David" (Mark 10:47). God promised King David that he would have an eternal line of kings, even though there was an interruption for centuries. So most Jews were expecting it to resume with the coming of the Messiah, an ancestor of David, who would first set up an earthly kingdom to rule the world. The assumption was that when the world was destroyed, the Messiah would rule in heaven forever.

Do As They Say, but Not As They Do (Matthew 23:1–36)

Jesus told the crowds at the Temple that day—as well as his own disciples—that they should respect the teachings of the Scribes and Pharisees, simply because they knew the law so well. But when it came to practicing that law the way they did, he told them, don't do it—because many of them didn't practice what they preached.

Furthermore, they brought the people down with impossibly heavy provisions but wouldn't so much as lift a finger to help them meet those demands. Jesus was referring not to the law itself but to the oral traditions, which the Pharisees saw as being just as important as the written Scriptures. Keeping the written law itself was all but impossible for even the most pious people, let alone keeping the law *and* the oral tradition.

Jesus further denounced those who made a show of their religious practices so that everyone could see. They wore extra large *phylacteries* attached to their sleeves, and extra long tassels on their robes—both of which were considered outward signs of righteousness.

Let's Come to Terms

Phylacteries, which is the word used in most versions of the Bible for "prayer boxes," were small leather boxes containing passages of Scripture written on parchment. Members of the Jewish religious leadership fastened them with bands to the left arm or to the forehead in an attempt to obey literally the Old Testament command to "commit yourselves completely to these words of mine [God's]. Tie them to your hands as a reminder, and wear them on your forehead" (Deuteronomy 11:18). Some of the Jewish leaders wore bigger prayer boxes so that they could be easily noticed.

Jesus went on to assail those who seek out the most prominent places in social or religious settings and those who enjoyed being called "Rabbi" more than they enjoyed humbly serving God and other people.

The bottom line of Jesus' teaching about the Jewish religious leadership was that too many of the authorities had lost sight of the most important message of the Scriptures. They were, in short, caught up in "religious" practices while missing out on the message of compassion.

The Percentage (Not the Amount) Counts

When Jesus finished his teaching about the religious leaders, he went over to the Temple collection box and observed as people came by and dropped in their offerings. He watched as rich people left large amounts of money toward God's work while the not-so-rich gave what they could. But Jesus saw one of the people who stopped by the Temple that day as one giving an offering he considered bigger and more important than any others.

A widow who was apparently desperately poor passed by the collection box and left two *lepta*, which was the equivalent of two pennies. Seeing what this widow had given touched Jesus' heart, and he called his disciples together to talk to them about it. He told them that the poor widow had given more than anyone else that day. The others, he said, had given only a fraction of their surplus while she had given all she had.

To Jesus, the true value of a gift wasn't in what it was worth intrinsically, but in what it cost the giver. Even though that widow had given what was in practical terms an insignificant amount, her gift was of immeasurable value to God, simply because it cost her everything she had.

Let's Come to Terms

A **lepton,** a tiny copper coin that was the smallest denomination in circulation at the time of Jesus, was worth about $1/128$ of a denarius, which was the pay for a day's wages. That meant that the widow who left two lepta had given the equivalent of $1/64$ of a day's wages.

It's All Greek to Them (John 12:20–36)

Sometime during Jesus' last week in Jerusalem, some Greek pilgrims approached one of his disciples and asked if they could meet Jesus in person. They were probably Gentiles who had been born in the Greek-speaking part of the region—such as cities from the Decapolis—and had adopted the beliefs and practices of Judaism for themselves. They probably wanted to know how the teachings of Jesus fit in with Judaism.

Jesus did not respond directly to this request; instead he gave his final public sermon. After this scene, all of Jesus' teaching, with the exception of his encounters with the Jewish and Roman authorities on the day of his arrest, would be to his 12 apostles.

A Death That Produces Lives

Jesus told the disciples, as well as the crowd who was with him that day (presumably including the Greeks) that the time of his death was at hand. "The time has come for the Son of Man to enter into his glory," he said.

Jesus went on to illustrate what his death would mean by telling the crowd that unless a single kernel of wheat dies (or, literally, is buried), it will remain just that: a single kernel. But if it is buried, its "death" will produce many other kernels of wheat—or, as Jesus spelled it out, a "plentiful harvest of new lives."

Did I Hear Thunder, an Angel, or God?

As Jesus was speaking, he stopped and told the crowd that he was in turmoil. He knew what was ahead for him—namely his arrest, trial, and a long, painful death on a cross—and he wondered aloud whether he should pray that his Father in heaven would save him from his fate.

But as Jesus was speaking, he reminded his followers that his trial and death on a cross was the ultimate reason he had come in the first place. He prayed, "Father, bring glory to your name."

Just then, a voice came from heaven and said, "I have already brought it glory, and I will do it again." Everyone in the crowd heard the voice, but not all of them were sure exactly they had heard. Some thought it was thunder, while others thought it was the voice of an angel speaking to Jesus.

Jesus told the crowd that what they had heard was indeed a voice from heaven, and that it had spoken for their benefit and not his. He went on to explain that the time of judgment for the world had come and that he, the Son of Man, was going to be nailed to a cross and die just a few days later. In suffering that way, he told them, he would bring everyone—Jews, Greeks, Romans, and others alike—to himself.

A Short-Lived Messiah

Of course, the people who heard him say this were perplexed. They believed that their Messiah would come into Jerusalem and set up his eternal kingdom on Earth. This whole "dying on a cross" thing wasn't supposed to be a part of the program. Why was the Son of Man going to die, they asked—and while they were on the subject, *who* is this "Son of Man?"

Jesus didn't answer their questions directly, but instead told them that he would be with them for just a short time longer. He told them that they should believe in "the light" (Jesus himself) while he was still with them.

Undercover Believers (John 12:37–50)

Jesus had known all along that his work and message would be met with unbelief on the part of most of the people, even many of those who had followed him for a great portion of his earthly ministry. They had seen him do many miracles and heard him teach with authority like none they'd ever heard. But they couldn't accept his claim that he was going to die and that his death would be a benefit to the entire world.

However, there were many people in Jerusalem who believed in Jesus at that time. Among those believers were members of the Sanhedrin. (While this passage of John's gospel doesn't name them, two of the Sanhedrin members who believed were Joseph of Arimathea and Nicodemus.) But they kept quiet about what they really thought about Jesus for fear that the Pharisees would throw them out of the Sanhedrin.

One last time, Jesus gave the crowds a chance to understand his message and believe in him and what he had come to do. He shouted to them, "If you trust me, you are really trusting God the Father who sent me. For when you see me, you are seeing the one who sent me."

With that, Jesus was finished addressing the crowds in Jerusalem. Now, he would turn his attention to his disciples and to preparing them—and himself—for what would be taking place in the next few days.

The Least You Need to Know

- ◆ Jesus dealt successfully with a series of attempts to trap him into saying something they could use to condemn him.
- ◆ Jesus revealed in a number of examples what true allegiance to God really means.
- ◆ In Jesus' final public teaching, he told the crowds what his mission on earth really was.

Chapter 18

Getting Ready for a Return Visit

In This Chapter

- ◆ Predictions of the destruction of Jerusalem and Jesus' second coming
- ◆ Jesus' "end times" instructions to his disciples
- ◆ Plans to arrest Jesus and the betrayal that aided them

As the end of his final week in Jerusalem grew near, Jesus knew that most of the people in the city didn't believe he was the Messiah sent from God. He also knew that he was facing the arrest by the Jewish religious leaders, then an execution at the hands of the Roman authorities.

Jesus was in anguish over what was ahead for him, but he was downright heartbroken at what he knew was ahead for the city and the people he so dearly loved.

At this point in the story, it is important for us to remember that Jesus was, first and foremost, a Jew who deeply loved his God and loved his people. As he saw what was going on in the capital city of the nation of Israel, he was grieved, probably to the point of tears.

Know Jesus, Know Peace; No Jesus, No Peace

Standing close to the Temple in the Holy City, Jesus addressed Jerusalem as a loving father would persuade a rebellious child he wanted to call back home and protect: "O Jerusalem, Jerusalem, the city that kills the prophets and stones God's messengers! How often I have wanted to gather your children together as a hen protects her chicks beneath her wings, but you wouldn't let me." In one of the Psalms, King David says to pray for the peace of Jerusalem, and Jesus believed that as Messiah, he was the ultimate answer to that prayer.

As you may remember from Chapter 16, Jesus cried openly when he first rode into Jerusalem. He wanted more than anything for the Holy City and its people to choose the way of peace, but he knew what the future held for the city, and it caused him incredible inner agony.

Jesus had just left the Temple, where, using very strong language, he had denounced the religious leadership for its hypocrisy. Now Jesus turned his attention to the apostles, teaching them of the things ahead for them, their people, and their nation as a whole.

The Must-See Temple Attraction (Mark 13:1–2)

As Jesus and the disciples left the Temple, one of the 12 looked at the magnificent buildings in front of him and marveled aloud, "Teacher, look at these tremendous buildings! Look at the massive stones in the walls!" The disciples were amazed at the stonework of the Temple, as well as the decorations on its walls. We mentioned earlier that King Herod the Great had begun the rebuilding of the Temple in around 20 B.C.E.

That Temple was a replacement for a smaller temple the Jews had constructed following their return from the Babylonian exile. The Babylonians had destroyed the original Temple when they sacked Jerusalem in around 595 B.C.E. At the time of Jesus, the Temple building itself had been completed, but renovations continued right up until 66 C.E., when the Jewish people in Jerusalem revolted against Roman rule.

The disciples' awe over the appearance of the Temple was shared by others who saw it at that time. It was impressive both in its construction and in the fact that it was adorned with gold plating, which gave it a gleam that could be seen from great distances from the city. The beauty of the Temple inspired one rabbi to later write, "He who has not seen the temple of Herod has never seen a beautiful building in his life."

The Stones Will Be Rolling

But Jesus, standing before this awesomely beautiful structure, shocked his disciples that day when he told them that it wouldn't be long before the Temple they were looking at would be destroyed: "These magnificent buildings will be so completely demolished that not one stone will be left on top of another," he said.

No doubt, Jesus' prediction that the Temple would be destroyed troubled the disciples deeply. As Jews themselves, the disciples saw the Temple as central to their whole way of life and system of belief. They also knew that if the Temple itself was destroyed, it meant that the city of Jerusalem would be in big trouble as well.

It's Not the End of the World, or Is It? (Matthew 24:3–26:15)

After telling the disciples that the Temple would be destroyed, Jesus left the Temple area and went to the Mount of Olives. Of course, the disciples had been with Jesus long enough to know that there was more he had to tell them, so they followed him to the mount, where they asked him two key questions: When would the destruction of Jerusalem and the Temple take place, and what would be the signs that would point to Jesus' return?

Jesus' answers to those questions must have been difficult for the disciples to hear. He began telling them in great detail the things they and others in the city of Jerusalem would soon face.

The Times They Are a'Changing

Jesus warned the disciples that many "false christs" would appear after he had left them and that they should be careful not to pay any attention to them. He further told them that these frauds would come in his name claiming to be the Messiah and that a lot of people would follow them.

He told them that they would hear of wars breaking out in their part of the world as well as other places. There would also be famines and earthquakes throughout the earth. But that was only the beginning of the horrors to come, Jesus said.

No Profit from False Prophets

Jesus told the disciples that they and others of his followers would face incredible persecution on account of his message, that they would be arrested and killed simply because of their allegiance to him. At the same time, false prophets would appear on the scene and try to lead people away from him. Many people, he said, would follow those false prophets and abandon him rather than face the persecution. Jesus said that before the fall of Jerusalem sin would run rampant and the love of God would grow cold within people.

Those who endured these things and held to their faith, Jesus said, were the ones who would be "saved," meaning that they would see the kingdom of heaven.

Jesus assured the disciples that the end would come only after the Good News of Jesus' message of salvation was preached to the ends of the known world.

The Future? Let's Not Go There!

Jesus spoke very specifically about the destruction of the Temple and Jerusalem, and it wasn't a very pleasant picture. It was a horrible scene of suffering unlike anything the disciples themselves, or the rest of humanity, had ever seen—or likely could have even imagined—which would be carried out by the Romans within this same generation.

Jesus told them this event would fulfill a prophecy in the book of Daniel: "Then as a climax to his terrible deeds, he will set up a sacrilegious object that causes desecration …" (Daniel 11:31). This meant that the sacredness of the Temple would be defiled by pagans.

> **W.W.J.K. (What Would Jesus Know?)**
>
> During the time of the Maccabean Revolt, which took place around two centuries before Jesus' end times discourse, it was believed that Daniel's prophecy referred to the actions of Antiochus Epiphanes, who tried to put an end to all Jewish religious practices and who set up an altar to the pagan god Zeus in the Holy Temple and sacrificed a pig on it.

Flee, or Go on an Unwanted Vacation

Jesus spoke of that prophecy as a yet-to-be-fulfilled event, one where the Temple would again be desecrated. Jesus told the disciples that when that happened, those who were in Jerusalem at the time should flee for the surrounding wilderness if they wanted to survive and those who were in the outlying towns and villages should stay out of the Holy City. Jesus said that during this time many people would be brutally killed or taken away to other nations as slaves. Jesus told the disciples to pray that these horrible events didn't take place during the winter or on the Sabbath.

Winter rains caused the rivers and streams in Palestine to swell, which would have made an escape from Judea even harder. Being attacked on the Sabbath would have meant an interruption in a sacred observation for the Jewish people. It has also been said that since the city gates of Jerusalem were locked during the Sabbath, an escape would have been all the more difficult, if not impossible.

The Wrong Roman Solution

Jesus' predictions surrounding the destruction of Jerusalem and the nation of Israel were fulfilled to the letter a little over three decades after he made them. In 66 C.E. the Jews revolted against Roman rule, and in 67 C.E., the Roman army, at the orders of Cestius Gallus, the Roman ruler of Syria, encircled the city of Jerusalem. At that time, the Christians who lived in Jerusalem fled the city and crossed the Jordan River into Perea.

The Jewish historian Josephus witnessed and wrote about the things he saw in Israel during that time, and it was a horrible picture that included acts of cannibalism as well as bloody fighting against the Roman forces and "internal" fighting between factions of the Jewish people. Finally, on August 10, 70 C.E., the Romans stormed the city, massacred more than a million people, and took around 100,000 survivors and sold them into slavery. At that time, the Holy Temple was destroyed.

Enough Is Enough Already!

Jesus described this time of "tribulation" as being so horrible and bloody that no one would survive it if not for God himself stepping in and putting a stop to it. That, he said, would be done for the sake of "God's chosen ones," which meant those who believed in Jesus.

Jesus told the disciples that during this time of crisis, there would be "false christs" who were very convincing in that they performed miracles. But Jesus told them not to pay attention to those who claimed to be the Messiah or who pointed to his coming, "For as the lightning lights up the entire sky, so it will be when the Son of Man comes," meaning, simply, that when Jesus returned, there would be no question about who he was.

Who Turned Out the Lights? (Matthew 24:29–31)

Jesus had answered the disciples' question concerning the destruction of Jerusalem and the Temple and the events surrounding these things. He then moved on to tell them—using some very colorful (and possibly figurative) language—about his return, or *"second coming."*

> ## Let's Come to Terms
>
> The **second coming** is the term used in the world of Christianity for the return of Jesus and his gathering of believers from all over the face of the earth. The apostle Paul painted a very vivid picture of Jesus' return when he later wrote in the book of 1 Thessalonians that all Christians living and dead will be caught up in the clouds to meet the Lord in the air and remain with him forever (1 Thessalonians 4:16–17). The destruction of this world, final judgment, and the makings of a new heaven and earth will also take place.

Jesus told the disciples that "immediately" after the destruction of Jerusalem and the dispersion of the Jewish people a series of events leading to his return would begin unfolding. In describing for the disciples his return to earth, Jesus painted a spectacular word picture for them:

> ### His Name Is Jesus, a.k.a.
>
> "The Sun of Righteousness" (Malachi 4:2). Though the sun and moon will be darkened in the last days, Jesus is seen in the book of Malachi as a perfect sun which, as it shines, brings healing. The book of Revelation also says that heaven will need no light because Jesus will shine forth and illuminate everything.

"Immediately after those horrible days end, the sun will be darkened, the moon will not give light, the stars will fall from the sky, and the powers of heaven will be shaken."

And down here on earth the nations will be in turmoil, perplexed by the roaring seas and strange tides." In other words, they couldn't count on anything in the universe to remain stable.

If Jesus' words were taken literally then they would be pointing toward a series of cataclysmic events in the heavens that would take place immediately before or at the very time he returned. Some experts on the subject believe that these words were to be taken literally, that Jesus' return would be accompanied by just these kinds of "natural" events.

However, many scholars believe that Jesus was speaking figuratively, that he was actually describing spiritual and political upheavals that would take place over a long period of time before he returned.

One thing that is certain, however, is that Jesus described his second coming as a spectacular event:

> "The sign of the coming of the Son of Man will appear in the heavens, and there will be deep mourning among all the nations of the earth. And they will

see the Son of Man arrive on the clouds of heaven with power and great glory. And he will send forth his angels with the sound of a mighty trumpet blast, and they will gather together his chosen ones from the farthest ends of earth and heaven" (Matthew 24:30–31).

See Me on Center Stage (Matthew 24:32-43)

Finally, Jesus taught, he would return in such a way that everyone on earth would see him. That would be a time of mourning for those who didn't know him and a time of celebration for those Jesus calls his own as they were gathered from every part of the earth.

No doubt the disciples were feeling a little overwhelmed at what Jesus was telling them. He was talking about the destruction of their very own homeland. And if they are like most people (which they were), they wanted to know when these things would happen so they could get ready.

To Get There, Watch the Signs

But Jesus refused to tell them when the end would come. In fact, he told that no one knew when it would happen, not even him, but only the Father. For that reason, he said, it was important that those who followed Jesus make sure that they were ready at all times, even when it didn't look like the time for the end to come.

While Jesus didn't tell the disciples the exact time of his return, he likened it to a fig tree coming into leaf and into bud, both sure signs that summer was close. In other words, when they saw all the signs of the end of this age, they could know that Jesus' return was near.

> ### His Name Is Jesus, a.k.a.
>
> "Our Hope" (1 Timothy 1:1). Jesus is given this title in the context of a hope for eternal life through the resurrection of the body when he returns as judge of the living and the dead. The event itself of his second coming is spoken of as the "blessed hope" by Timothy's contemporary in the book of Titus.

Talkin' 'Bout *My* Generation (Matthew 24:34)

When it came to the "when" of Jesus' return, he said something that has puzzled people for many centuries when he said that his generation would not pass from the scene before all these things would take place.

Some believe that when Jesus said that, he was referring to the fall of Jerusalem. That would make sense, since Jerusalem fell within the timeline of that particular generation.

But others believe that he was referring to his return but that when he used the word *generation*, he was referring to the Jewish race as a whole. That also would make sense, because even though the nation of Israel ceased to exist in 70 C.E., the Jewish people survived as a distinct race for more than 18 centuries: from the fall of Jerusalem until 1948, when the nation of Israel was reestablished as an independent state.

No Rain Check for This Party

Jesus told the disciples that they could know that his coming was close when they saw the "signs of the times." But he also told them his coming would be so sudden that it would catch most people off guard.

Just as the great flood had caught the people of Noah's day unawares, so would his second coming catch people off guard. In the days of Noah, he told the disciples, people were living pretty normal and happy lives—enjoying weddings and parties. But before they knew what hit them, the rains came and they were underwater.

How can we understand both points of view? In today's world we have order, routine, and prosperity amidst violence and natural disasters. But at any time, Jesus is saying, the latter can get out of control and become the real thing—the signs of his coming again.

His Name Is Jesus, a.k.a.

"The Bridegroom" (Matthew 9:15). In this parable of the bridesmaids the bridegroom is a veiled reference by Jesus to himself, with his followers, the church, being the bride—based on our intimate love relationship with him for eternity. He refers to the first event in heaven as "the marriage feast of the Lamb" with Jesus being the Lamb of God (see name in Chapter 8) and ourselves as the bride at this great heavenly celebration.

The Real Party Comes Later

Jesus illustrated the disciples'—as well as others who believe in him—need to be alert and ready for his return using a "mini-parable" that pointed out how if a man knew that someone was going to break into his home and when he was going to do it, the man would be ready and therefore able to keep the robbery from happening.

But Jesus didn't just tell his disciples to watch for his return but also warned them to make sure they were ready when it came. To further drive this point home, Jesus told them that they needed to be like faithful servants who continued working diligently even though their master had temporarily left them alone to work.

Jesus contrasted those kinds of servants with the "evil" ones—those who assumed that the master wouldn't be home for a while and therefore spent their time mistreating other servants, partying, and getting drunk. Those servants, Jesus said, would be kicked out of the master's home (and worse) when he returned and found them slacking off.

Some Very Talented Servants (Mark 13:34–36)

Jesus was very clear with his disciples that he would be leaving them soon but that he would also be returning for them one day. He also told them that as they waited and prepared for his return, they were to keep themselves busy spreading his message of love and compassion.

In telling the disciples that, he used what has come to be known as the Parable of the Talents, which, as you will see, has a very interesting double meaning when it comes to the use of the word *talents*.

This parable is the story of an obviously wealthy man who gave each of his three servants a large amount of money—some more than others—which they were to put to use in such a way that it increased his wealth. He gave five talents to one, two talents to the second, and one talent to the third, then left on his trip.

Let's Come to Terms

A **talent** wasn't a measure of currency, such as a coin or a bill of a certain denomination, but a piece of precious metal of a specific weight. A silver talent weighed around 75 pounds and had a value of 6,000 denari (remember, a denari was equivalent to a day's wage for the typical Jewish worker). In modern terms, the man in Jesus' parable of the talents had distributed nearly $2 million to his three servants.

It's Safer Than in a Mattress, but That's All

The two servants who had been given charge of five talents and two talents, respectively, both made good investments and doubled the rich man's money for him. But the servant who had received one talent was afraid of losing the money, so he took it and buried it in the ground for safekeeping, a common practice in that place and culture.

When the rich man returned from his trip, he called his three servants together to see what they had done with the money he had given them. The first two announced that they had invested his money well and made a 100 percent profit. Of course, the man was pleased with both of them and not only gave both of them additional responsibilities but celebrated with them.

No Talent for Finances or Flattery

The third servant, however, reported to his boss that he was afraid he would lose the money so he had buried the one talent. Of course, he hadn't lost any of it, but he also hadn't made his boss any profit. Furthermore, he insulted his boss by implying that he was a harsh, unfeeling man.

W.W.J.K. (What Would Jesus Know?)

According to Jewish religious law, it was not permissible for Jews to collect interest on loans from other Jews. It was lawful, however, to collect interest from Gentiles. In the scenario of Jesus' parable of the talents, someone would be allowed to collect "interest" by investing his money with moneychangers, who charged foreigners a fee to exchange their currency for Jewish money.

Of course, the man was angry at what he had just been told. He told his servant that he was wicked and lazy and that the very least he should have done was put his money in the bank so that he could earn some interest on it.

Jesus pointed out that the third servant had not served his master faithfully. He had been asked to take a risk—and not even with his own money but the master's—but he refused to do it. As a consequence, the master took the 1 talent he had been given and gave it to the one who had invested the master's money wisely and who now had 10.

Use It or Lose It

The one who had the most talents but had used them in a way that brought the man the most profits would receive even more. But the one who wasted the master's time would have what little was given to him taken away.

The message Jesus was giving his disciples when he told them the Parable of the Talents was that God had given each of them useful "gifts" and had also given them the responsibility of using those gifts for the benefit of his kingdom while Jesus was away from them. Mainly, they were to use their gifts to bring in a rich harvest of followers.

Here Comes the Judge (Matthew 25:31–46)

Jesus finished his "end times" teaching by telling the disciples that when he returned, he would separate "the sheep from the goats"—the sheep being those who showed his kind of compassion and love for others and the goats being those who did nothing about what he had taught and shown people during his time on earth.

In telling this story, Jesus refers to himself as "the king," the only time he does that in any of the gospel accounts, outside of when he was teaching in parables. And he does so in the capacity of a judge administering final justice.

Jesus told the disciples that the sheep, those who would be at his right hand come judgment day, were those who fed him when he was hungry, gave him a drink when he was thirsty, showed him hospitality when he was a stranger, clothed him when he was naked, and visited him when he was in prison.

When the sheep asked him *when* they saw him hungry, thirsty, in need of hospitality, naked, or in prison, he told them, "I assure you, when you did it to one of the least of these my brothers and sisters, you were doing it to me!" He so cared about and identified with the outcasts that they were helping him when they ministered to these people.

The goats, Jesus taught, were those who didn't meet the king's needs in any way. Jesus said they might be piously saying, "Lord, Lord" and calling themselves his followers, but they were ignoring these same people that Jesus wanted to help. Jesus would ask these "goats" to depart from his presence, because they really didn't acknowledge his Lordship in their lives.

Jesus' teaching of the "sheep and goats" was in many ways a synopsis of much of his other teaching. Jesus held that true righteousness before God wasn't achieved through religious acts with a selfish motivation to earn a reward, but through a heart that had been so changed by his love that it was motivated toward showing compassion toward others for their own sake—just as Jesus had always done.

His Name Is Jesus, a.k.a.

"The Judge" (2 Timothy 4:1). When Jesus performs his role of separating the sheep from the goats at the end of time he is acting as "judge of the living and the dead," which is a role given to him by the Father. He states that in his earthly life, however, he first comes to save the world, not judge it, offering forgiveness and new life to those who believe.

Make It Thirty, and It's a Deal (Luke 22:1–6)

When Jesus was finished teaching the disciples, he told them that it was only a few days until the Passover celebration. When the Passover came, he said, he would be arrested then handed over to the Romans to be crucified.

At that very moment, some Jewish religious leaders were meeting at the palace of the high priest, Caiaphas, finalizing their plans to have Jesus arrested. They knew that arresting him during the Passover might mean causing a riot among the people, so part of their plan was to arrest Jesus quietly and without a lot of public attention.

That night, Judas, the treasurer for Jesus and the disciples, approached the chief priests and asked them what they would give him if he would set up the arrest of Jesus. Of course, they were delighted that one of Jesus' own followers was willing to help them out. They agreed to pay Judas a bounty of thirty silver coins.

From that time forward, Judas began looking for the best time to betray Jesus and turn him in to the authorities.

The Least You Need to Know

- ◆ Jesus said that the Temple and the city of Jerusalem would one day be destroyed.

- ◆ Jesus said that he would return after his death, and he gave his disciples the signs of his coming.

- ◆ Jesus told the disciples that as they waited for his return, they were to keep themselves busy doing the work he had given them.

- ◆ The chief priests were aided in their plans to arrest Jesus by Judas Iscariot, who agreed to betray him.

Chapter 19

The Final Hours

In This Chapter

- ◆ Jesus and the disciples take part in "the Last Supper"
- ◆ Jesus gives his farewell address to the disciples
- ◆ Jesus' parting prayer—for himself, the disciples, and other believers
- ◆ Jesus is betrayed and arrested in the Garden of Gethsemane

As the Passover approached, Jesus' time on earth with his disciples was down to a matter of hours. Nearly everything we think of as his "earthly ministry" was now in the past, with the future holding betrayal, arrest, and death for Jesus.

It was always part of Jesus' plan to be in Jerusalem for the Passover meal and to spend it with his disciples. They had been spending their evenings following his triumphal entry in Bethany, and he sent Peter and John ahead into Jerusalem to make arrangements for the meal.

When the two disciples asked him where specifically they were to go, Jesus told them that as they entered the city they would meet a man carrying a pitcher of water. They were to follow that man to a house, and when they got there, they were to ask the owner if they could use the guest room, which was located upstairs.

W.W.J.K. (What Would Jesus Know?)

Unleavened bread, bitter herbs, and the sacrificial lamb were the three foods central to the Passover meal. In addition, four cups of wine were also used in the celebration—the first at the opening prayer over the Passover day, the second after the explanation of the meaning of the Passover and the singing of a hymn called the "Hallel," the third after the meal itself, and the fourth after the singing of the final portion of the Hallel.

A Dinner Scene Worthy of da Vinci (Mark 22:7–16)

Peter and John went to Jerusalem, and just as Jesus had told them would happen, they met a man carrying a picture of water. Once they had been led to the room Jesus had told them about, they went about preparing the Passover meal for him and the rest of the disciples. That meant obtaining a Passover lamb and other items needed for dinner (spices, bread, and wine), finding a "friendly" priest to oversee the sacrifice of the lamb, then actually preparing supper. Later, when all the preparations had been made, Jesus and the disciples left Bethany and headed to Jerusalem, to the "upper room," where they were to see and hear Jesus' final teaching before his arrest and death. It was teaching they would desperately need, as he would not be with them much longer.

Some of Us Are More Equal Than Others? (Luke 22:24–26)

Because there are four gospel accounts of Jesus' Passover supper with the disciples, it is very difficult to put the events of that night in perfect order. However, many Bible scholars believe the first thing that happened when Jesus and the disciples got together was an argument among the 12 about who would be greatest in the kingdom of heaven.

Many believed that this argument started as a result of who was seated where at the table. In Jewish culture, the place someone took at the table during a meal was important, as it signified a social "pecking order." If that was what started the disciples' argument, then what they were concerned about was probably who sat closest to Jesus.

You're Head Honcho ... No, You Are!

Jesus didn't settle the argument but instead told the disciples that they weren't to worry themselves over who would be "greatest." He pointed out that in the world's system, people with power and authority liked to tell others what to do, but that they, as those who would take his message to the world after he was gone, were to take a different approach. Each of them was to humble himself and look at the other apostles as more important than himself.

Jesus also told the disciples that it was typical for the master or leader among any group to sit at the head of the table and let his servants tend to him. But it wasn't going to be that way here! As the supper was getting started, Jesus didn't just tell the disciples what kind of servants he was and they were to be.

What's Stubborn and Has Twenty-Four Feet? (John 13:1–17)

Jesus got up from the table, took off his robe and tied a towel around his waist, as if he was "girding his loins" for some menial labor. He then put some water into a wash basin and began doing something that the 12 apostles themselves saw as unthinkable: He moved from one of the men to the next, washing and drying their feet as he went.

In Jewish culture, it was a common practice for hosts to have the feet of their guests washed. People in those days wore sandals and walked nearly everywhere they went on dusty roads and trails, and that meant that their feet were in need of a good washing when they arrived at someone's home.

However, the washing of a visitor's feet was seen in that world as too demeaning for even the lowliest of Jewish servants, let alone someone in the position of disciple. Usually, the one who did the foot washing was a non-Jewish servant or slave. But what made this scene all the more incredible (and obviously uncomfortable) to the disciples was that it was Jesus, their teacher and master, who was washing their feet. To them, this scene was backwards and upside-down.

An "All or Nothing" Kind of Guy

Peter was always the one apostle of the 12 who was willing to say what he was thinking—and what the other eleven were probably thinking too—even if it meant contradicting Jesus a little bit. When his teacher came to him and stooped down to wash his feet, Peter asked why he was washing his feet in the first place. Jesus told him that he couldn't have understood it just yet, but that he soon would. But that wasn't good enough for Peter. "No!" he protested. "You will never wash my feet!"

But Jesus replied with a simple but loving ultimatum. He said that if Peter wouldn't allow him to wash his feet, then he couldn't be one of his disciples. That was all Peter needed to hear. He eagerly told Jesus to wash not only his feet, but his hands and head as well.

Teacher, Lord, and Chief Foot Washer

Once Jesus had finished this lowly chore, he put his robe back on and sat down, then looked at the disciples and asked them if they understood what he was trying to prove by washing their feet.

When his question was met with silence, Jesus pointed out to the disciples that they had rightly called him "Teacher" and "Lord." He then explained that he washed their feet so that he could set an example for how they were to serve one another.

Jesus had lived a life of humble self-sacrifice and service to others. Yes, he had some tough teaching for his disciples and for others. But he wanted the disciples to know that he had come first and foremost to give and to serve.

Raise Your Hand If You're with Me ... Not So Fast, Judas (John 13:18–31)

Jesus told the disciples that the message he gave and the example he set in washing their feet was an important one for all of them—except for one. He then made an announcement that must have stunned them.

Speaking with a very heavy heart, Jesus told them that one of them who was sitting there at the table and sharing a meal with him was going to betray him. He explained that this betrayal was a part of God's plan as announced in an Old Testament prophecy and that in seeing it fulfilled they would believe that he was the Messiah.

The disciples looked around the room at one another, wondering who could even think of doing such a thing. Each of them, including Judas Iscariot, even asked Jesus if he was the one who would give their teacher up to the authorities. At that point, Peter motioned to John, who was sitting next to Jesus, to quietly ask him who the betrayer was. John, who referred to himself in his gospel as "the disciple Jesus loved," leaned over and asked Jesus "Lord, who is it?"

Jesus answered by giving the disciples a sign. He told them that the betrayer would be the one he gave a piece of bread dipped in sauce. Jesus dipped a piece of bread in the sauce, then handed it to Judas. As soon as Judas had eaten the bread, "Satan entered into him." Matthew reports that Judas, knowing what he had earlier agreed to do, looked at Jesus and very deceitfully asked, "Teacher, I'm not the one, am I?"

Jesus looked at Judas and told him, "You have said it yourself," then said, "Hurry. Do it now." Judas got up from the table and left the upper room and headed out to meet with those who wanted to arrest Jesus.

Let's Come to Terms

The Lord's Supper, as this scene in Jesus' life has come to be known, is still commemorated in services in Christian churches around the world as Jesus commanded. Besides the Lord's Supper, it is called "Communion" (union with Christ) in many Protestant congregations and "the Eucharist" (feast of thanksgiving) in Catholic circles. Some Christians believe Christ is physically present in the bread and wine, some believe they are merely symbols of his presence.

I Give You Myself (Matthew 26:26–30)

Once Judas had left, Jesus took a loaf of bread and asked God to bless it. He then broke it into pieces and gave them to the disciples and told them, "Take it and eat it, for this is my body." In the Gospel of Luke, we see that Jesus was speaking figuratively when he said that the bread was his body and that eating the bread would be an act of commemoration: "Do this in remembrance of me."

After the disciples had eaten the bread, Jesus took a cup of wine and blessed it, then gave it to the disciples and told them to pass it around and take a drink. "Each of you drink from it, for this is my blood, which seals the covenant between God and his people. It is poured out to forgive the sins of many," he told them.

Jesus told the disciples that in a very short time he was going away and leaving them. When that happened, he said, they would long to see him but wouldn't be able to. Therefore, Jesus said, he was giving the disciples a "new" commandment: that they love one another in the same way he had loved them—sacrificially, humbly, and unconditionally.

His Name Is Jesus, a.k.a.

"The Passover Lamb" (1 Corinthians 5:7). The Israelites consumed a lamb at the original Passover meal as they were fleeing Pharaoh in Egypt. They also slaughtered a lamb and smeared the blood on their doorposts that night to protect them from a destroying angel who killed the firstborn sons of Egypt. Jesus was the new lamb who shed his blood in this new Passover—the "passing over" from death to eternal life through the forgiveness of sins.

Going AWOL at the Worst Time (Mark 14:27–31)

The Bible doesn't tell us of any response on the disciples' parts concerning Jesus' command that they love one another, but it does tell us that his statement that he would be going away really caught their attention.

Rather than asking him about his command to love one another, Peter asked him, "Lord, where are you going?" Jesus told him that he couldn't go with him—at least not right now. But Peter persisted. He asked Jesus why he couldn't come with him now, then told him that he was willing to die for him if it came to that.

That is when Jesus dropped what the disciples must have considered a big bomb. As if Jesus' saying that one of them would betray him wasn't enough, he shocked them even further by telling them very plainly that all of them would desert him that night. He also told them that their desertion of him would be a fulfillment of the Old Testament prophecy: "God will strike down the Shepherd, and the sheep of the flock will be scattered" (Zechariah 13:7).

You Won't Be Crowing About Your Courage

Jesus assured the disciples that their leaving him alone to face arrest, trial, and execution wasn't going to be the end of him or the end of their missions. In fact, it would really be a new beginning of their relationship with him. He told them that after he had been raised from the dead he would meet them in Galilee, where they had spent most of their time with him.

That, however, just wasn't going to do for Peter. "Even if everyone else deserts you, I never will," he promised. But Jesus knew what was ahead for him and for his disciples. He told Peter that before he heard a rooster crow the next morning, he would deny even knowing Jesus three times.

There's No Other Route to Heaven (John 14:1–14)

With just a few precious hours remaining with his disciples, Jesus was filled with sadness over what was ahead, including having to leave these eleven men who had been his constant companions, helpers, and students for the past three years.

Humanly speaking, if there was anyone who needed comforting that night, it was Jesus. But instead of turning to the disciples for consolation, he looked beyond his own pain and encouraged them with the promise that one day they would be with him forever: "Don't be troubled. You trust God, now trust in me," he said. "There are many rooms in my Father's home, and I am going to prepare a place for you. If this were not so, I would tell you plainly. When everything is ready, I will come and get you, so that you will always be with me where I am" (John 14:1–3).

Jesus told the disciples that they knew where he was going and how to get there. But at least one of them, Thomas, was confused. "No, we don't know, Lord," he said. "We haven't any idea where you are going, so how can we know the way?" Jesus responded by speaking what would become one of the better-known verses in the gospels: "I am the way, the truth, and the life. No one can come to the Father except through me" (John 14:6).

Jesus went on to tell Thomas that had he really understood who he was, then he would also have known who his Father was. But he also promised him that from this time forward, he would fully know and understand Jesus' and God the Father's true identity.

But yet another disciple—this time Philip— was confused and asked Jesus, "Lord, show us the Father and we will be satisfied." Jesus then gently rebuked Philip by asking him how, after all they had been through, he didn't fully understand who he was, then said very directly, "Anyone who has seen me has seen the Father!"

> **His Name Is Jesus, a.k.a.**
>
> "The Gate" (John 10:7). Jesus told Thomas that he himself was "the Way" to the Father. Likewise, in his illustration of the Good Shepherd, Jesus said he was the gate as well as the shepherd of the sheep. They could go in and out and find green pastures; in other words, feed off the bounty of God's love and life.

My Name Will Work Miracles (John 14:16–26)

Jesus told the disciples that they, as people who believed in him, would do the same kinds of things he had done, that in some ways the things they would do would be even greater than what Jesus himself had done. That, Jesus told them, was because he was going to his Father, who would do anything they asked him to do, if they simply asked in his name.

Jesus warned the disciples that the road ahead wasn't going to be easy for them. He said that people would hate them just because they identified themselves with him. "When the world hates you," Jesus encouraged them, "remember it hated me before it hated you" (John 15:18).

But Jesus promised the disciples that he wasn't going to just leave them to handle all these difficulties on their own.

When I Leave, You'll Need Counseling

Jesus promised the disciples that when he returned to heaven, he would send "another Counselor" who would never leave them. Jesus was referring to the *Holy Spirit*, who he said would teach disciples all truth and remind them of the things Jesus had said to them while he was alive on earth.

Let's Come to Terms

The **Holy Spirit** is the third person of what Christians call "the Trinity," which is the revelation of one God who identifies himself in three distinct persons: the Father, the Son, and the Holy Spirit. In the Old Testament, King David made reference to the Holy Spirit: "Do not banish me from your presence, and don't take your *Holy Spirit* from me" (Psalm 51:11). The prophet Isaiah wrote, "But they rebelled against him [the Lord] and grieved his *Holy Spirit*" (Isaiah 63:10). The New Testament, on the other hand, makes many references to the Holy Spirit, identifying him as the one who would live within those who had faith in Jesus, giving them the guidance, gifts, and wisdom it took to make them suitable ministers for Jesus.

Jesus wanted to tell the disciples many more things before he left them, but the time was just too short. But he told them that when he sent the Holy Spirit to them, the Spirit would teach them the same way Jesus had: as one speaking on behalf of God in heaven. The Holy Spirit, he said, would be one who was beholden to the Father and to the Son and would bring glory to Jesus by speaking only what Jesus spoke to him. The Holy Spirit would also be the one to convince the world of its sin, of God's righteousness, and of the coming judgment (John 16:12–16).

Peace in the Heart, Not on Earth (John 14:27–30)

Jesus knew that the disciples were about to face bitter disappointment and incredible sadness as they saw and heard what would happen to him during the next several hours. But in spite of that, he told them that he was leaving them another gift: peace of heart and mind, a peace unlike any the world could have given them.

He told them not to be worried or afraid, but to be happy for him, because in a short time he would be returning to heaven to be with his Father. It wasn't going to be an easy road for him or for them, he said, because the authorities were coming for him and coming soon. But he told them that those authorities had no real power over him and that he was going to die willingly, just as God had ordained.

Getting Ready to Branch Out (John 15)

Jesus had referred to his relationship with his disciples many times using the metaphor of the relationship of a shepherd to his sheep. But in speaking his final words of encouragement to them, he called himself "the true vine" and God the Father "the gardener." He then told them, "I am the vine; you are the branches" (John 15:5).

In likening himself to a vine and the disciples to branches, Jesus was stressing to them the fact that they were to be dependant on him for everything. He told them that unless they remained close to him—even after he was gone—they couldn't accomplish anything in the spiritual world. Conversely, if they stayed close to him and remembered and treasured the things he had taught them through his words and actions, they would produce much "fruit"—meaning souls—for the kingdom of God.

> **W.W.J.K. (What Would Jesus Know?)**
>
> In the Old Testament, vines and vineyards are often used as symbols for "God's chosen people," Israel, with God being the one who tends to the vineyard so that it bears fruit. Isaiah 5 and Psalm 80:8–16 are examples. When Jesus referred to himself as "the true vine," he was saying that he had come to fulfill Israel's destiny as God's vineyard.

Jesus went on to explain to the disciples that he had loved them in the same way that God had loved him and that they were to remain in his love. That meant obeying the things he had been telling them to do that night and over the course of their three years together with him.

As Jesus explained to the disciples just what kind of love he had for them, he told them that he was saying those things so that they would have "overflowing" joy. He also further defined his love for them when he said, "Greater love has no one than this, that one lay down his life for his friends" (John 15:13).

Jesus had never before called his disciples "friends"—at least not as recorded in the gospels. Also, the disciples had always called him "Lord," "Master," and "Teacher," but never "friend." But Jesus showed the disciples just how he felt about them when he called them his "friends." He told them that he didn't see them just as servants but as friends, simply because a master doesn't tell his servants the kinds of things he had told them about himself and his Father in heaven.

Be Back Shortly! (John 16)

Jesus told the disciples that although he would be leaving them soon, he would also be returning a short time later. He told them that he would no longer speak to them in parables but tell them plainly about his Father in heaven. He also promised them that they would be able to approach God in prayer—just as Jesus always had—knowing that he loved them simply because they had believed Jesus had come from God and because they loved him.

Finally, Jesus told the disciples that although they would abandon him and leave him alone, he would not truly be alone, because God the Father would be with him.

My Friends Need a Helping Hand (John 17)

After Jesus had given the disciples his final teaching and words of encouragement and comfort, he turned his attention toward his Father and prayed for himself, his disciples, and the others who would know and serve him from that time forward.

"Father," Jesus prayed, "the time has come. Glorify your Son so that he can give glory back to you" (John 17:1). Jesus then acknowledged that he had been sent to Earth so that all people could have eternal life through knowing the Father and knowing Jesus himself.

Jesus prayed for the remaining disciples, the eleven men who had followed him faithfully so far. He prayed that God would care for them once he was gone and that he would continue to teach them the truth and keep them safe from "the evil one"—the devil. Just as God had sent him into the world, Jesus prayed, so he was sending them.

One Big Happy (Future) Family

Jesus also prayed for others who would believe in him because of the work his disciples would do after he was gone. He prayed that those who followed him would be united in love in the same way that Jesus and God had always been united. "Then the world will know that you sent me and will understand that you love them as much as you love me," he prayed.

Jesus had now completed his ministry on earth. He was finished teaching the disciples about himself and about his Father in heaven. Now it was time for him to head out to the place where he would meet up with his destiny and with the mission for which he had come to Earth.

Gut-Wrenching Prayers (Luke 22:39–46)

After the Passover meal and the teaching and prayer that followed, Jesus and his disciples made their way from the city of Jerusalem and headed east over the Kidron

Valley to the Mount of Olives. Once they were there, they entered what was probably a wall-enclosed olive grove called the Garden of *Gethsemane.*

Jesus and the disciples had been through an emotionally and spiritually wrenching evening. The disciples were exhausted from all they had been through, and Jesus himself needed some time alone to pray.

Jesus told eight of the disciples to stay at the edge of the garden and took Peter, James, and John with him into the garden. As they made their way into the grove, Jesus was struck with deep feelings of anguish and horror. He stopped the three disciples and told them, "My soul is crushed with grief to the point of death. Stay here and watch with me" (Matthew 26:38).

Let's Come to Terms

Gethsemane, the name of which literally means "olive press," is traditionally believed to have been at the site of a church now called Gethsemane Church of All Nations, which is located on the western slope of the Mount of Olives. It is the latest in a series of churches built on this spot, all of which had been destroyed over the years.

Strengthened for Suffering

Jesus left the three and went on a little further and fell face-down on the ground and prayed an anguished prayer: "Father, everything is possible for you. Please take this cup of suffering away from me. Yet I want your will, not mine" (Mark 14:36). Luke tells us that an angel came to Jesus as he was praying to strengthen him and that Jesus was so anguished and prayed with such intensity that "his sweat fell to the ground like great drops of blood" (Luke 22:43–44).

These Aren't Bedtime Prayers

Three times Jesus got up from this time of anguished prayer and went to the three disciples and found them asleep. He pleaded with them to stay awake and to pray not for him but for themselves. He told them to pray that they would not fall to temptation in the next several hours. "Though the spirit is willing," he told them, "the body is weak." Then he want back to his private place of prayer, where he continued pleading with God.

The last time Jesus returned to his exhausted and sleeping disciples, he roused them and told them that the time had come for his arrest.

W.W.J.K. (What Would Jesus Know?)

There is a lot of centuries-old tradition surrounding the events during Jesus' last few hours before his crucifixion, and at least two of them involve John Mark, the author of the Gospel of Mark. One of these traditions is that the "upper room" where Jesus and the disciples had the Passover supper—and where they would again meet after his resurrection—was in the home of Mark's parents. The other is that the young man who fled the scene of Jesus' arrest minus his robe was Mark himself.

Not Your Garden-Variety Betrayal (Matthew 26:47–56)

From out of the darkness in the garden that late night came a big crowd intent on taking Jesus into custody. The authorities who had sent the mob must have believed that Jesus still had a large number of people following him and that arresting him just might incite violence. They sent a battalion of Roman soldiers and Temple guards, all carrying torches, swords, and clubs.

Jesus knew full well why the mob had come. He stepped up and met the men and asked "Whom are you looking for?" When they said that they were looking for Jesus of Nazareth, Judas stepped forward to give them the signal as to who Jesus was so they could arrest him. "Teacher!" he exclaimed, then gave Jesus a kiss of betrayal. "Judas," Jesus asked, "how can you betray me, the Son of Man, with a kiss?"

The Disciples' Last Stand

With the signal given, the soldiers and guards rushed Jesus and grabbed him, intent on taking him away immediately.

When the disciples saw what was happening, they asked Jesus if he wanted them to try to fight off the mob. It was a brave offer, but also very foolish and futile. The disciples were eleven men from different backgrounds (at least four of them fishermen), and as far as we know, none of them had backgrounds as soldiers or guards. They wouldn't have stood a chance against this mob, which included experienced warriors and guards.

The Bad News That Reached His Ears (Luke 22:49–53)

But Peter wasn't waiting for the command to fight. He jumped up, drew out his sword, and started swinging wildly. However, he obviously wasn't as skilled as a swordsman as he was as a fisherman. He could only cut off the ear of the high priest's servant, a man named Malchus. Jesus stopped Peter and the rest of his disciples from fighting, telling them that those who fought by the sword would die by the sword—good teaching, especially given the fact that they were so outnumbered. Besides, he said, if he wanted to keep the mob from arresting him, all he had to do was call on God to send thousands of angels, and the situation would be taken care of instantly.

The First of Many Dark Moments

Jesus performed his final healing miracle prior to his death and resurrection by touching Malchus's ear and healing him, then turned to the crowd and said, "Am I some dangerous criminal, that you have come armed with swords and clubs to arrest me? Why didn't you arrest me in the Temple? I was there teaching every day. … [But] this is your moment. The time when the power of darkness reigns." (Luke 22:52–53).

With his disciples still listening, Jesus told the leaders of the mob that everything that was happening that night was a fulfillment of the words of the Old Testament prophets about his coming. Even if the crowd didn't want to hear it, Jesus' message to them was clear: He was going with them quietly and willingly.

Jesus had openly identified himself as the one the crowd wanted to arrest, and he also asked the soldiers and guards to let his disciples go. After all, *he* was the one they wanted, not them. As Jesus was tied up and taken into custody, the disciples fled the scene, just as he—as well as an Old Testament prophet—had said they would.

As Jesus had known would happen all along, he was about to be tried, convicted, and sentenced to die. And he was going to do these things as he and the Old Testament prophets had said he would: willingly … and alone.

The Least You Need to Know

- Jesus instituted "the Lord's Supper" or partaking of his body and blood in the form of bread and wine, to remember his death for us.

- In the "upper room" the disciples learned, among other things, about being humble servants.

- After the Passover meal, Jesus offered a final prayer that God would preserve the disciples, and give them a spirit of love and unity.

- Jesus was human like us and felt great weakness as he prayed about the gruesome ordeal he would face.

Part 5

A Life with an Ultimate Purpose

A sense of purpose is very important for any human being, and that was especially true for Jesus. But unlike most people, Jesus never questioned his purpose for being.

He told his disciples repeatedly that one day he would be arrested, tried, falsely convicted, and put to a violent, ugly death on a cross. After Jesus' death, the disciples—all of them a little dull of understanding about all these things—must have wondered about their own reason for being. But Jesus put those questions out of their minds for good when he did what no other had done: defeated death itself.

Chapter 20

A *Very* Speedy Trial

In This Chapter

- ◆ Jesus appears before Annas, the former high priest, then before Caiaphas the current high priest

- ◆ Jesus is tried and convicted on charges of blasphemy before the Sanhedrin and condemned to die

- ◆ Peter denies Jesus three times, just as he had been told would happen

- ◆ Judas Iscariot, in a fit of remorse after Jesus' arrest and conviction, commits suicide

After months of planning and scheming, the Jewish religious authorities in Jerusalem finally had Jesus in their custody. Amazingly, although the people in the Holy City had welcomed Jesus, celebrated his arrival, and hung on his teaching, the religious leaders were able to arrest Jesus without causing much public uproar—at least none that is written about in the gospel accounts.

The religious leaders had fully intended to have Jesus executed when they finally arrested him. So to them, it wasn't a matter of *what* they wanted to do with Jesus but *how* they were going to go about it.

Their first step in dealing with Jesus was to bring him in for a series of "interviews" that would turn out to be his actual trial and sentencing.

No One Can Pass *This* Exam (John 18:13, 19–23)

After Jesus was arrested, he was taken first to Annas, the former high priest and father-in-law of the current high priest, Caiaphas. This interrogation took place in the wee hours of the morning on Friday, the eve of Passover, shortly after Jesus' arrest.

Remember, despite the fact that Jewish law and tradition said that a high priest was to serve for life, the Romans had removed Annas from office in 15 C.E. and replaced him with Caiaphas, who held the office until 36 C.E.

John is the only gospel writer to record Jesus' appearance before Annas, but he doesn't tell us specifically *why* he was taken to the former high priest. It is believed that though Annas didn't hold the office of high priest in an official capacity, he still held a lot of "behind the scenes" influence over Caiaphas.

No Skeletons in His Closet

It may be that Annas's interrogation of Jesus was what we might think of in modern legal terms as a "preliminary examination," more to gather information than to actually convict Jesus of anything or to sentence him.

W.W.J.K. (What Would Jesus Know?)

As Jesus fielded Annas's questions about what he had been teaching his disciples, he was actually doing what anyone well versed in Jewish law would have done. Jesus knew that the law required the truthful testimony of two witnesses in a capital trial, and that's exactly what he told Annas to find.

Annas began questioning Jesus about his followers and what he had been teaching them. Jesus didn't directly answer Annas's question but told him that he had done all of his teaching and miracles right out in public view and that all he needed to do was talk to some of the many witnesses to find out what he had been teaching.

Just then, one of the Temple guards stepped forward and slapped Jesus on the face and asked him, "Is that the way to answer the high priest?" But Jesus answered him by telling him that if he had said anything wrong, then the authorities, not him, had to bring the evidence.

Annas's questioning of Jesus was getting him nowhere, so he sent him to the palace of Caiaphas (actually, it is likely that Caiaphas and his father-in-law lived in different quarters of the same palace), where Jesus would face another grilling, this time by Caiaphas and the rest of the Sanhedrin.

Let's Execute Him (I Mean "This") Quickly (Matthew 26:57–67)

As Jesus faced the high priest Caiaphas and the rest of the Sanhedrin members in attendance at his trial, he was facing a group of men who had already decided that they would find a reason to have him executed.

Earlier, we pointed out that the Jewish leaders were deathly afraid that Jesus' teachings and miracles would incite a nationwide rebellion that could have grave consequences, namely an invasion by a Roman army bent on stopping any kind of rebellion against the empire's rule of Palestine and by any means necessary.

Just prior to Jesus' "triumphal entry" into Jerusalem, Caiaphas and the rest of the Sanhedrin had met to discuss the situation. It was during that meeting that Caiaphas had told his colleagues that it would be better that one man—Jesus—die than have the whole nation destroyed at the hands of the Romans (John 11:49–52).

Now, with Jesus in their custody, these religious leaders looked for a way to make that happen.

A Sham of a Farce of a Mockery of a Trial

The Sanhedrin, wanting desperately to find grounds to have Jesus executed, tried to find witnesses who could give them something to work with. Many people came forward and testified concerning Jesus' teachings, but none of what they had to say was useful to the council. It is very likely that they simply told the Sanhedrin members about Jesus' teachings and miracles, none of which were grounds to condemn him to die.

Finally, two men came forward who had heard Jesus make what they believed was an outrageous—and dangerous—claim. They told the Sanhedrin, twisting Jesus' words slightly, that they had heard Jesus say he was able to destroy the holy Temple in Jerusalem and rebuild it in three days.

The men were referring to what Jesus had said after he had cleared the Temple of merchants and moneychangers early on in his ministry. After some religious leaders in Jerusalem challenged Jesus to prove his authority to cleanse the Temple by doing a miracle, he told them, "Destroy this temple, and in three days I will raise it up" (John 2:19).

Body Rebuilding in Three Days?

These witnesses had misrepresented what Jesus had actually said, and they also had what he had meant all wrong. It is likely that these witnesses tried to paint a picture of a radical who was intent on doing actual physical damage to the Temple and to the city of Jerusalem.

In his gospel account of that scene early in Jesus' earthly ministry, John pointed out that when Jesus said "this temple," he was referring to his own body and not the Temple in Jerusalem. In other words, he was telling the religious authorities that if they killed him, he would be raised from the dead three days later.

But there was another problem with this bit of testimony concerning Jesus' words about the destruction of "the temple," and that was that the two witnesses couldn't get their own stories straight (Mark 14:59).

Still, Caiaphas pressed Jesus on these false accusations. He stood up and challenged Jesus, "Well, aren't you going to answer these charges? What do you have to say for yourself?" But Jesus didn't answer. In fact, he didn't say anything at all.

The "Yes" That Shook the World (Matthew 26:63–68)

Caiaphas was losing his patience. Finally, he got down to asking the one question he and his cohorts on the Sanhedrin wanted Jesus to answer: "I demand in the name of the living God that you tell us whether you are the Messiah, the Son of God."

In other versions of the Bible, this passage reads, "I charge you under oath by the living God ...." Caiaphas wasn't making it a secret that he wanted to corner Jesus by getting him to answer him concerning who he thought he was. If Jesus said "no," then that would be the end of the problem. However, if he held his ground and answered "yes," then the Sanhedrin would have grounds to get rid of him.

Jesus finally broke his silence and told Caiaphas that, yes, he was indeed the one who the priest had just said he was: the Messiah and the Son of God. But that wasn't all he said. In words that these religious leaders must have found not just blasphemous but outwardly defiant, Jesus boldly told them, "And in the future you will see me, the Son of man, sitting at God's right hand in the place of power and coming back on the clouds of heaven" (Matthew 26:64).

W.W.J.K. (What Would Jesus Know?)

We know that there were some Sanhedrin members and other Jewish leaders who believed in Jesus and some who were at least sympathetic with him (for example, the Pharisee Nicodemus, who met with Jesus on the night when he was in Jerusalem and argued on Jesus' behalf at one meeting of the Sanhedrin). But where were they during Jesus' "trial?" Some scholars believe that since the whole Sanhedrin didn't need to be in attendance at a particular criminal trial, those who didn't want to see Jesus executed chose not to attend the proceedings that night.

Caiaphas Comes Undone at the Seams

That was all Caiaphas needed to hear. He tore his clothing—an outward display of resentment and anguish in the Jewish culture—and exclaimed, "Blasphemy! Why do we need other witnesses? You have all heard his blasphemy." Caiaphas then asked the rest of the Sanhedrin for a verdict, and in unison came not only the verdict but the sentence: "Guilty! He must die!"

With that, the Sanhedrin ended this "special session" they had called to deal with Jesus. They turned him over to the Temple guards, who took him away, abusing him and taunting him. They blindfolded Jesus—who had already been tied up—spat in his face, and slapped and punched him. Some even mocked him by slapping him and saying, "Prophesy to us, you Messiah! Who hit you that time!"

The Sanhedrin had already passed judgment on Jesus and sentenced him to die. All that remained was for them to affirm that decision the way they were required by the law to do: in the light of day.

Jesus' trial.

(Copyright © 2001 Tyndale House Publishers)

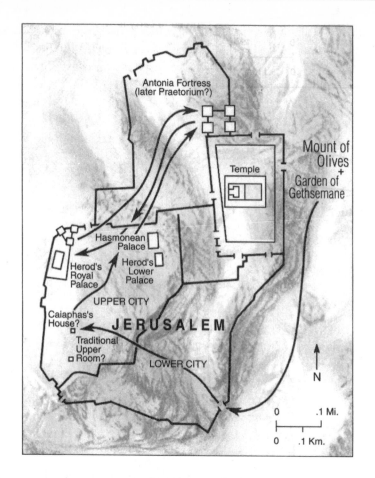

Peter Gets Sudden Amnesia (Mark 14:54, 66–72)

While all this was going on, Jesus' disciples weren't doing so well themselves. All of them had scattered, except for Peter and John, who followed at a distance to see what was happening to Jesus without being arrested themselves.

After Jesus was arrested, Peter and John had entered the court of Caiaphas's palace. John had been acquainted with the high priest, so he was allowed to enter the court-yard immediately. As he walked through the gate, he spoke to a woman who was watching the gate and persuaded her to let Peter go in with him.

A short time after Peter had entered the courtyard, he stepped close to a group of the high priest's guards and servants who were warming themselves close to a charcoal fire they'd built. As Peter squeezed in close to the fire and began warming himself, one of the high priest's servants, a young woman, looked at him closely and told him that she recognized him as one of the people who had been following Jesus. But Peter told her, "I don't know what you're talking about."

But the girl was sure she had seen Peter with Jesus before and told people standing around the fire that he was one of Jesus' followers. When they began asking him about his relationship with Jesus, Peter again denied knowing him.

Amnesia Turns to Paranoia

Finally, about an hour later, a group of people, including a servant of Caiaphas—who just happened to be a relative of Malchus, the man whose ear Peter had lopped off with his sword in the garden that night—asked Peter if he was one of the men he'd seen at the olive grove when Jesus was arrested. The people had heard Peter talking that night and recognized his thick Galilean accent and became convinced he was the same man they'd seen in the garden just a few hours earlier.

This time, Peter was more vehement in his denial. He cursed and swore by God—meaning he essentially took an oath—that he didn't know Jesus. As the words of Peter's third and final denial of Jesus came out of his mouth, he heard the rooster crow. At that moment, Jesus must have been within eyeshot of Peter, as Luke records, "… the Lord turned and looked straight at Peter" (Luke 22:61).

Three Strikes, You're Out ... for Now

On several occasions during his time with Jesus, Peter had demonstrated himself to be a brave, even impetuous, follower who was willing to do (and say) things the others wouldn't have dreamed of doing. He had tried walking on the water when Jesus called him to do so. And, as you may remember from Chapter 19, he bravely (if not foolishly) drew his sword and began swinging it in an attempt to fight off Jesus' arrest at the Garden of Gethsemane.

> **W.W.J.K. (What Would Jesus Know?)**
>
> Some experts on the Bible have held that the references to the rooster or "cock" crowing after Peter's denial of Jesus don't refer literally to the early morning call of a male chicken but to a trumpet blast given at the end of the "third watch" (midnight to 3 A.M.), which was called "cockcrow." It was, in fact, against Jewish law for people to raise chickens or other fowl in Jerusalem, although it is likely that many Jews ignored this prohibition.

> **W.W.J.K. (What Would Jesus Know?)**
>
> It might seem easy to see Peter as being a bit on the cowardly side for not standing up for Jesus after his arrest. But, as you will read later in this book, Jesus later restored and forgave Peter, then commissioned him to lead in the establishment of the early church in Jerusalem and to take several missionary journeys to the outlying areas. During that time, Peter bravely spoke Jesus' message, oftentimes in the face of dangerous opposition and persecution.

But now, with Jesus in the hands of his enemies and, as far as he knew, at their mercy, Peter lost his nerve. He remembered what Jesus had told him just a few hours earlier after he had promised to stand by Jesus, if it meant dying with him, and he remembered how Jesus had told him that he would deny even knowing him not once but three times that night. When the realization hit Peter that he had done that very thing, he went outside the courtyard and wept bitterly.

Change the Verdict and Keep Your Change (Matthew 27:3–10)

In the last chapter, we pointed out that before Jesus was arrested, he had some very unpleasant predictions for two of the disciples. One was Peter, who Jesus said would deny him that very night. The other was Judas, who by the time of the Passover supper was already in the process of betraying him.

Early in the morning after Jesus' arrest, Judas found out that Jesus had been tried and sentenced to die, and he was filled with remorse over what he had done. In an attempt to ease his guilt—or maybe to see if he could stop Jesus' execution—he went to the Temple and tried to return the money to the religious leaders who had given it to him in exchange for his leading them to Jesus. "I have sinned," he told them, "for I have betrayed an innocent man."

A High-Strung Response

But as far as these religious leaders were concerned, Judas's remorse just wasn't their problem. He was going to have to face the consequences of his actions on his own, and there was nothing they would do about it. Judas took the "blood money" he had received and threw it on the Temple floor, then went out and hanged himself.

> ### W.W.J.K. (What Would Jesus Know?)
>
> While Matthew's gospel tells us that Judas hanged himself in a fit of remorse over having betrayed Jesus, the Acts of the Apostles tells the story this way: "he fell head-long, his body burst open and all his intestines spilled out" (Acts 1:18). There are three different theories as to why these accounts seem to differ: (1) Judas's body hung so long that it burst when it was cut down; (2) when Judas hanged himself, the rope or tree limb broke and when Judas's body fell on the rocky ground it burst open; or (3) Judas "hanged" himself on a spear or other sharp object, meaning he actually impaled himself.

Blood Money

The chief priests and leaders gathered the money that Judas had thrown on the Temple floor. They knew it was not lawful for them to put the money into the Temple treasury. So after some discussion about what do with it, they decided to use it to buy a field previously used by potters (the land wasn't worth much after it had been put to that use) and use the land as burial ground for foreigners. That field came to be known as "the Field of Blood."

> **His Name Is Jesus, a.k.a.**
>
> "The Power of God" (1 Corinthians 1:24). When Jesus answers the Sanhedrin about his role as Messiah he states he will come back sitting at God's right hand in the place of power. He is the agent of God's power—in creation, in salvation, and in ruling for eternity.

Deja-Vu Demands (Luke 22:66–71)

On the same day that Judas had come back to the Temple in an attempt to return the thirty coins he'd received for betraying Jesus, the Sanhedrin reconvened to affirm the decision they'd made only hours before.

Again, they asked Jesus to tell them if he was the Messiah. Jesus had already answered that question very directly just a few hours earlier, and he wasn't going to answer it again. Instead, he told them, "If I tell you, you won't believe me. But the time is soon coming when I, the Son of Man, will be sitting at God's right hand in the place of power" (Luke 22:68–69).

Then the Sanhedrin took the questioning yet another step, this time shouting angrily at Jesus, "Then you claim you are the Son of God?" Again, Jesus didn't back down from his claims but instead turned these leaders' words against them: "You are right in saying that I am" (Luke 22:70).

When the Sanhedrin heard this, in their minds Jesus' fate was sealed. As far as they were concerned, they didn't need to call any more witnesses; Jesus' words themselves had condemned him.

> **His Name Is Jesus, a.k.a.**
>
> "My Witness" (Isaiah 55:4). Throughout his life Jesus, claiming to be one with the Father before the world began, thus claimed to "witness" to the person, words, and works of the Father. In the case of this trial, he was acting as a witness to who he was in relation to the Father—the Son of God who would be revealed fully at his second coming.

The Trial That Was a Tribulation

All of the events surrounding Jesus' arrest and trial took place in a time and in a culture that was a lot different from ours. In our modern world, even the worst of criminals are treated fairly and humanely. But it wasn't like that in Jesus' day.

For centuries, people have made the case that the way Jesus' "trial" before the Sanhedrin was handled was a violation of law as written in the Pentateuch (the books of the law, or the first five books of the Old Testament) and in the Mishnah, a systematized collection of both the "Oral Torah" of the Old Testament era and political and civil laws in Judaism.

Let's Come to Terms

The Mishnah, the name of which means "repeated study" in Hebrew, was compiled around 200 C.E. by the greatly loved and respected Jewish rabbi and political leader Judah (or Yehudah) ha-Nasi (135–220), then the leader of the Sanhedrin. It was a six-volume collection of Oral Law and Jewish political and civil laws. The six volumes dealt with agriculture, Jewish festivals, issues involving women, civil and criminal law, religious sacrifices, and ritual purity.

Rules Were Made to Be Broken?

Here are a few of the "legal problems" many scholars cite in the gospel accounts of Jesus' trial before the Sanhedrin:

- Trials involving capital punishment were to be held during the daylight hours and not during the night, as Jesus' first and second trials were.

- These trials were not to be held on the eve of the Sabbath or of a festival, and they were to be held at the Temple, not in the home of the high priest.

- These trials were to begin with people giving reasons for acquittal and not for execution. This is similar to our own criminal justice system, which is set up to err on the side of innocence.

- The accused in a capital trial was to be given legal representation and was not to be asked self-incriminating questions, which Jesus was when he was asked if he was the Messiah.

- "Not guilty" verdicts in capital cases could be reached on the same day of the trial, but "guilty" verdicts had to be affirmed after a night's sleep.

- Death sentences could only be handed down on the basis of multiple witnesses. When witnesses contradicted one another, their testimonies canceled one another out.

- In a capital trial, each member of the Sanhedrin was to vote individually whether to convict or acquit a defendant, but Jesus was convicted by the words of Caiaphas and the other members present.

Some people have pointed to these "illegalities" as proof that the Sanhedrin was so intent on getting rid of Jesus that they would ignore their own law if that is what it took.

However, many scholars hold that it is likely that the laws we referred to earlier either weren't strictly enforced at the time of Jesus' trial or that many of them hadn't yet been instituted.

Terminator Too? Not the Jews

There were, however, obviously legal problems with the way Jesus was tried before the Sanhedrin. But the biggest legal obstacle the Sanhedrin faced in their plans to have Jesus executed wasn't a matter of Jewish law but of the Roman law they were forced to live under.

By the time Jesus had come on the scene, the Romans had made capital punishment their prerogative—one they used often and savagely—and had stripped the Jewish legal system of the right to mete out the death penalty, even for the worst of crimes.

Even if the Sanhedrin had the right to convict Jesus of blasphemy and condemn him to die the way they did, they had no legal right to carry out his execution. That right in this case belonged to Pontius Pilate, the Roman governor of Judea under Emperor Tiberius Caesar at the time of Jesus' arrest, trial, and conviction.

And it was before Pontius Pilate that Jesus would face the next phase of his trial.

The Least You Need to Know

- Jesus is accused of blasphemy, or claiming to be God, after other confusing accusations.

- Jesus was tried, convicted, and sentenced to die by the high priest Caiaphas and the rest of the Sanhedrin.

◆ As Jesus had said he would, Simon Peter denied knowing him three times during Jesus' trial before the Sanhedrin.

◆ Jesus' trial was marked by a series of legal problems that affected its outcome.

21

Jesus Is Sentenced to Death

In This Chapter

- Jesus appears before Pontius Pilate, who finds no reason to have him crucified
- Pilate sends Jesus to Herod Antipas, governor of Galilee
- Pilate attempts to persuade the Jewish religious leaders to free Jesus
- Pilate reluctantly hands Jesus over to be crucified

In this chapter, we want to cover Jesus' appearance before Pilate—as well as Herod Antipas, the governor of Galilee, who also had a chance to "try" Jesus following the Sanhedrin's death sentence on him. But first, let's take a quick look at the man history remembers as the one who ultimately sent Jesus to die on the cross.

A Pilate Flying High (for a While)

Pontius Pilate, the son of an influential Roman equestrian family, had probably risen through the ranks of Roman leadership under Tiberius Caesar, who appointed him to the post of governor of Judea in 26 C.E. Pilate held that position until around 36 or 37 C.E. As governor of Judea, it was Pilate's job to command Roman military units, oversee various construction projects and the collection of imperial taxes, and to stand in judgment over civil and criminal cases.

Not a lot is known for certain about Pilate's reign. All the gospels tell us about Pilate prior to Jesus' trial is that he was the governor of Judea at the time when John the Baptist started his ministry and that Jesus later received a report that he had murdered some Galileans who were making sacrifices at the Temple in Jerusalem.

I'm Your Boss, Not Your Friend

But according to some ancient historians (particularly Flavius Josephus, who wrote after the time of Jesus; and Philo of Alexandria, a Jewish philosopher who lived in Egypt and who was a contemporary of Jesus), Pilate could hardly have been considered any friend of the Jewish people in Judea. While some historians believe that the writings of both Josephus and Philo were at least a little bit tainted by their own biases (they were, after all, Jews living under Roman domination), some also believe that Pilate was at best crassly insensitive to the Jewish people's way of life and belief systems and at worst cruel and harsh when it came to dealing with what he perceived as a threat to the status quo of Roman dominion. Philo's writings described Pilate as a prideful, greedy, and power-hungry—all to the extreme—man who often judged his subjects with harshness and violence. He exacted the harshest criminal penalties, including the death sentence, oftentimes without the benefit of a fair trial.

> ### W.W.J.K. (What Would Jesus Know?)
>
> In his book *Antiquities of the Jews*, Josephus made reference to Jesus and his crucifixion: "At this time there was a wise man who was called Jesus, and his conduct was good, and he was known to be virtuous. And many people from among the Jews and the other nations became his disciples. Pilate condemned him to be crucified and to die. And those who had become his disciples did not abandon their loyalty to him. They reported that he had appeared to them three days after his crucifixion, and that he was alive. Accordingly they believed that he was the Messiah, concerning whom the Prophets have recounted wonders."

A Leader with Image Problems

According to Josephus, one of Pilate's first acts as the governor of Judea was to have images of the Roman emperor mounted on the walls of the Fortress of Antonia, which faced the Temple. Pilate did this in the dark of night and in contradiction to Caesar

Augustus's order giving Jerusalem immunity from these images. According to Josephus, the posting of these images in plain sight of the Temple outraged Jews, who considered the images of the emperor idolatrous.

Pilate had prepared his soldiers for any possible rebellion or uprising over the images, but it never came. Instead, a large group of Jews went to Pilate's base in Caesaria, where they openly protested what he had done. When Pilate threatened to kill the protesters, they didn't disperse but instead knelt and prayed, which told him they were willing to accept death before they accepted the idolatrous images he had erected in Jerusalem. Rather than slaughter the protesters, Pilate gave in and had the offensive images in Jerusalem removed.

Go Ahead, "Punch Us" Pilate!

Later, Pontius Pilate again offended Jewish religious sensibilities when he built an aqueduct to bring water into Jerusalem. The problem wasn't with the aqueduct itself but with the fact that Pilate used Temple funds to build it. Of course, the Jews didn't approve of this plan, and tens of thousands of them gathered in protest during one of Pilate's visits to the Holy City.

Pilate responded to the protest by sending a large number of soldiers, dressed in Jewish civilian clothing, to surround the protesters. At Pilate's signal, the soldiers attacked the protesters with clubs they had hidden under their garments. Sadly, the attack was more fierce and violent than Pilate had intended, and many of the Jews were killed, some by the soldiers' blows and some by the stampede away from the scene that ensued.

Pilate's Eventual Crash

Finally, according to Josephus, in 36 C.E., after his dealings with Jesus, Pilate went too far. That year, a Samaritan who claimed to be the reincarnation of Moses gathered an armed following near Mount Gerizim. Pilate, seeing this as a threat to the stability of his government, sent in military forces to disperse the gathering and to execute its ringleaders.

The Samaritans saw the violence of Pilate's troops in that incident as excessive and reported it to Lucius Vitellius, the Roman governor of

> ### His Name Is Jesus, a.k.a.
>
> "Emmanuel" (Matthew 1:23). Emmanuel means "God is with us" and was the name given to Jesus at his birth by Matthew, stemming from the prophet Isaiah in the Old Testament. Though this trial pretended to be about Jesus being a king in opposition to Rome, it was really about his claiming to be the Son of God, or "God with us" in front of the high priest Caiaphas the day before.

Syria at that time. Vitellius, in turn, sent Pilate back to Rome, where he would give an account for what had happened. He was removed from office and exiled to Vienne, France. That was the last historians tell us about Pontius Pilate, although one tradition has it that in 39 C.E. he committed suicide at the orders of Emperor Caligula, who ruled the empire from 37–41 C.E.

It was about six years before the end of the administration of Pilate as Judean governor—in 30 C.E.—that he met face to face with Jesus.

Pilate's Rude Awakening (Matthew 27:1–14)

Once their own trial of Jesus was completed after dawn, the members of the Sanhedrin tied Jesus up again and took him to Pilate's Jerusalem headquarters, hoping that he would approve and carry out their sentence of death. It may have been about seven o'clock, or even a bit earlier in the morning, when Pilate went out to meet Jesus' accusers. That Friday morning the most important trial in all history was about to begin.

> **W.W.J.K. (What Would Jesus Know?)**
>
> The Fortress of Antonia was located at the northwest corner of the Temple Mount in Jerusalem. It stood about 115 feet high and was partially surrounded by a 165-foot-wide ravine. It was constructed around 35 B.C.E. by Herod the Great, who named it after Marc Antony, Cleopatra's lover and aspiring emperor. It was used as a palace and as headquarters for Roman soldiers, who watched the Temple from the fortress so that they could keep order.

Pilate spent most of his time at his palace in Caesarea Maritima, the Roman seat of government in Judea, which was located on the coast of the Mediterranean Sea. However, as he always had done during Jewish celebrations, he traveled to Jerusalem for the Passover Feast—mostly to keep order in the city.

While Pilate was in Jerusalem, he stayed in a place called the "Praetorium," which was located either at the Fortress of Antonia or (more likely) at the palace of Herod the Great, which was located at the western part of the city or what is called the "upper city."

We Wouldn't Be Caught Dead in Here

The Jewish religious leadership wouldn't set foot in Pilate's headquarters themselves because according to their reading of Jewish law, doing so would have "defiled" them, meaning that they wouldn't be able to take part in the remainder of the Passover celebration.

Pilate stepped outside his headquarters to meet with the Jewish leaders and ask them the nature of their charges against Jesus. But they didn't answer directly, only telling him that they wouldn't have brought Jesus to him if he weren't a criminal.

Pilate, however, wasn't interested in getting involved in the situation and told the Jewish religious leaders that since it was a Jewish law Jesus had allegedly broken, they needed to deal with it through the Jewish legal system.

The Sanhedrin's Revolutionary Approach

But the Sanhedrin persisted, accusing Jesus of spreading revolution against the Roman Empire. They told Pilate that Jesus had encouraged his followers not to pay their taxes to the Roman government and had claimed to be the Messiah and a king. They also pointed out to Pilate that under Roman law they were not permitted to put anyone to death for any reason—even for encouraging rebellion against the Roman government. They knew that if they framed the charges this way it made this a "Roman" issue that Pilate himself needed to address.

> **W.W.J.K. (What Would Jesus Know?)**
>
> Jews in Jesus' time believed any contact at all with a Gentile—even entering his home—made them "ceremonially unclean." In this case, they equated contact with a Gentile to be the equivalent of contact with a dead body, with an unclean animal, or with another human who is for any reason "unclean" (Leviticus 22:4–6). That meant they were disqualified from participating in any part of the Passover celebration.

These were very serious charges that the Roman government considered worthy of the death penalty, charges that had led to many executions in the empire. Pilate had no chance to investigate them further, so he brought Jesus into his quarters and began asking some questions of his own.

This Is Not Rome's Battle

Once he had Jesus in his own quarters, Pilate "cut to the chase" and asked him very directly if he considered himself the king of the Jews. Jesus didn't answer directly but instead asked the governor, "Is this your own question, or did others tell you about me?" (John 18:34).

Pilate had no doubt heard about Jesus and about his conflicts with the Jewish religious leadership. But since he wasn't a Jew himself, he saw those conflicts as being between the Jewish leaders and Jesus. "Am I a Jew?" Pilate rhetorically asked Jesus. "Your own people and their leading priests brought you here" (John 18:35). However, Pilate's question for Jesus remained, and that was what he had done to motivate the Sanhedrin to give him the death sentence.

My Kingdom Is Out of This World

Jesus wouldn't answer Pilate concerning the accusations of inciting rebellion against Rome. Rather, he told Pilate that his was not an earthly kingdom, and that if it had been, his followers would have drawn their swords and fought when the Jewish leaders had him arrested in the Garden of Gethsemane.

Pilate, probably wanting to make sure he understood what kind of kingdom Jesus was talking about, asked him, "You are a king then?" Jesus told him, "You say that I am a king, and you are right. I was born for that purpose. And I came to bring truth to the world. All who love the truth recognize that what I say is true."

Rebel with a Very Different Cause

Pilate then very flippantly and cynically asked Jesus, "What is truth?" At that point, Pilate may have come to the conclusion that Jesus was just a mystical religious fanatic whose "outside the box" approach to the Jewish faith was stirring up trouble at the Temple.

Pilate had seen a lot of insurrectionists and other rebels during his reign in Judea, and as far as he could see, there was no real reason to believe that Jesus was one of them. To Pilate, this was obviously a matter of religion and not one of a possible uprising among the people, as the Sanhedrin had charged.

No Crime in Pursuing Truth

To Pilate, the evidence was clear. If Jesus was leading a revolution, it was a religious one based on what he considered "truth" and not one that would lead to violence. Otherwise, the situation in the Garden of Gethsemane would have escalated and there would have been bloodshed. That hadn't happened ... other than from an already healed wounded ear on one of the high priest's servants.

Satisfied that Jesus posed no threat to Roman rule in Judea, Pilate went back out to the Sanhedrin and told them that he found no reason to put Jesus to death. But the Jewish religious leaders answered that Jesus had been stirring up the crowds, starting in his home of Galilee and working his way to Jerusalem.

This Is *Herod's* Hot Potato

When Pilate heard this accusation, he asked the Sanhedrin if Jesus was a Galilean. When he was told that Jesus was indeed from Galilee, he realized that this situation just might fall under the jurisdiction of Herod Antipas, who was the governor of that region at the time.

To Pilate, this might have seemed like a good way out of a sticky situation. As far as he knew, Jesus had done nothing in Judea to deserve the death penalty, but maybe Herod would see the situation differently. Like his father—King Herod the Great—before him, Herod Antipas considered himself a faithful Jew; at least he wanted people to see him that way. It is possible that Pilate wanted to get legal advice from a Jewish perspective.

A "Re-Headed" John the Baptist? (Luke 23:6–12)

Although Herod and Jesus had never met face to face before that day, there was history between them. A few years earlier, Herod had ordered the imprisonment and execution by beheading of John the Baptist, the man Jesus knew had come to prepare the people for his arrival as Messiah.

But there was more. Later, when some of Herod's associates heard of the miracles and teaching Jesus was doing in Galilee, they wondered aloud if Jesus was John the Baptist come back to life or if he was the "second coming" of Elijah the prophet, which the Jewish people believed would come prior to the arrival of the Messiah. At that time, Herod himself wondered who Jesus was and wanted to meet him in person to find out.

Later, some Pharisees warned Jesus that Herod wanted to have him killed too. Jesus responded to that reported death threat by telling the Pharisees that he would continue teaching and doing miracles in Galilee.

The Messiah? Show Me the Miracle

The seat of government for Galilee and Perea, Herod's provinces, was a city called Tiberius, which was within 10 to 15 miles of the bulk of Jesus' earthly ministry and only a few miles south of Capernaum, Jesus' "home base." However, it was Herod's practice as a professing Jew to travel to Jerusalem for the Passover feast, and he was in the Holy City during the time of Jesus' trial.

Herod, who served as governor of Galilee from the time of his father's death in 4 C.E. until 39 C.E., was more than happy to see Jesus early that day (probably by 7:30 A.M.), but it wasn't so much that he wanted to accuse him of anything or condemn him to death. Rather, Herod was hoping more than anything that Jesus would perform a miracle for him. In other words, Herod wanted to see a "magic show," not talk to Jesus about what he was doing and why.

This Is Not a *Show* Trial

Herod questioned Jesus thoroughly, probably asking him over and over again to perform some kind of miracle purely for his entertainment. But Jesus refused not only to perform a miracle but also to answer Herod's questions at all. Herod Antipas was probably disappointed that Jesus refused to entertain him with a miracle. But like Pilate, he found no basis for the death penalty for Jesus.

With the chief priests and Scribes still hurling their accusations at Jesus, Herod and his soldiers began ridiculing him. They dressed him in a royal robe, which mocked Jesus' claims of being a king, and sent him back to Pilate.

W.W.J.K. (What Would Jesus Know?)

The gospel account of this scene tells us that Herod and Pilate had been enemies before but became friends that day, probably because Pilate had shown Herod the courtesy of sending him a prisoner who was under his jurisdiction. Luke doesn't tell us why Pilate and Herod had been enemies before, but historians tell us that they had plenty of reason to be suspicious of one another. Pilate was governing Judea, which was Herod the Great's Jewish kingdom, and Herod very likely had designs of taking over the leadership of Judea for himself.

He's Innocent, Twice Over (John 18:39–40)

Pilate was probably encouraged by the fact that Herod found no reason to condemn Jesus. He called together the priests and other religious leaders, along with a crowd of people they had gathered to the scene, and told them that Herod had affirmed what he himself had said about Jesus in the first place: that there was no real reason to execute him.

How About a *Real* Criminal?

Now Pilate had another idea. It was his custom on the Passover holiday to have a prisoner released—one of the Jewish leaders' choosing—during the Passover. That morning, probably around 8 A.M. or even a little earlier, he gave them a choice: release Jesus or release a notorious criminal named Barabbas, who had been sentenced to death for murder and for inciting an insurrection. No doubt, he believed that the crowd would choose to release Jesus and condemn a dangerous man like Barabbas.

By now believing that the religious leaders' desire to have Jesus executed was out of jealousy—maybe over the fact that he had such a huge following of people—Pilate told the crowd that he would have Jesus flogged and then release him. But the crowds grew more restless than ever, insisting that Jesus be crucified.

Don't Disappoint a Wife's Dreams

It wasn't usually standard practice for Roman rulers to bring their wives to the posts they ruled. But Pilate's wife— Claudia Procula, the granddaughter of Caesar Augustus and the illegitimate daughter of Tiberius—was not only with Pontius Pilate in Caesarea, but with him that week in Jerusalem. Claudia further complicated matters for Pilate, himself a very superstitious man, when she told him that she'd had a dream about Jesus and that he should leave him alone because he was innocent.

What made things even worse was that Jesus' enemies had persuaded the crowds—allies that they had very likely called to the scene that morning to intimidate Pilate into giving in to their demands—to call for the release of Barabbas and the crucifixion of Jesus.

W.W.J.K. (What Would Jesus Know?)

Matthew tells us that Pilate sat before the people on the "judgment seat" (Matthew 27:19). This was the seat or platform the Roman judge sat on as he passed down judgment. It was traditionally held in a public place—as was Jesus' trial before Pilate. It has been suggested that Pilate, believing that he would be able to set Jesus free, sat at the judgment seat as if he was about to affirm his decision before Jesus' enemies.

W.W.J.K. (What Would Jesus Know?)

For centuries it has been debated just what happened to the crowds of people who had just days earlier welcomed Jesus into Jerusalem. In other words, where were Jesus' supporters (and there were many of them) as he was about to be sentenced to death? Many scholars believe that Jesus' supporters had had no knowledge of Jesus' arrest at this early hour of the morning and that the crowds who demanded his crucifixion were those the Sanhedrin members knew would support whatever they decided.

The Poorest Choice on Earth

Pilate, trying desperately to persuade the people standing before him to let Jesus go, asked them again, "Which of these two do you want me to release to you?" But the crowd hadn't changed its mind: "Barabbas!" they called back.

Pilate asked the crowd what he should do with Jesus once he had released Barabbas, and in unison the crowd demanded that he crucify him. Pilate asked the crowd on what charges Jesus should be crucified, but that got him nowhere. In fact, what had before been a raucous but mostly peaceful gathering was about to break out into an all-out riot.

An Alternative to Reading the Riot Act (John 19:1–16)

Pilate had dealt with insurrections and uprisings among certain Jewish groups before, but he knew that there couldn't have been a worse time than this for a riot. It was time for the Passover and more than a million Jews were in Jerusalem. If there had been a big disturbance in Jerusalem, it would have been reported to Rome and Pilate wouldn't have been able to give an acceptable answer as to why he allowed such a thing to happen.

With that, Pilate gave his approval—at least for the time being—for Jesus' execution. But as he did, he sent for a bowl of water, then washed his hands in it, declaring, "I am innocent of the blood of this man. The responsibility is yours!" (Matthew 27:24).

Jesus was about to face the darker side of Roman criminal justice, and it started with what historically has been seen as one of the most cruel forms of punishment ever devised.

Let's Come to Terms

Roman flogging was a horrible, cruel form of punishment that oftentimes brought the condemned near death, even before the crucifixion itself. In the Roman flogging, the victim was tied to a wooden post and beaten, usually on the back, with a whip (or *flagellum*) made of several leather straps, each interwoven with pieces of bone and metal, some of which were shaped into hooks.

A Cruel and *Very* Unusual Punishment (John 19:1–3)

According to Roman capital law, a *flogging* was always part of an execution. According to Jewish law, a flogging was limited to 40 lashes (Deuteronomy 25:3). But there was no limit to the number of lashes the condemned person received according to Roman law.

The repeated lashes of the Roman flogging cut through the skin and literally left it hanging in shreds. The punishment often left the victim's bones and innards exposed and sometimes the victim lost so much blood in the flogging that he (it was not legal for women to be flogged) was critically weakened or even dead before he could be crucified. This was such a terrible and brutal form of punishment that even many of the most hardened military leaders of that time were horrified by it.

Elements of a Mock Trial

After flogging Jesus, some of Pilate's soldiers took him to their headquarters, where they put a purple robe on him and placed a "crown" of long, sharp thorns on his head and a stick in his hand. They bowed down to him in mock worship and shouted "Hail! King of the Jews!" They spit on him and took the stick from his hand and beat him on the head with it.

When that was finished, the soldiers brought Jesus back to Pilate, who tried one final time to have him released—his hope being that the terrible punishment Jesus had already endured would be enough.

Pilate presented Jesus—now beaten and bleeding very badly and dressed in the mock robe and crown of thorns—to his accusers. He reiterated his contention that Jesus was an innocent man not deserving of the death penalty and that he should be released.

Who Are You ... Really?

When the chief priests and Temple guards saw Jesus, they repeated their demands that he be crucified. When Pilate again told them that he found him not guilty, the Jewish religious leaders shouted back, "By our laws he ought to die because he called himself the Son of God."

Hearing that frightened Pilate. He already believed he was condemning an innocent man to death, and his wife's message about her dream still haunted him. But was there more to it than that? Was there something about this man that Pilate needed to know? He had to find out.

Pilate took Jesus back into the palace and asked him where he was from, but Jesus wouldn't say anything more. Pilate wanted desperately for Jesus to say something he could use as a reason to release him, so he told Jesus, "Don't you realized that I have the power to release you or to crucify you?" But Jesus told Pilate, "You would have no power over me at all unless it was given to you from above" (John 19:8–11).

Playing "the Friend of Caesar" Card

Pilate now wanted more than ever to release Jesus, so he went outside again to appeal again to his accusers. But the Jewish leaders simply went over Pilate's head, telling him that if he released Jesus, he was no friend of Caesar's.

Hearing what Jesus had to say as well as some of the accusations against him had troubled, even frightened, Pilate. But he was even more afraid of having his actions—or lack thereof—in the face of a possible uprising reported to Rome.

Finally, after attempting all that early morning to dodge the decision put before him, Pilate gave in and had Jesus led away to be crucified.

Pilate: Competing Interests Combine with True Motives

Over the centuries, the subject of exactly why Pilate attempted to release Jesus has been debated over and over. Why, goes the question, when Pilate had proved himself more than willing to deal harshly with those he saw as a threat to peace and security in Judea, would he have even a second thought when it came to executing some rabble-rouser like Jesus?

It has been suggested that Pilate didn't care one way or another about Jesus and that he was more concerned with how his execution might have been taken among the "common people." Pilate knew that Jesus had a large following among the Jews, and he may have feared that either decision he made would lead to rioting in the streets of Jerusalem.

That would have spelled the end for Pilate, who was already "skating on thin ice" with the emperor. In the end, even though he really believed Jesus was innocent, sending him away to be crucified was the politically expedient thing for him to do.

On the other hand, some believe that while Pilate was tough on Zealots and others who tried to create problems for the Romans in Judea, he also had a sense of fairness and justice. After all, it is argued, he wouldn't have lasted as long as he did as governor of Judea if he wasn't somewhat fair with his Jewish subjects.

Leaders with Cross Purposes?

Finally, it is believed in some quarters that Pilate actually saw something different about Jesus, that he thought there just may have been something about his claims to being the Messiah and the Son of God. He also greatly resented the Jewish leaders trying to use him as a puppet to achieve their own ends.

Yet no matter what motivated Pilate—first to defend Jesus then to give in to demands that he be executed—in the end, he will always be remembered as the man who consented to the demands of the religious leaders and sent him away to die on a cross.

In the long run, both Roman and Jewish leaders felt that this carpenter from Nazareth upset the status quo too much and that only death on a cross would solve the problem.

The Least You Need to Know

- After being sentenced to death by the Sanhedrin, Jesus was taken to Pontius Pilate, the Roman governor of Judea.

- Finding no reason to condemn Jesus to death, Pilate sent him to Herod Antipas, governor of Galilee.

- Jesus was brutally flogged and mocked by the Roman soldiers.

- After arguing for Jesus' release, Pilate finally gave approval to his crucifixion.

22

Behold the Man of Sorrows

In This Chapter

♦ The horror and history of crucifixion

♦ Jesus taken out to be crucified

♦ Jesus' words on the cross

♦ Jesus breathes his last on the cross

While all four of the gospels tell us that Jesus was crucified, none of them gives any details about the crucifixion itself—probably because their intended readers lived in the Roman Empire and were quite familiar with this awful practice.

It's an extreme understatement to say that crucifixion was a horrible way to die. It was excruciatingly painful and humiliating at the same time. It was, as Josephus wrote, "the most wretched of deaths."

TGIF: A Friday We (Eternally) Thank God For

Crucifixion was a ghastly and grisly form of capital punishment in which the condemned was stripped naked and then nailed and/or tied to a

W.W.J.K. (What Would Jesus Know?)

Most depictions of Jesus' crucifixion show him being nailed to the cross by his hands and feet. However, most experts believe that if a man were nailed to a cross in that way he wouldn't stay fastened on the cross. Jesus was probably also tied as well as nailed to the cross through his wrists and there may have been a small seat affixed to the upright on which he sat for more stability.

crossbeam. The executioners then lifted the crossbeam until the victim's feet cleared the ground, and fastened it to a permanent upright stake. Then, his feet were nailed to the upright, using thick spikes that measured up to 7 inches long.

The condemned man's death was slow—taking anywhere from hours to a matter of days—and painful beyond measure. Death came as a result of the loss of blood, exposure to the elements, suffocation, shock, or a combination of the above.

The victim had to forcibly lift his chest for each breath and when his strength gave out, suffocation was the result.

A More Civilized Death Crossed Out

Roman philosopher and playwright Lucius Annaeus Seneca, who lived at the same time as Jesus, once suggested in a letter that suicide could be preferable to suffering through the horrors of crucifixion: "Can anyone be found who would prefer wasting away in pain dying limb by limb, or letting out his life drop by drop, rather than expiring once for all? Can any man be found willing to be fastened to the accursed tree, long sickly, already deformed, swelling with ugly weals on shoulders and chest, and drawing the breath of life amid long-drawn-out agony? He would have many excuses for dying even before mounting the cross."

In another of Seneca's writings, he indicated that there were many variations of crucifixion, each of them incredibly horrible, painful, and humiliating: "… some hang their victims with head toward the ground, some impale their private parts, others stretch out their arms on a fork-shaped gibbet; I see cords, I see scourges, and for each separate limb and each joint there is a separate engine of torture!"

Crossroads in History

The first historical record of crucifixion was from around 519 B.C.E., when Persian king Darius I crucified 3,000 political opponents following the Persian Dynasty's conquest of Babylon. Crucifixion was later practiced by the Greeks, Seleucids, Carthaginians, and several other civilizations. The Romans later adopted the practice—historians say they "inherited" it from the Carthaginians—and used it as punishment for slaves, non-Romans, and citizens found guilty of treason.

Crucifixion first appeared in Palestine during the Hellenistic times. In fact, historians say that Alexander the Great was the one who introduced the practice to his empire and used it liberally. Later, according to Josephus, Antiochus IV Epiphanes, the cruel Seleucid king whose actions precipitated the Maccabean Revolt, crucified Jews in Palestine who rebelled against his efforts to Hellenize their homeland.

The Romans practiced crucifixion all over the empire, and that included Palestine. At that time, Roman citizens were seldom crucified, and it took direct approval from the emperor for that to happen. However, many Jews—mostly insurrectionists and others seen as dangers to the stability of a particular region of the empire—were crucified during that time.

The Romans—during, before, and after the time of Jesus—used crucifixion often and with morbid and cruel creativity. Roman executioners had learned how to hasten death and how to delay it so that the condemned would suffer longer.

> **W.W.J.K. (What Would Jesus Know?)**
>
> The cross used for crucifixion was made of two parts: an upright stake that was permanently embedded in the ground, and a crossbeam. During a crucifixion, the crossbeam was placed on top of the upright in a "T" shape, or fastened lower on the stake in the traditional shape of the cross †. A third kind of cross, one put together in an "X" shape, was also used in some crucifixions.

An Ancient Campaign of Shock and Awe

The Romans, like others who had used crucifixion before them, used it not only as a means of punishing criminals but to shame and humiliate the condemned and intimidate or frighten the masses into compliance. For that reason, Roman crucifixions were always held near busy roads, ensuring that a greater number of witnesses would be shocked and intimidated by what they saw.

A Roman rhetorician named Quintilian, who was born about five years after Jesus' execution, once wrote of the "deterrent" effect of public crucifixion: "… whenever we crucify the guilty, the most crowded roads are chosen, where most people can see and be moved by this fear. For penalties relate not so much to retribution as to their exemplary effect."

A Christian End to Crucifixion

The practice of crucifixion in the Roman Empire came to an end by order of Emperor Constantine, who ruled during the fourth century C.E. and who himself had converted to the Christian faith. That meant that crucifixion, in one form or another, was part of the system of "criminal justice" in the then-known world for around nine centuries. During that time, many thousands—maybe hundreds of thousands—of people died by this cruel and barbaric method of execution.

But out of those many thousands of cruel deaths by crucifixion, one stands out, and it was the one suffered by Jesus in the year 30 C.E.

The Way of the Cross.

(Copyright © 2001 Tyndale House Publishers)

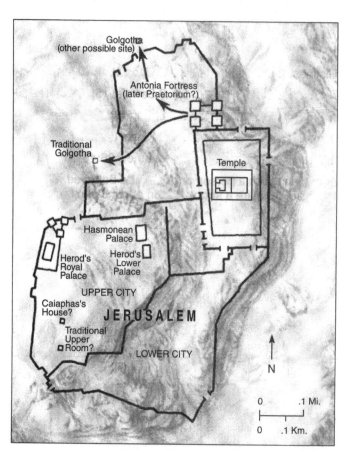

The "Via Dolorosa" (Way of Sorrows) (John 19:16)

The Roman soldiers who took charge of Jesus had likely taken many prisoners away to their deaths. To them, he must have seemed like just another criminal who deserved what was about to happen to him. They removed the robe they had put on him earlier, put his own undergarment back on him, then led him away to be crucified at a place outside the city called "Golgotha."

It was standard practice during a Roman crucifixion for the condemned person to carry his own cross to the execution site. At first, Jesus carried—or more likely *dragged*—his cross toward the site of the execution. But he was exhausted and his body was a bloody mass of torn flesh from being beaten, flogged, and given a crown of thorns that day—not to mention the fact that he hadn't slept the night before—and he sank under the weight of the cross.

The Load Lightens ... Just a Little (Mark 15:21)

It was about nine in the morning when the Roman soldiers led Jesus out of Jerusalem, and they couldn't stand around and wait all day for him to rest enough so that he would be able to continue on. So they recruited (or, as the original language suggests, *forced*) a man named Simon of Cyrene (now Libya) to carry the cross for Jesus. Simon was a Jew who had just arrived in Jerusalem at the time, probably for the Passover celebration.

W.W.J.K. (What Would Jesus Know?)

Most every dramatic reenactment or artist's renderings of Jesus' walk to the place where he was crucified shows him carrying a complete cross. However, according to Roman historical sources, people condemned to be crucified never carried a complete cross. They instead carried only the crossbar, which was fastened to the upright of the cross after the victim was nailed or tied to it. One reason for that may be that wood was scarce in Jerusalem, making it necessary for the Roman executioners to reuse the upright.

W.W.J.K. (What Would Jesus Know?)

Mark's gospel identifies Simon of Cyrene as the father of two men named Alexander and Rufus but doesn't tell modern readers who they were. According to the Christian writer Papias, Mark originally wrote his gospel for a community of Christians in Rome, which might mean that Mark took it for granted that his readers knew who Alexander and Rufus were. It has been conjectured that Simon of Cyrene had himself become a Christian after his experience with Jesus and that his sons had also become believers. Coincidentally, the apostle Paul makes mention of a man named Rufus in his letter to the Romans (16:13).

Still Behind Him—All the Way (Luke 23:27-31)

Jesus still had a lot of supporters and followers at the time of his trial and crucifixion, and many of them followed him as he made his way to the cross. Among those supporters were women of the city of Jerusalem whose grief over what was happening to Jesus showed in their crying and tears.

Jesus, however, told them not to cry for him but for the coming destruction of the city of Jerusalem in the very near future. Even as Jesus was enduring one of the ugliest and most violent forms of death ever devised, his heart was broken over what lay ahead for the city and the people he so dearly loved.

Let's Come to Terms

The exact location of Jesus' crucifixion isn't known for sure, but the name of the place is—**Golgotha.** In Hebrew, *Golgatha* literally means "The Place of the Skull." The Latin equivalent of the word *Golgatha* is *calvaria*, which is where the English word *Calvary* comes from. It is believed that the site of Jesus' crucifixion was called that either because (1) there was a rock formation there that resembled a human skull, (2) it was a place where executions were done, or (3) it was a place of execution that also included tombs or graves.

W.W.J.K. (What Would Jesus Know?)

When someone was about to be crucified, it was common for Jews sympathetic with that person to give him a drink of wine laced with a grain of frankincense in order to lessen the senses and the pain of being crucified. But some scholars say that in this case, the Roman soldiers—hardly the most sympathetic characters on the scene—were more likely faking their sympathy and actually offering him a drink of mere sour wine that would only make his already severe thirst worse.

The First Passion Play: The Final Act

Finally, after what must have seemed like an endless journey—but what was in actuality probably only a several-minutes walk from the city—Jesus, badly beaten and perhaps already near death, was at *Golgotha,* the place where he was to be crucified.

As it was during his ministry, there was a large crowd of people following Jesus that morning— Roman soldiers, Jewish religious leaders, his supporters, and two other men who were to die that day.

This time, however, it was different. Those who supported Jesus and opposed what was happening that day—including his mother Mary and the apostle John—were grieved to the core over what was happening. Their teacher, leader, and friend was about to die a horrible death, and there was nothing they could do to stop it.

As Jesus had repeatedly told them would happen one day—and *why* it would happen—he was about to be put to death on a cross by the Romans.

The Heart of the Passion of the Christ (Mark 15:22–31)

Before the Roman soldiers crucified Jesus, they offered him a drink of wine drugged with gall, which he tasted but refused to drink.

After that, the soldiers nailed Jesus by the wrists to the crossbar (probably also tying his arms) and raised it up and attached it to the upright stake, then nailed his feet to the upright. At that same time, they crucified two criminals and put them on crosses stationed on either side of Jesus' cross.

As Jesus was being crucified, he pleaded with God on behalf of his executioners and for the people who had condemned him to die: "Father, forgive these people, because they don't know what they are doing."

Appearances Can Fool You

Ironically, many of them *didn't* understand what they were doing and thought they were fulfilling Jewish law by putting a false Messiah to death. Most Jews focused on the triumphant Scripture passages regarding the Messiah, where he defeats their earthly enemies (Christians believe this happens at the Second Coming of Jesus) and weren't as familiar with a passage about the Messiah in the Book of Isaiah. At least it gives a rationale for why Jesus would voluntarily suffer this way and why his persecutors wouldn't understand him.

"There was nothing beautiful or majestic about his appearance; nothing to attract us to him. He was despised and rejected—a man of sorrows, acquainted with bitterest grief ... Yet it was our weaknesses he carried; it was our sorrows that weighed him down. And we thought his troubles were a punishment from God for his own sins. But he was wounded and crushed for our sins. He was beaten that we might have peace. He was whipped and we were healed ... From prison and trial they led him away to his death. But who among the people realized that he was dying for their sins—that he was suffering their punishment?" (Isaiah 53:3–8)

> ### His Name Is Jesus, a.k.a.
>
> "Redeemer" (Job 19:25). The promise of a redeemer in the Old Testament began in the Garden of Eden. Job, the man who suffered so much in ancient Jewish history, was aware even then of the need for a redeemer who could achieve what he couldn't, even if he suffered as a relatively good man. He said, "I know that my Redeemer lives, and that he will stand upon the earth at last. And after my body has decayed ... I will see God."

"King" in a Language Everyone Understands

Pontius Pilate had prepared a sign that read "Jesus of Nazareth, the King of the Jews." This was written in Aramaic, Greek, and Latin—the most commonly spoken languages in that part of the world at that time—so that more passersby could read what it said.

After seeing the sign, the Temple priests went and protested to Pilate that the sign should have read "He *claimed* 'I am King of the Jews'" and they asked him to change it. But Pilate told them, "What I have written, I have written. It stays exactly as it is."

Humiliation ... Another Cross to Bear

As Jesus hung naked and bleeding on the cross, he endured not only the pain and humiliation that was always a part of this kind of execution, but also the mocking and torments of those at the scene who had opposed him.

There were four soldiers at Golgatha that day, and after they had crucified Jesus they divided up most of his clothes among themselves. The exception was his robe, which would have been ruined if they had divided it. So the soldiers began throwing dice to decide who would get the robe. The sole remaining possession of Jesus was being "auctioned" in a game of chance.

A Savior Who Can't Save Himself?

People passing by the crucifixion scene on their way into and out of the city shook their heads at Jesus in mockery. Someone in the crowd, maybe one of Jesus' accusers who had appeared at his trial, shouted out, "So! You can destroy the Temple and build it again in three days, can you? Well then, if you are the Son of God, save yourself and come down from the cross!" Ironically, this very scene is exactly what Jesus was talking about when he had told the Jewish leaders, "Destroy this temple, and in three days I will raise it up" (John 2:19).

> ### His Name Is Jesus, a.k.a.
>
> "The Man of Sorrows" (Isaiah 53:3). Isaiah says in this verse that the sorrows he carried were not his but our own sins, diseases, and death; and once borne by him, he would set us free forever of their consequences and bring us eternal joy. To Jesus, it was worth the price.

The priests and Scribes also insulted Jesus with great sarcasm, saying, "He saved others, but he can't save himself! Let this Messiah, this king of Israel, come down from the cross so that we can see it and believe in him!"

But, of course, that would have defeated the very purpose Jesus said the Father assigned for his own life—the one who was sinless would bear the punishment of sinners.

Two Views from the Cross (Luke 23:39–43)

Even the two criminals crucified on either side of Jesus—who many scholars believe were associates of Barabbas, the criminal who had been released earlier that morning—joined in the mocks and insults. However, one of them had a serious change of heart that morning.

One of these lawbreakers scoffed, "So you're the Messiah, are you? Prove it by saving yourself—and us, too, while you're at it!" But the criminal on the other side of Jesus was more humble and contrite. He might have seen Jesus and heard his teaching, for he seemed to believe that Jesus just might be who he said he was. "Don't you fear God even when you are dying?" he asked his partner in crime, then told him that the two of them were getting what they had coming because of their own misdeeds.

No Paradise for You ... Until Later Today!

But this obviously penitent criminal saw Jesus as being different from them: "This man hasn't done anything wrong," he stated. He then looked over at Jesus and said, "Jesus, remember me when you come into your Kingdom." Jesus saw that this man had obviously had a change of heart as he prepared to die and told him, "I tell you the truth, today you will be with me in paradise."

Jesus' earthly ministry had been all about compassion and caring for others who saw their own need for help. And even as he hung on the cross in agony, he looked after the spiritual needs of a penitent criminal who had the nerve to ask him for salvation.

Jesus also took the time to tend to the needs of the most important woman in his life: his mother, Mary.

A New Mother-Son Relationship (John 19:25–27)

As Jesus hung dying on the cross, the apostle John, Jesus' mother and her sister, Mary Magdelene, and another Mary who is identified as the wife of a man named Clopas, stood nearby, probably nearly overcome with tears.

When Jesus saw his grieving mother standing there next to John, the narrator of this account,

> **W.W.J.K. (What Would Jesus Know?)**
>
> Mary Magdelene was a woman from whom Jesus had cast out seven demons (Luke 8:2) and who apparently had followed him after that time. As you will read in Chapter 23, it was Mary Magdelene who first discovered that the stone in front of Jesus' tomb had been moved and that Jesus' body was no longer there. She was also the first to see Jesus after his resurrection. Contrary to legend, it doesn't say she was a sexually immoral woman.

he told Mary, "Woman, he [John] is your son" and told John "She [Mary] is your mother." After that day, John took Mary into his home and cared for her.

At this point, Mary is almost universally believed to have been widowed, probably around fifty years old, and now without her first-born son, Jesus. In caring for his mother, even as he was dying, Jesus was being obedient to Jewish law concerning honoring his remaining parent.

A Cry of Despair, or Hope? (Mark 15:33–39)

By noon, Jesus had been on the cross for about three hours. At that time, "… darkness fell across the whole land until three o'clock." (Jesus had been crucified at 9 A.M., which was referred to at that time as "the third hour." Noon was called "the sixth hour."). At three o'clock that afternoon, after Jesus had been on the cross for six hours, he cried out, *"Eloi, Eloi, lema sabachthani?"* which meant, "My God, my God, why have you forsaken me?"

Jesus was quoting directly the words of King David (Psalm 22:1), but Christians believe that there was more to his words than a cry of pain and anguish at having to die on the cross. It was at this time that Jesus not only suffered physical pain that defies human description but also the emotional and spiritual pain of being separated from God.

By going to the cross, Christians believe that Jesus had taken on the sins of all humankind, and since God was holy and couldn't look on that sin, for a time he couldn't look on his only Son. Yet in later verses of Psalm 22 there is much hope, just as Jesus said this wasn't the end of the story. In verse 24, Jesus knew these words: "For he [God] has not ignored the suffering of the needy. He has not turned and walked away. He has listened to their cries for help." So though Jesus knew the Father turned his back (so to speak) at that moment, he would listen to his cry for help, and ultimately, vindicate Jesus.

Did He Say "Eloi" or "Elijah"?

Some of those at the crucifixion scene misunderstood what Jesus had said and thought that he was calling on the prophet Elijah to come and rescue him. (Many of the Jews believed that Elijah would come to the aid of those in trouble.) Some people even stood and watched to see if Elijah would indeed make an appearance.

As the very moment of Jesus' death drew near, he said, "I am thirsty." Someone took a sponge and soaked it in sour wine (perhaps some of the same wine Jesus had been offered just before he was crucified), then put it on the end of a hyssop branch and held it up to Jesus' lips. When Jesus tasted the bitter wine, he cried out, "It is finished!" then breathed his last breath.

Maybe We Made a Mistake ... (Matthew 27:51–54)

At the moment of Jesus' death, some very strange things began happening in and around Jerusalem. The curtain of the Temple was torn from top to bottom. An earthquake strong enough to split rocks and open tombs hit the area. As the tombs broke open, the bodies of righteous people who had died in the past came to life and headed into the city, where they were seen by many.

The soldiers at the scene of Jesus' crucifixion—the very men who had probably driven the nails into his wrists and feet only hours before—were terrified, and the officer in charge of them said, "Truly, this was the Son of God!"

> **W.W.J.K. (What Would Jesus Know?)**
>
> The Temple curtain that was torn in two at the moment of Jesus' death may have been the veil between the Holy Place—which was illuminated by a golden candlestick only (no outside light could get in) and held the table of showbread and the golden altar of incense—and the Most Holy Place (or holy of holies)—which could only be entered by the high priest, and then only once a year. The curtain itself was made of the most expensive and colorful materials available. It may also have been the curtain that was placed over the entrance to the Holy Place.

The Piercing Truth: He's Truly Dead (John 19:31–37)

By the time Jesus had died, it was getting late in the day, and the Jewish religious leaders didn't want the bodies of the three men who had been crucified to be left on their crosses after sundown. It was Preparation Day for the Sabbath, and it was against Jewish law for the dead to be left on crosses overnight.

The Jewish leaders asked Pilate to hasten their deaths by breaking their legs—a common practice in Roman crucifixions that made it impossible for the condemned to breathe and thus speeded up their deaths.

Pilate gave the order for the legs of Jesus and the two criminals to be broken, and the soldiers did just that to the two. But when they came to Jesus, they found that he was already dead. The soldiers didn't break Jesus' legs, but one of them took a spear and pierced his side. When the soldier did that, water and blood came out of the wound.

A Broken Heart for His Enemies

It has been long debated why this happened, and one of the most popular theories is that Jesus died on the cross of a ruptured heart that was brought on by the trauma he suffered that day.

John's gospel is the only one of the four that told this part of the story of Jesus' death. John doesn't explain the medical reason for this incident, but he does tell us that it was a part of Jesus' fulfillment of Old Testament Messianic prophecies: "Not one of his bones will be broken" (Numbers 9:12 and Psalm 34:20) and "They will look on him whom they pierced" (Zechariah 12:10).

Most of the things Jesus had told his disciples would happen had now come to pass. But as you will see in the next chapter, according to these and other eyewitnesses, Jesus' story wasn't close to being finished.

The Least You Need to Know

- ◆ Crucifixion was a horrific form of execution often used in many parts of the ancient world.

- ◆ At nine o'clock in the morning on Sabbath eve, Jesus was led away to be crucified at a well-traveled place just outside the city of Jerusalem.

- ◆ Jesus, along with two criminals, was crucified at a place called Golgatha.

- ◆ At three o'clock that afternoon, Jesus cried out "It is finished," then died.

Chapter 23

You Can't Keep a Perfect Man Down

In This Chapter

◆ One brave Sanhedrin member receives permission to bury the body of Jesus near the site of his crucifixion

◆ The women followers of Jesus find his tomb empty on Sunday morning following the Sabbath

◆ Jesus appears to Mary Magdalene, then the other women

◆ The religious leaders circulate the story that his disciples stole Jesus' body

The few days following Jesus' death must have been an agonizingly depressing time for his disciples. It was the Passover, usually a time of celebration for the Jews. But those who followed Jesus probably saw little if anything to celebrate.

They had in just the past few days seen their beloved teacher betrayed by a man they had counted as one of them, falsely convicted of blasphemy and sedition in a mock trial before the Sanhedrin, and sentenced to a horrible death on a cross.

What made it all the worse for the disciples is that they had all failed Jesus in his time of need. As the authorities closed in on Jesus, the 11 disciples who remained had scattered (with the possible exception of John and Peter, who followed, but at a distance out of fear of being arrested themselves), leaving Jesus to face his accusers alone.

The Darkness Before the Dawn

It's hard to imagine the kind of disappointment the disciples must have felt in those few days after Jesus' death. They believed that he would be their Messiah and their King, the one who would redeem their homeland. But now Jesus was gone. At that point, the disciples must have been preparing themselves to return to the lives they lived before they met him.

Even though Jesus had told them—as late as on the very night he was arrested— that he would be taken into custody and tried and convicted by the Jewish religious leaders, put to death by the Romans, then later rise from the dead, the disciples somehow didn't connect with what he had told them over and over.

Now the disciples were living in a state of grief and fear, both so deep that they didn't even think to attend to their Master's burial.

No Body Would Want to Stay Here Long

It was the Romans' standard practice to hand over the bodies of those they had executed to the "next of kin," who would make arrangements for a proper burial. The exception to this was crucifixion. In those cases, the Romans, in an effort to increase the "shock value" of a crucifixion, usually left the bodies on their crosses, where they were exposed to decay due to the elements and to the harassment of birds and other natural scavengers.

W.W.J.K. (What Would Jesus Know?)

The Roman practice of leaving dead bodies on their crosses was in conflict with Jewish beliefs and practices when it came to handling the burial of those who had been crucified. Jewish law stated very explicitly that those who had died that way were to be buried before sundown: "If someone has committed a crime worthy of death and is executed and then hanged on a tree, the body must never remain on the tree overnight. You must bury the body that same day, for anyone hanging on a tree is cursed of God" (Deuteronomy 21:22–23).

In trying to keep their own religious law, the Jews at the time of Jesus sought to have the bodies of those who had died by crucifixion taken down from their crosses and buried before nightfall. This was especially important to them on the eve of the Sabbath, since the Jews could do no work on that day. If it was offensive to the Jews to leave a dead body hanging on a cross overnight, it was even more so to leave one there for two days.

The friends or family of someone who had died by crucifixion would typically request the body so that they could give it a proper Jewish burial. Sometimes these requests were granted, but usually only to the more influential of Jews, those who had enough access to the Roman authorities to be able to make that request in the first place.

It wasn't members of Jesus' family or even one of his disciples who went to the authorities to request the right to bury him. Instead, it was someone with some power and influence in Jerusalem: a member of the very Sanhedrin that had convicted him and sentenced him to death early that day.

Not Your Average Joe (Luke 23:50–56)

One of Jesus' disciples (not one of the original Twelve) was a rich and powerful man named Joseph of Arimathea, a highly regarded member of the Sanhedrin who kept his belief in Jesus a secret because he feared what might happen to him if he publicly confessed his faith.

Joseph wanted to make sure that Jesus got a proper burial, and he approached Pontius Pilate and asked for permission to put Jesus' body in a tomb before sundown. Joseph had to gather his courage before he boldly approached Pilate and asked for permission to bury Jesus.

It only makes sense that approaching Pilate for that purpose was dangerous for Joseph. After all, Jesus had been put to death partially on the charges of sedition against Roman authority. Although Joseph hadn't consented to the execution of Jesus, he knew full well that associating himself with Jesus in any way could spell trouble for him.

Finding More Than Common Ground

At first, Pilate was skeptical as to whether or not Jesus was already dead, so he called for the soldier in charge of the crucifixion to tell him if Jesus had died. When the soldier confirmed that Jesus was dead, Pilate—probably wondering what a member of the Sanhedrin wanted to do with Jesus, even after his death—gave Joseph permission to take the body down from the cross and give it a burial that was in accordance with Jewish law.

In first-century Palestine, most Jewish "commoners"—meaning the poor—were buried in very much the same way the dead are buried today in our culture: in the ground with rock or concrete over the grave to protect it from scavengers or grave robbers.

The rich at that time, on the other hand, could afford burial in tombs cut into rock hillsides (man-made caves). These tombs, many of which are still in place in and around Jerusalem, included a main burial chamber, and an entrance low enough that people needed to stoop down to enter it.

Grave Matters (John 19:38–42)

When Joseph headed to Golgatha to take charge of Jesus' burial, he was joined by his fellow Sanhedrin member, the Pharisee Nicodemus—the same Nicodemus who had spent an evening taking to Jesus earlier in his ministry (see Chapter 9).

The gospels don't tell us whether these two men handled all the work of burying Jesus themselves. It is likely that they didn't, because according to Jewish law coming in contact with a dead body rendered them "ceremonially unclean" for a period of seven days, meaning that they could not take part in the rest of the Passover celebrations. It is more likely that they took slaves or servants with them to do the actual work.

Nicodemus brought about 75 pounds of embalming ointment made of myrrh and aloes, which were used in the burial process at that time to help keep down the odor of decomposition. Nicodemus and Joseph (or their servants) took the body of Jesus down from the cross and took him to a new tomb in a garden near the site of the crucifixion.

They wrapped Jesus in a long linen cloth—giving him the appearance much like that of a mummy—put him in a "cave tomb," and sealed it by having a huge rock placed at the entrance. The tomb they buried Jesus in was Joseph's family plot.

W.W.J.K. (What Would Jesus Know?)

It was the custom among first-century Jewish families to practice "two-stage" burials for their dead. They would lay the body to rest in tombs cut in rocks. The bodies were laid in holes cut in the rock walls of the tomb or on a shelf carved next to the wall. Once the flesh of the dead had decomposed, the bones were gathered and laid with those of other deceased family members or placed in a burial box (or ossuary). That allowed the families to reuse the tombs. Jesus' tomb, however, had never been used before.

This wasn't just a decent Jewish burial for Jesus but one that was in accordance with Jewish law concerning handling the bodies of the dead. It was also a burial that fulfilled the Messianic prophecy: "he was put in a rich man's grave" (Isaiah 53:9).

Mary Magdalene and a woman the gospels call "the other Mary" (probably the mother of Joses and the apostle called "James the Younger") were both there when Jesus was buried, and it would be after the Sabbath that they and some other women would return to the tomb with burial spices.

Let's Keep a Lid on This Thing (Matthew 27:62–66)

Early on the morning following Jesus' death and burial—on a very special Sabbath, because it was the Sabbath of the Passover week—some members of the Sanhedrin, remembering Jesus' repeated promise that he would be raised from the dead on the third day after his death, realized that they needed to make sure nothing happened to make Jesus' followers believe that he had come back from the dead.

> ### W.W.J.K. (What Would Jesus Know?)
>
> Although the place of Jesus' burial—as well as the place of his crucifixion, which the gospels tell us was near his tomb—isn't known for certain, one long-held tradition is that it was at the current site of the Church of the Holy Sepulchre (or "holy grave" and also known as the Holy Resurrection Church), which was first built by Roman emperor Constantine in the fourth century C.E., and which is located in the northwestern part of the city. The church stands within the modern city walls but it was outside the walls of the city during Jesus' time, making it possible that this really was where he was crucified and buried.

In order to keep that from happening, the leading priests and Pharisees went to see Pilate and asked him to seal the tomb of Jesus, who they called "the deceiver." That way, they argued, the disciples wouldn't be able to come and steal the body and then tell everyone that Jesus had been raised from the dead.

Pilate agreed with the religious leaders and granted them the use of some Roman guards to watch over the tomb. They also put a seal on the tomb, which scholars believe was some kind

> ### W.W.J.K. (What Would Jesus Know?)
>
> The third day in the account of Jesus' resurrection doesn't refer to the end of three 24-hour days but to a period including parts of three Jewish "days." In other words, since Jesus was in the grave on Friday evening, all day Saturday (the Sabbath), and into Sunday morning, he had, by Jewish computation of time, been in the grave three days.

of official security device such as a cord attached to both entrance to the tomb and the rock that sealed it with a wax imprint of some Roman seal at both ends of the cord. That would mean that if anyone tampered with the tomb, the religious leaders and Roman authorities alike would know.

Ahead of a Good Man Is a Good Woman (Luke 24:1–12)

Women played a huge role in the life of Jesus. As you may recall from Chapter 5 of this book, it was women who first received the announcement of the coming of Jesus the Messiah (as well as his forerunner, John the Baptist). Now, about 33 years later, it would again be women who would first recognize another event in Jesus' story: his resurrection.

This part of Jesus' story has been seen for centuries as one piece of evidence as to the authenticity of the resurrection accounts in the gospels. In Jewish culture at that time, women weren't seen as reliable—or even valid—witnesses to much of anything. Why, goes the argument, would a group of Jewish writers tell a story that put women in such prominent roles if it weren't true? If they wanted to make the story more "palatable" for their readers, the gospel writers would have put men in the roles of "witnesses."

W.W.J.K. (What Would Jesus Know?)

The four gospels don't name all the women who went to the tomb that morning following the Passover. However, they tell us that Mary Magdalene, Mary the mother of Jesus, Mary the mother of the apostle James (not John's brother but "James the younger") and Joses, Salome the wife of Zebedee and mother of James and John, Joanna the wife of a man named Chuza, and a woman named Susanna were all among the group that morning.

Spices Only a Dead Person Can Handle

Early in the morning following the Passover (Sunday, which was considered the first day of the Jewish week), close to that morning's sunrise, a group of women who were close to Jesus headed out from Jerusalem to take some burial spices they had purchased the night before to Jesus' tomb.

There were no men with them that morning, and somewhere along the way it occurred to them that there might not be anyone to move the stone for them once they got there. It was a huge rock, and they knew there was no way they were going to be able to move it without some help.

As it turns out, however, the women wouldn't have to worry about moving the stone at all. This time, they didn't need any men to do the job, because they had angels on the scene.

An Earth-Shattering Experience

When the women arrived at Jesus' tomb, they found that the stone had already been rolled away from the entrance. Thinking that the stone had been moved by grave robbers, Mary Magdalene immediately turned and ran back to Jerusalem to tell Peter and John.

At that point, Mary had no idea why the stone had been moved or who had done it. Just before the women arrived at the tomb, there had been a big commotion (Matthew's gospel calls it an earthquake) when an angel of God had come and rolled the stone away.

Lying Down on the Job

The women looked in astonishment and fear as they saw the soldiers who had been sent to guard the tomb lying on the ground unconscious. The angel himself was a spectacular and terrifying sight, so terrifying that the guards fainted when they saw him.

Actually, there were two angels at the scene that day—perhaps one to do the stone moving and the other to do the talking. One of the angels asked the women, "Why are you looking in a tomb for someone who is alive?" (Luke 24:5).

Yes, We Have a Vacancy

"Don't be afraid," the angel went on. "I know you are looking for Jesus, who was crucified. He isn't here! He has been raised from the dead, just as he said would happen. Come, see where his body was lying."

When the women looked inside the tomb, they found it empty. The angel then told them to go back to town and tell the disciples that Jesus had been raised from the dead and that he would meet up with them in Galilee, just as he had said he would before his death.

The Case of the Missing Corpse (John 20:2–18)

When Mary found Peter and John, she told them that someone had taken Jesus' body out of the tomb and that she didn't know where it was. When the two disciples heard Mary's story, they were at first skeptical. But they knew that grave robberies were common in that place and time, so they took off running toward the tomb with Mary following them.

John was apparently a little fleeter of foot than Peter, because he arrived at the entrance of the tomb first. He didn't go in right away, but instead just stooped down and looked inside and saw Jesus' burial wrappings but no body.

When Peter arrived at the tomb, he didn't just wait outside. He barged right in and found that Jesus' body was indeed missing. All he saw was Jesus' burial clothes—the linen wrappings and the headcloth Joseph of Arimathea and Nicodemus had wrapped Jesus' body in—sitting where the body should have been. John followed Peter and went into the tomb himself.

> ### His Name Is Jesus, a.k.a.
>
> "Firstborn" (Revelation 1:5). Jesus is the "firstborn" among all who, by putting their faith in him, will also rise from the dead to eternal life, and be given a new incorruptible body. The Resurrection, then, is part of the faith that includes all believers in Jesus, not just Jesus himself.

After seeing the empty tomb and the burial wrappings inside it, John and Peter went back home. In his own gospel, John tells us that when he saw the empty tomb, he believed that Jesus had indeed risen from the dead. Peter, on the other hand, wasn't quite sure what to make of what he had seen. At least not yet.

Turning Tears to Joy (John 20:11–18)

After John and Peter had gone, Mary stayed at the tomb. She was crying bitterly and wondering what had happened to Jesus' body. *How could someone do such a thing to the body of her Lord?* she wondered. She stooped down to look inside the tomb for herself and saw two angels sitting where Jesus' head and feet would have been if he were still in the grave.

The angels asked Mary why she was crying, and she told them what she had told Peter and John earlier: because someone had taken away her Lord's body and she didn't know where it was.

Just then Mary glanced over her shoulder and saw a man standing there looking at her. "Why are you crying?" the man asked. "Who are you looking for?" Believing that it was the gardener standing there, she somewhat accusingly asked him to tell her if he had taken Jesus away so that she could go get him and put him back in his tomb.

But it wasn't a gardener standing there talking to Mary. It was Jesus! "Mary!" he said to her. She recognized that voice. She knew it was Jesus! "Teacher!" Mary exclaimed, then fell at Jesus' feet.

He's Now Your Father, Too

Jesus told Mary not to cling to him, because he still had to return to his Father in heaven. But Jesus had an important mission for Mary that morning: She was to go back to town immediately and tell the disciples that she had seen him alive and that he was going to ascend back to heaven to be with "my Father and your Father, my God and your God."

Mary rushed back to town, and after she had found Peter and John (and the rest of the disciples), she excitedly told them, "I have seen the Lord!" then told them exactly what Jesus had told her.

The Proof Is in the Person (Matthew 28:8–10)

Just a short time after Jesus talked to Mary (maybe only a matter of minutes) the other women who had gone to Jesus' tomb that morning—all of them feeling a mixture of fear, excitement, and joy at what they had seen and heard—ran back to Jerusalem to tell the disciples what the angel had said.

Before they made it to Jerusalem, however, they came face to face with living proof that Jesus was alive: Jesus himself! "Greetings!" Jesus said to the women, who were so overjoyed to see him that they ran to him then fell at his feet and clung to him and worshipped him.

W.W.J.K. (What Would Jesus Know?)

Jesus made five different appearances to his followers on the day of his resurrection. The first was to Mary Magdalene (John 20:11–19), followed by his appearances to the other women (Matthew 28:9–10), to Peter (Luke 34:34), to a pair of his disciples on their way to a city called Emmaus (Luke 24:13), and to the apostles in Jerusalem (John 20:19).

You Missed the Son Rise, but You'll See Him in Galilee

Jesus told the women not to be afraid but to go to his disciples—whom he called "my brothers"—and tell them exactly what the angel had told them a few minutes ago: that he would meet up with them in Galilee.

The women got up and continued into Jerusalem, where they told the disciples what they had seen and heard for themselves—that Jesus was alive!

Jerusalem, We Have a Problem (Matthew 28:11–15)

Not everyone was overjoyed with the news that Jesus' tomb was empty. With the body now missing, both the Jewish religious leaders and the Roman soldiers sent to guard the tomb had a serious problem.

> **His Name Is Jesus, a.k.a.**
>
> "The Last Adam" (1 Corinthians 15:45). The first Adam (first human) began with a natural body and passed this on to us. The last Adam, Jesus (both human and divine), who was the first born from the dead, takes on a spiritual body, and also passes this on to all who believe in him. This heavenly body, will nonetheless be a solid body that will encase our spirits, or true selves, for all eternity in a new heaven and new earth.

The day after Jesus' crucifixion, the priests and Pharisees had told Pilate that they would be worse off than they were before if the disciples took Jesus' body then started spreading rumors that he had been raised from the dead.

Now, at least as the Jewish religious leaders saw it, that is exactly the situation they faced.

At the very moment that the women were on their way to Jerusalem to tell the disciples that Jesus' body was gone and that an angel had told them that he had risen from the dead, some of the guards who had been sent to guard the tomb rushed to tell the leading priests that his body was gone.

The Son Rising Might Cause an Uprising

The Jewish religious leaders feared that if the people heard and believed that Jesus was raised from the dead, then they might face a rebellion or uprising among the many Jews who had supported Jesus before his death. Even worse, those who hadn't believed in Jesus might now believe that he really was the Messiah and that he had proved it by being raised from the dead.

The guards, on the other hand, faced certain death if the report got back to Pilate that they had been sleeping on the job and allowed someone to come and steal Jesus' body. Falling asleep on the job was a very serious charge for a Roman guard, one punishable by death.

A Story That Began Under the Table

The priests had to do something to nip this problem in the bud. They called a meeting of the rest of the religious leaders so they could figure out what to do next. After talking the situation over, they decided to bribe the soldiers into saying that they had fallen asleep at their post and that Jesus' disciples had come and taken his body.

The guards took the bribe and began circulating the religious leaders' story, which took on a life of its own at the time. Matthew, who wrote his gospel about 30 years after Jesus' death, reported that the story was still widely circulating among the Jews at the time of his writing.

Scared Men Don't Die for a Lie

Over the centuries, it has been pointed out repeatedly that the story the Roman guards—and others—took to the people was full of holes. To start with, the disciples hadn't exactly shown themselves to have the kind of courage it would take to carry out an operation like that. Would it make sense that a bunch of disciples who had fled the scene when Jesus was taken into custody would have the kind of courage it took to try to sneak by trained Roman guards and steal the body?

It has also been pointed out that all but 2 of the 12 disciples had died violently as martyrs for the cause of Jesus (more on that in Chapter 26). Certainly no one could expect these men to die for something they knew to be a lie, especially if they were afraid to even stand by their Messiah when he was under pressure. They needed nothing short of a resurrection to give them the assurance that Jesus was the Messiah and that their own deaths would not be wasted but that they, too, could be ultimately raised from the dead.

Jesus planned to meet with his disciples in Galilee, just as he had said he would before his crucifixion. But before that happened, Jesus gave the disciples a little taste of what lay ahead for the next several weeks.

> ### His Name Is Jesus, a.k.a.
>
> "The Great Shepherd of the Sheep" (Hebrews 13:20, 21). Jesus called himself the Good Shepherd, but in these verses he is "promoted" by his followers with the term "great" in the context of being brought back from the dead. The writer of Hebrews indicates that his Resurrection is what gives the Shepherd the power to help us (the sheep) do God's will.

The Least You Need to Know

- After Jesus' death, Joseph of Arimathea and Nicodemus—both members of the Sanhedrin—laid Jesus in a tomb owned by Joseph.

- Jesus' mother Mary, Mary Magdalene, and other women returned to Jesus' tomb the day after the Sabbath, only to find that his body was gone.

- Jesus made his first post-resurrection appearance to Mary Magdalene.

- Jesus appeared to the other women as well and told them to let the disciples know that he was alive.

- The religious leaders, along with the Roman soldiers, circulated a story that his disciples had stolen the body of Jesus and invented the story of the Resurrection.

Chapter 24

He'll Be with Us Always ... to the End of Time

In This Chapter

- ◆ Jesus meets with two disciples (not 2 of the 12) on the road to Emmaus

- ◆ Jesus appears to 10 of the 11 disciples in Jerusalem, then to "doubting Thomas"

- ◆ Jesus "reinstates" the apostle Peter

- ◆ Jesus gives his followers "the Great Commission"

- ◆ Jesus ascends to heaven

For nearly 2,000 years, *the* key question surrounding the belief system called the Christian faith has been whether or not Jesus was actually raised from the dead. In other words, was Jesus *really* bodily resurrected, or was the empty grave just the result of a cleverly concocted scheme by the apostles to make it appear that way?

The early Christians understood the importance of dealing with the question of where Jesus' body was that morning when the women came to visit his grave. Like the apostles, they knew that if Jesus hadn't been raised from the dead, then there would be no such thing as what later came to be known as Christianity. Writing to a church located in the Greek city of Corinth, the apostle Paul (introduced in the next chapter) made this very point:

> "For if there is no resurrection of the dead, then Christ has not been raised either. And if Christ was not raised, then all our preaching is useless, and your trust in God is useless. ... And if Christ has not been raised, then your faith is useless, and you are still under condemnation for your sins."
>
> —1 Corinthians 15:13–14, 16–17

A couple decades later, Paul knew that there was a lot riding on the belief that Jesus had been raised from the dead; in fact, he felt that *everything* rode on it. So did the 11 remaining apostles who followed Jesus from the start of his earthly ministry through his arrest.

At the end of Chapter 23, we left off with Jesus' appearance to some of the women who had followed him and their report to the disciples that the tomb was empty. John, the writer of the gospel that bears his name—believed that Jesus had been raised from the dead.

The others? Let's just say that at least one had doubts. At least until Jesus arrived on the scene with bodily remnants of his wounds visible for all to see and touch.

Rumors of My Life After Death *Weren't* Exaggerated (Luke 24:13–34)

On the same day Jesus had been raised from the dead, he sidled up to a couple of disciples who were on their way on the road from Jerusalem to a nearby village called Emmaus. One of the disciples was a man named Cleopas. His traveling companion is unnamed, and could have been a family member—maybe even his wife. The two were likely on their way home from the Passover feast.

Cleopas and his companion were involved in some deep and serious conversation, and when Jesus got close to them, he asked them what they were talking about. At first, these two disciples seemed shocked that Jesus could have been in Jerusalem and not know what had happened over the past few days.

W.W.J.K. (What Would Jesus Know?)

The exact location of the town known as Emmaus isn't known for certain. It has been identified as being the modern town of el-Kubeibeh (the name of which means "little dome"), which is over seven miles northwest of Jerusalem. Another possibility is the modern town of Khurbet Khamasa, which is about eight miles southwest of Jerusalem.

If Jesus didn't know what was at the center of everyone's conversation that day, they told him, then he was the only one.

Of course, Jesus knew what had happened in Jerusalem over the past few days. These things had, after all, happened to him! But he wanted to engage these disciples in a conversation, so he asked them what exactly what happened in Jerusalem to have all the people buzzing.

A Stranger, or a Friend You Have Met Before?

Cleopas and his companion told this seeming stranger that there had been a great prophet by the name of Jesus of Nazareth in Jerusalem during the week of the Passover. They told him that he was an amazing man who God and all the people loved. He had done some incredible miracles and taught like no one they'd ever heard. They went on to tell him, however, that the Jewish religious leaders had arrested Jesus and handed him over to the Romans, who crucified him.

It's not known whether these two disciples themselves believed that Jesus had been raised from the dead. Cleopas and his traveling companion had simply heard the reports that some of the women who followed Jesus had gone to the tomb early the morning after the Sabbath, found that his body was missing, and heard from angels that Jesus was alive. The reports of the men who had followed Jesus, these two said, confirmed the fact that Jesus' body was indeed missing that morning.

His Appointment Amidst Their Disappointment

These two disciples then got to the crux of their own disappointment and the disappointment that many of Jesus' followers felt when he was put to death. They had believed that Jesus had come to be the liberating and conquering Messiah for the nation of Israel, but they were bitterly disillusioned when he was tried and put to death on a cross, ending their hopes of freedom.

The gospel account of this scene tells us that the two disciples on their way to Emmaus didn't recognize Jesus as they talked with him on the road. But it wouldn't be long before they knew that the man they would spend a big part of their day visiting with was the very same Jesus they had been talking about.

No Pain, No Gain

Jesus chided both of these disciples, telling them that they had missed at least part of the Old Testament prophecies of the coming Messiah: "Wasn't it clearly predicted by

"The Scepter" (Numbers 24:17). Though Jesus was known as the "suffering servant" while on Earth, as the heavenly king he would eventually conquer all his enemies. The book of Numbers states that this symbol of a ruler, a scepter, would emerge and crush all evil and deliver his own suffering people.

the prophets that the Messiah would have to suffer all these things before entering his time of glory?" Jesus asked them, then began quoting and explaining the passages concerning the "suffering servant" side of the Messiah.

When the two disciples arrived in Emmaus, they hospitably invited Jesus to stay with them that night. Jesus had planned to move on, but Cleopas and his companion begged him to stay with them. It was getting late in the day, so Jesus accepted their invitation.

End of a Warm-Hearted Meeting

As the two disciples and Jesus sat down for their evening meal, Jesus took a small loaf of bread, blessed it, and gave it to them. Suddenly, they realized just who was having dinner with them that night. It was Jesus! But, just as suddenly, Jesus was gone.

Cleopas and his companion then remembered that their hearts had been "strangely warmed" as they listened to what Jesus told them on the way to their home. To them, this wasn't news that could wait. They had to go tell the apostles what had happened, and they had to do it *right now*. Rather than wait until the next morning to go tell them what had happened that day, they headed for Jerusalem "within the hour."

W.W.J.K. (What Would Jesus Know?)

It isn't known for certain when and where Jesus made his first appearance to Simon Peter. The apostle Paul makes reference to this appearance as well as another appearance to 500 believers at once, most of whom were alive at the time of Paul's writing in 1 Corinthians 15:5–6.

It Already Appears He's Appeared (John 20:19–25)

That night, 10 of Jesus' apostles (Thomas wasn't there) were gathered in a home in Jerusalem. They had locked their doors out of fear of the authorities. Obviously, they had some very serious things to talk about among themselves.

Suddenly, the two disciples from Emmaus burst into the house. But they quickly found out that what they had to tell the apostles was no longer news. The 10 apostles greeted them with: "The Lord has really risen! He appeared to Peter!"

Frightfully Good of You to Come!

The room that night must have been buzzing with people telling their stories of the things they had seen and heard that day. But as the two disciples from Emmaus began telling their story of how Jesus had appeared to them on the road and had come to their home, he suddenly appeared in the room. "Peace be with you," Jesus greeted them.

At first, everyone in the room was terrified, thinking they were seeing a ghost. Jesus asked them what had them so frightened and why they doubted that it was really him standing there. To prove that it was really him, he told them to look at his hands and feet, which bore the marks of the crucifixion.

That was pretty compelling evidence for most of them, but some of them still weren't sure what they were really seeing. Then, to further prove to them that he was actually alive in the flesh, Jesus asked them for a bite to eat. The disciples gave him a piece of broiled fish, and he ate it right in front of them.

Perfect Man, Now with a Perfect Body

All of this was proof to the disciples in the room that night that Jesus wasn't a ghost but the same Jesus they had known for three years, only with a new, resurrected body. They didn't know everything that went on in the spirit world, but they knew that ghosts don't have hands and feet, as Jesus did, and they certainly don't eat fish.

Jesus then reminded the disciples that when he was with them before his death, he had told them many times that everything written about the Messiah in the Old Testament must come true, and that included his arrest, death, and resurrection three days later.

Once Jesus had proved to the people in the house that he was the resurrected Son of God, he told them that he would be sending them out into the world just as God the Father had sent him. They were to take his message of eternal life through him to the world, starting in the city of Jerusalem. But first, they were to wait in the Holy City for the coming of his Holy Spirit, who he would be sending soon and who would be their power source to help them do the things Jesus had sent them to do.

Always a Doubting Thomas in the Bunch (John 20:26–31)

The gospels don't tell us why Thomas wasn't with the other 10 apostles and the 2 disciples from Emmaus, only that he wasn't there.

When the 10 who had seen Jesus that night told Thomas about it, he was deeply skeptical. In fact, even though he was outnumbered 10 to 1, he just wasn't going to buy their story unless and until he had some physical proof. "I won't believe it," Thomas said, "unless I see the nail wounds in his hands, put my fingers into them, and place my hand into the wound in his side."

During his earthly ministry, Jesus had specialized in winning people over to him by meeting their needs. If they had honest questions, he answered them. If they were hungry, he fed them. If they were sick or crippled, he healed them. If they were demon-possessed, he gave the evil spirits a one-way ticket to the netherworld.

And since Thomas—one of Jesus' beloved apostles—had some honest doubts, Jesus gave him the physical proof he needed in order to believe that his Lord was indeed alive again.

A Locked-Room Mystery Solved

In our culture, when something happens that is beyond our wildest expectations—something we've hoped for but dare not expect—we say, "It's just too good to be true."

That's exactly how the apostle Thomas saw the resurrection of Jesus. Over the week since Peter and John had seen the empty grave, the possibility that Jesus just might have been raised from the dead was probably at the top of their list of things to talk about. Thomas himself had heard all this talk, but he just wasn't buying it.

One week after meeting with the 10 apostles in a house in Jerusalem, Jesus appeared to them again. This time, all 11 of them—Thomas included—were locked in a room, probably the same room and probably again out of fear of the authorities, when Jesus instantly appeared before them again.

"Peace be with you," Jesus greeted the apostles as a group, then turned to his doubt-filled apostle, who probably felt the same kind of fear the others felt when they first saw the resurrected Jesus. "Put your finger here and see my hands," Jesus told Thomas. "Put your hand into the wound in my side. Don't be faithless any longer. Believe!"

Believe It When You *Haven't* Seen It

In honestly stating his doubts about Jesus' resurrection, Thomas had in a way thrown down the gauntlet and challenged Jesus to prove that he was really alive again. Thomas wanted more than anything for the reports he had heard to be true, and Jesus met his specific needs and physically showed him what he wanted to believe in the first place.

Thomas had no choice but to believe: "My Lord and my God!" he exclaimed.

"You believe because you have seen me," Jesus told Thomas. "Blessed are those who haven't seen me and believe anyway."

Get a Commission *Before* You Sell the Idea (Mark 16:14–18)

From the time they started following Jesus, the disciples were being prepared for the time when they would take his message to those who, unlike Thomas, couldn't see him. With his time to return to heaven drawing near, Jesus gave the disciples what has come to be known as "the Great Commission": "Go into all the world and preach the Good News to everyone, everywhere."

Jesus told them that anyone who believed in him and was baptized would be saved but that those who refused to believe would be condemned. He also told the disciples that they and others who believed in him would be able to perform many spectacular miracles of their own. They would be able to cast out demons in Jesus' name, and heal the sick by *laying hands* on them.

It was now over a week since Jesus had been raised from the dead, and the apostles, now fully convinced that Jesus had indeed been raised from the dead, were ready to take the next step. The 11 of them headed for Galilee, where Jesus had told them he would meet up with them and give them—as well as other disciples—some final instructions.

> **Let's Come to Terms**
>
> The **laying on of hands** was an important religious rite, not only in the Christian faith but in the Jewish faith as well. It was considered a way of passing on a special divine blessing as well as for anointing or ordaining someone for a special work. One Old Testament example was Moses laying his hands on Joshua, his successor as leader of the people of Israel (Deuteronomy 34:9). In the New Testament, church leaders and missionaries were devoted to service by the laying on of hands. Christians also laid hands on newly baptized believers (Acts 8:16–19).

International Ambassadors for King Jesus (Matthew 28:16–20)

When Jesus told the 11 apostles to go to Galilee, he gave them a specific time and place—neither of which are recorded in Matthew's gospel, other than the place was "a mountain." What Matthew does tell us is that when the disciples saw him, they worshipped him but that "some doubted."

W.W.J.K. (What Would Jesus Know?)

The 11 apostles had all seen Jesus alive prior to the meeting at the mountain in Galilee, yet Matthew's gospel says that "some doubted." But why would they doubt if they had already seen ample proof that Jesus was alive again? It is supposed by some scholars that this meeting with the disciples wasn't just with the 11 apostles but also with the 500 other "disciples" as recorded by the apostle Paul in 1 Corinthians 15:6: "After that, he was seen by more than five hundred of his followers at one time ..." If that is the case, then the ones who doubted were those who hadn't yet seen Jesus alive.

But Jesus assured them that he really was alive and that God had given him complete authority in heaven and in Earth, meaning that from that time forward, he would be king and judge of all people and nations. Because he had that authority, he told them, he was sending them out so that they could "go and make disciples of all the nations, baptizing them in the name of the Father and the Son and the Holy Spirit."

Earlier, Jesus had commissioned his apostles to take his message to the Jews only. This time, however, his instructions were different. This time, he told them that they were to go to "all the nations" and not to just their homeland of Israel.

This command the disciples would later follow as they began was taking Jesus' message not just to the city of Jerusalem and not just to the areas surrounding Judea, but to the "Gentile" or non-Jewish world. (We'll cover that in more detail in Chapter 25.)

Now for Your Assignment, Class ...

Jesus told the disciples that part of their job of reaching the nations for him was to teach them the very things he had taught them over the previous three years. It was a message of the need for holiness before a God who would judge every living person, but it was also one of compassion and forgiveness through Jesus himself.

It was a huge assignment Jesus was giving his disciples, but he assured them that although he was leaving them physically, he wouldn't leave them to do it alone: "... be sure of this: I am with you always, even to the end of the age," he told them.

While there is some debate at the order of Jesus' appearances to his disciples in Galilee, there was one other Galilean appearance recorded in the gospels, one that would be of special importance to the man who would turn out to be the most influential apostle of the 11: Simon Peter.

Something's Fishy About That Stranger (John 21:1–23)

One day, as seven of the disciples—Peter, James and John, Thomas, Nathanael (a.k.a. Bartholomew), and two others who were not named in John's gospel—were in Galilee waiting for Jesus, Simon Peter decided he was going fishing, and the other disciples said they'd go with him.

All seven of the men piled into the boat, headed out onto the Sea of Galilee, and spent the night fishing. Nighttime was seen as the best time to fish on the Sea of Galilee, but this particular night wasn't a very productive one. After spending the whole night fishing, the disciples didn't have so much as one fish in the boat to show for their efforts.

Around sunup, the disciples looked toward the shore and saw Jesus standing there, but they didn't recognize him. Jesus called out, "Friends, have you caught any fish?" and the disciples, probably with at least a hint of aggravation in their voices, especially at being bothered by a stranger, told him they hadn't caught anything.

The "Right" Way to Fish

Then the "stranger" standing on the shore made quite an audacious request: "Throw out your net on the right-hand side of the boat, and you'll get plenty of fish!" Most of the disciples on the boat were experienced fishermen who'd no doubt had many unproductive nights on the lake, and they knew that it didn't make a lick of difference which side of the boat they put their nets out on.

We can imagine seven exasperated disciples thinking—and saying—"Yeah, right!" as they put the nets out on the right-hand side of the boat. *Who does this guy think he is, telling us how to catch fish?* they must have thought. But when they did as the stranger on the shore had told them, they soon found that their nets were so full of fish the seven of them together could not summon the strength to pull them to the boat.

The "All You Can Eat" Fish Breakfast

Suddenly the disciples caught on to who this "fishing consultant" really was, and John himself exclaimed to Peter, "It is the Lord!"

When Peter heard John's announcement, he knew he couldn't wait for the boat to make its way to the shore so he could get close to Jesus. Peter stood up, put on his outer garment, and jumped over the side of the boat and started swimming.

The other six disciples stayed with the boat and rowed it, with the net full of fish in tow, to the shore—a distance of about a hundred yards—where they met up with Jesus and Peter.

By the time the disciples made it to the shore, Jesus already had a fire going. He had cooked up some fish and also had some bread for breakfast, but he asked Peter to go to the boat and bring back some more fish. Peter went and discovered that there were 153 large fish in the net and brought some back to Jesus. "Now come and have some breakfast!" Jesus said, and all eight of them sat down and started eating the fish and bread.

As they finished eating, Jesus turned his attention toward Peter. It was time for some reconciliation.

A Second Chance Three Times Over (John 31:15–33)

Before Jesus' arrest, crucifixion, and resurrection, Peter really believed he had the guts to stand up for him, even if it meant he had to die. But, just as Jesus had told him would happen, at the moment of truth Peter cowered and denied knowing him three times.

Before that morning on the shore of the Sea of Galilee, there is no record of Jesus speaking with Peter about what had happened on the night of his arrest, but now was the time.

W.W.J.K. (What Would Jesus Know?)

It has been debated what Jesus was referring to when he asked Peter if he loved him more than "these." Some believe he was talking about the other disciples, but others believe he was referring to the fish and to the equipment with which he used to catch them, which had been Peter's occupation in life before he met Jesus.

Finally, in what most people believe was Peter's "reinstatement" as Jesus' servant, Jesus took Peter aside and asked him, "Simon son of John, do you love me more than these?" Peter told Jesus that he knew that he loved him, and Jesus replied by telling him, "Then feed my lambs," meaning that Peter was to tend to the people who would believe in Jesus after he was gone.

But Jesus wasn't finished. Twice more he asked Peter if he loved him, and twice more Peter told him that he did. Peter was deeply hurt that Jesus would ask him that question a third time, and he told him, "Lord, you know everything. You know I love you."

Why would Jesus ask Peter such a question, not once but three times? It has been suggested that it was to counteract in Peter's mind the fact that on the night of Jesus' arrest he had denied Jesus three times in an effort to save his own skin.

Receiving Death with Open Arms

After Jesus asked Peter three times if he loved him and told him three times to tend to his followers, it seems that he went on to tell him that he would die as a martyr for the Christian faith: "The truth is, when you were young, you were able to do as you liked and go wherever you wanted to. But when you are old, you will stretch out your hands, and others will direct you and take you where you don't want to go," Jesus told him.

When Jesus used the words "stretch out your hands" it coincided with an expression that was understood in the ancient world as referring to death by crucifixion. Jesus may have been symbolically telling Peter that he would die a violent death on his behalf—something Peter had already said he was willing to do—and that he would glorify God in the process.

When Peter heard this message, he turned and saw John following him and Jesus and asked Jesus, "What about him?" But Jesus told Peter not to worry about what would happen to John or anyone else but just to follow him and do the things Jesus had assigned him to do.

> **W.W.J.K. (What Would Jesus Know?)**
>
> It is generally accepted that Peter did, in fact, die by crucifixion at the hands of the Romans. Bishop Clement of Rome, who lived in the first century C.E. and was believed to be the third bishop of the Roman Christian church, wrote in 96 C.E. that Peter had been martyred. Later, Tertullian, the Christian writer who lived from around 155 to 225 C.E., asserted that Peter had been crucified. Another historical version is that he was crucified upside down because he didn't feel worthy to die like his Lord.

This Message Will Go Far (Mark 16:19–20, Acts 1:3–11)

Jesus had spent a total of 40 days on Earth following his resurrection, and it was now time for him to return to his Father in heaven, just as he had said he would one day do all along. But before he left the disciples, he gathered them together near Bethany to say farewell and to give them some final instructions.

Before Jesus left, the disciples had some questions of their own to ask him. They repeatedly asked him if it was time for him to free Israel and restore their kingdom, as the Old Testament prophecies had said would one day happen.

> **His Name Is Jesus, a.k.a.**
>
> "The Mediator" (1 Timothy 2:5). Where did Jesus go after he went up to heaven? He sits at the right hand of the Father and is a mediator, or "goes between" ourselves and God. He offers our prayers on his behalf to the Father and seeks our protection and blessing.

But just as he had said before, Jesus told the disciples that the Father in heaven alone knows when those things would happen. He told them that in the meantime, they were to go about the business of taking his message to the entire world—to Jerusalem and the rest of Judea, to Samaria, and "to the ends of the earth."

Now You See Me, Now You Don't

These were Jesus' last words to his disciples. Not long after that, he bodily rose up to heaven to take his place at the right hand of God the Father. The account of this scene in the first chapter of the Acts of the Apostles tells us that Jesus was "taken up into the sky while they [the disciples] were watching, and he disappeared into a cloud."

As the disciples watched Jesus' "ascension" as it is called, two angels (the Bible calls them "white-robed men) appeared among them and said, "Men of Galilee, why are you standing here staring at the sky? Jesus has been taken away from you into heaven. And someday, just as you saw him go, he will return!" (Acts 1:11)

A Done Deal Offered to Everyone

Jesus had done everything he'd come to Earth to do. He had spent three years teaching, doing miracles, and preparing his disciples to take his message to the world around them once he had left them. He had suffered and died, then been raised from the dead three days later.

Now, it was time for the disciples to take what they had learned from Jesus and, with the help of his promised Holy Spirit, carry on Jesus' legacy of compassion and forgiveness of sins, teaching others to obey all of Jesus' commands. They were to offer the Good News of a new partnership with God the Father, and the deal had been completely accomplished and delivered by his son, Jesus.

The disciples knew they would receive both great acceptance and great resistance as they spread this message. What was perhaps most comforting were the final words of Jesus recorded by Matthew, "And be sure of this: I am with you always, even to the end of the age."

The Least You Need to Know

- Jesus appeared to two disciples on the Road to Emmaus, then to the apostles—except for Thomas.

- Jesus later proved to "doubting Thomas" that he had risen from the dead by showing himself physically.

- Jesus "reinstated" Peter to the position of apostle at the Sea of Galilee.

- Before he ascended to heaven, Jesus gave the disciples "the Great Commission" of making new disciples throughout the world.

Part 6

A Roman Empire ... Soon to Become the *Holy* Roman Empire

Jesus commissioned his disciplines to take his message of love and salvation "to the ends of the earth," and that was exactly what they did, as far away as Asia Minor (modern Turkey) and Greece. That would happen after the amazing conversion of one of this new movement's worst opponents, a man named Saul of Tarsus.

The Christian movement would continue expanding throughout the Roman Empire for several hundred years. It wasn't easy, though. For about three centuries, Jesus' followers would face sometimes fierce opposition. Eventually, however, the movement started by Jesus and continued after his death and resurrection by his apostles would transform the entire Roman Empire as well as the civilizations that followed, including our very own.

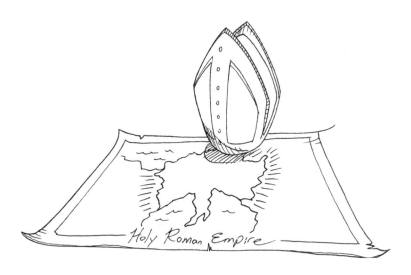

Holy Roman Empire

Chapter 25

The Legacy of Jesus and His Followers

In This Chapter

- ◆ The Christian faith takes root in Jerusalem
- ◆ The message of Jesus spreads, despite organized persecution against his followers
- ◆ The conversion of a Pharisee and opponent of the Christian faith named Saul
- ◆ Saul (the apostle Paul) spreads the message of Jesus into Asia Minor and Macedonia

Before his death and after his resurrection Jesus promised the disciples that he would send his Holy Spirit to help them, direct them, and strengthen them. It wasn't long after he ascended back to heaven that Jesus made good on that promise.

Exactly 10 days after Jesus returned to heaven, 120 of his closest followers—including the apostles, now joined by Judas's replacement, a man named Matthias—assembled in Jerusalem for what Christians now

Let's Come to Terms

Pentecost, which literally means "50th" in Greek, was the day of the Jewish "Feast of Weeks" (a week of weeks plus one day). Pentecost took place exactly 50 days after the Passover.

call the "day of *Pentecost.*" This was the day when the Holy Spirit came to them in spectacular fashion.

The second chapter of Acts describes the scene this way: "Suddenly, there was a sound from heaven like the roaring of a mighty windstorm in the skies above them, and it filled the house where they were meeting. Then, what looked like flames or tongues of fire appeared and settled on each of them. And everyone present was filled with the Holy Spirit and began speaking in other languages, as the Holy Spirit gave them this ability" (Acts 2:2–4).

Filled with the Spirit, Not Spirits (Acts 2)

There were devout Jews from all over the known world in Jerusalem on the day of Pentecost. When they heard the sounds of the Holy Spirit's arrival, they came running to see what was going on and heard something that amazed them: A bunch of simple Galileans were speaking to all of them in their own languages.

Some of these witnesses were in awe as they watched and listened to what was happening, but some assumed that the people who were "speaking in tongues" were babbling nonsense and were drunk. But Peter, now the unquestioned leader of Jesus' followers, quickly stepped in and pointed out that it was only nine o'clock in the morning and that none of the people had so much as touched even a drop of wine.

Peter went on to explain that what the people were seeing and hearing that day was the fulfillment of a prophecy by the Old Testament prophet Joel, who hundreds of years before had predicted that God would pour out his Spirit on people and that great miracles would accompany that outpouring (Joel 2:28–32).

Repent? You're Speaking My Language!

Having cleared up the issue of what, or more accurately, *who* exactly was causing people to speak in languages they didn't know, Peter went on to tell the crowd that Jesus was indeed alive and had sent his Holy Spirit as proof.

Peter's words cut to the depths of their hearts, and they asked him what they needed to do about what they had seen and heard. Peter told them that they must repent, or turn away from their sins and turn to God, and be baptized in the name of Jesus Christ for the forgiveness of their sins.

The response to Peter's words was nothing short of incredible. As a result of Peter's first sermon, some 3,000 people became followers of Jesus that very day.

A "Reinvented" Peter (Acts 3:1–4:30)

As the leader of this "new" religious movement in Jerusalem, Peter spoke with great power, authority, and courage. Even in the face of threats by those who opposed the Christian faith, he refused to back down from his claims that Jesus was the Messiah and the Son of God.

The results spoke for themselves. It wasn't long before the ranks of the believers had grown to 5,000—and that was just the men.

This growth in the number of believers really got the attention of the Jewish religious leadership. But while they wanted Peter's preaching and teaching to come to a stop, they were very careful in how they attempted to bring that about, simply because the large number of believers in Jerusalem represented to them the threat of an uprising if they came down too hard on the disciples.

Miracles Are to Be Seen but Not Heard (Acts 4:1–5:42)

The Sanhedrin attempted to quiet the apostles, first giving them some stern warnings about preaching the message of Jesus. When that didn't work, they resorted to threats, arrests, imprisonment, and beatings. But none of these things worked. In fact, they only seemed to encourage and embolden the apostles.

The persecution and opposition the apostles faced did nothing to keep the numbers of believers in Jesus from growing. However, it did later prove to be a factor in moving the message of Jesus out of Jerusalem and into the surrounding areas.

His Name Is Jesus, a.k.a.

"The Power of God" (1 Corinthians 1:24). Jesus was named the "power of God" and this was demonstrated beyond the miracles in his lifetime. He promised his disciples that they would do even greater things because he was going to plead with the Father on their behalf. We see a number of miracles by Peter, John, Paul, and Phillip in the expansion of the early church. All are in the name of Jesus, and the disciples are careful to give him the full credit based on his own divine power, not theirs.

You're Just Fanning the Flames (Acts 7:54–8:3)

For a time, there seemed to be a strained but somewhat peaceful co-existence between Jesus' followers and the authorities in Jerusalem. However, just as Jesus had said would happen, the new church in Jerusalem began suffering through intense persecution, starting with the stoning death of an outspoken believer named Stephen.

The opponents of the Christian movement wanted more than anything to stop it before it spread any further, but the opposition to the faith and to those who practiced it had the opposite effect. Yes, the persecution drove many of Jesus' followers out of Jerusalem. But that only served to expand the message of Jesus further, as the believers fanned out around Judea and Samaria, taking the *Gospel* message with them.

Now, Jesus' command that his disciples take his message outside Jerusalem and to the "ends of the earth" was beginning to happen. But it was just the beginning. Soon, there would be another apostle on the scene who would take the message of Jesus to areas *far* from Jerusalem. He would come to be known as the apostle Paul, and he would come from a background none of the original apostles could ever have expected.

W.W.J.K. (What Would Jesus Know?)

When Judea became a Roman province in 6 C.E., Roman law took away the Jewish Sanhedrin's right to inflict capital punishment. There was one exception to that law. When someone violated the sanctity of the Temple through words or deeds, the Sanhedrin was allowed to mete out the death penalty. According to Jewish law, it was necessary for two witnesses to have seen or heard what he did or said before the death penalty could be handed out.

Let's Come to Terms

The **Gospel** the apostles took to the Jews and later to the Gentiles doesn't refer to the four books about Jesus' life and work but to the message itself. The word *Gospel* in this context literally means "God's spell" or Good News. It is also called in the New Testament "the gospel of the kingdom," "the gospel of Christ," and "the gospel of salvation." It explains the death, resurrection, and ascension of Jesus to work out our eternal salvation.

'Saul Over? No, Just Beginning!

In some ways, the apostle Paul—or Saul, his Jewish name—was the kind of man many people would expect to be a great ambassador for Jesus. He was well educated in Jewish law, and he had an incredible zeal for the things of God.

Saul was born around 10 B.C.E. in Tarsus, the capital city of Cilicia, a Roman province in the southeastern part of Asia Minor. Tarsus was located in what is now the southern coast of Turkey. Saul was from a family of devout Jews. His father was a Pharisee who sent Saul to Jerusalem as a young teen to study under the highly regarded rabbi Gamaliel. Saul himself became a very strict Pharisee with a zeal for truth.

However, Saul was anything but a friend of the apostles and to the Christians living in Jerusalem. When he learned that Christianity was gaining a foothold in the Holy City, he began a campaign of persecution against Jesus' followers.

> **W.W.J.K. (What Would Jesus Know?)**
>
> One of the believers who fled Jerusalem during the wave of persecution was a man named Philip (not one of the original 12 disciples), who went to the city of Samaria, where he preached about Jesus, cast out demons, and healed the sick and lame by laying hands on them. As a result, there were many converts to Christianity in that city (Acts 8:4–8).

A Pharisee Who Makes House Calls

Saul was one of the men at the scene of Stephen's stoning. Although he didn't actually take part in the stoning itself, he clearly condoned the mob's action. Later, he continued his persecution of Christians in Jerusalem by going from house to house, taking men and women who believed in Jesus into custody and putting them in prison.

Saul was so intent on ending the Christian movement that he went to the high priest and asked for letters addressed to the synagogues in the Syrian city of Damascus so that he could go there and arrest Jesus' followers.

As Saul was on his way to Damascus carrying with him the list of the names of Christians he intended to arrest, something spectacular happened to him, something that would change not only the course of his own life but the course of the world as we know it even today.

I've Seen the Light, but Nothing Else (Acts 9:1–7)

As Saul neared the city of Damascus, he was suddenly struck blind by a brilliant light. Just then, he heard a voice asking him, "Saul! Saul! Why are you persecuting me?" Probably trembling in fear, Saul asked the voice who was talking to him. "I am Jesus, the one you are persecuting!" came the answer. "Now get up and go into the city, and you will be told what you are to do."

Saul's traveling companions were astonished at what had happened. They heard the voice themselves, but they couldn't see who it belonged to. After the voice was finished speaking, Saul picked himself off the ground, and his companions led him by the hand to Damascus, where he stayed three days.

With Friends Like These ...

Meanwhile, a man named Ananias, a Jewish believer who lived in Damascus, received a message from God telling him that he was to meet with Saul and take care of him. Ananias was perplexed at what he was hearing. Wasn't this the same Saul of Tarsus who had such a reputation for persecuting believers in Jerusalem? But God told Ananias to do as he had said and told him that Saul would be used to take Jesus' message to the Gentiles and the Jews as well.

Ananias must have wondered what God had in mind—or if he had heard correctly—but he obeyed anyway. Later, when Ananias met Saul, he placed his hands on him and something that looked like scales fell from his eyes and he could see again. Saul got up and was baptized, then had something to eat.

Let's Come to Terms

The word **apostle** refers to those Jesus gave the responsibility of organizing his church and taking his gospel "to the ends of the earth" after he left. Another part of Jesus' calling of the apostles was giving them authority to cast out demons and to heal sickness and other physical problems. When Saul was called as Jesus' thirteenth apostle (minus Judas plus Matthias) he was given the same responsibilities and authority.

Preach the Opposite, Brother!

Only a few days after his conversion, Saul began going to the synagogues in Damascus and telling people that Jesus really was the son of God. Of course, the people who heard him were amazed—and probably more than a little skeptical. They knew about Saul's reputation, and they knew that he had come to Damascus so he could arrest Christians there.

The people in Damascus soon became convinced that Saul was "for real," as his preaching became more and more powerful. In fact, his preaching was so effective that the people couldn't dispute his claims that Jesus really was the Messiah. But his preaching also got the attention of the religious leaders there, and they began planning to have him killed. When Saul found out about these plans, he left Damascus—with the help of some fellow believers—and headed to Arabia and then back to Jerusalem.

Cool Reception for a Former Hothead

Saul's reception by the *Christians* in Jerusalem was even cooler than the one he'd received in Damascus. At first, the believers there wouldn't even meet with him because they were afraid of him. However, a brave disciple named Barnabas helped convince them that Saul was a changed man.

Jesus' apostles accepted Saul into their ranks, and they soon found that they had a preacher who spoke as passionately about Jesus as they did. But it wasn't long before Saul's preaching got him in trouble with the religious authorities in Jerusalem.

Knowing that staying in Jerusalem put Saul in danger, the believers there took him to the coastal town of Caesarea and sent him on to his hometown of Tarsus. Later, Barnabas went to Tarsus and found Saul, then the two of them traveled to Antioch, a Syrian city about 300 miles north of Jerusalem, where they stayed for a year, teaching the ever-growing number of believers who lived there.

Let's Come to Terms

It was during Saul's stay in Antioch that the word **Christian** to describe a follower of Christ first came into use, by the Greeks or Romans (or both) who lived there. Up to that point, Jesus' followers had referred to themselves using terms such as "brethren," "saints," or "believers," while the Jews called them "Nazarenes" or "Galileans."

The Gospel Message Goes International (Acts 13:1–15:35)

Here are a few highlights of Paul's ministry to the Gentiles throughout Asia Minor and Macedonia during his three missionary journeys.

We'll Worship You; No, We'll Kill You

Like most cities in the Mediterranean region, Lystra was a place where the people worshipped a variety of pagan gods. After Paul healed a man with crippled feet in Lystra, the people there believed that the two men were the mythical Greek gods Hermes and Zeus come in the flesh.

W.W.J.K. (What Would Jesus Know?)

In the Acts of the Apostles, it is at this point that Luke stops referring to Saul by that name and uses the name Paul. Luke doesn't explain the reason for the name change, but many people think it was simply a matter of shifting from the traditional Hebrew name of Saul to a Greco-Roman variation of the name. From that time on, Paul would be ministering primarily to Gentiles.

Of course, Paul and Barnabas weren't happy about that, and quickly tried to set the record straight. But that wasn't going over well with the people, and to make matters worse, some of Paul and Barnabas's persecutors had come to Lystra from Pisidian Antioch and Iconium to stir up trouble for the apostles.

Before Paul and Barnabas knew what was happening, the crowds who had earlier been worshipping them as gods had been whipped into a rage and dragged Paul outside the city, stoned him, and left him for dead. However, Paul was still very much alive (but probably a little groggy at first) and he returned to Lystra that day. The next morning, Paul and Barnabas left Lystra and went to a city called Derbe. From there, they retraced their itinerary, stopping at each city they'd visited before and appointing elders in each city's church.

Adding Greece to the Mixture (Acts 16:1–5)

The Acts of the Apostles doesn't tell us what happened when Paul and Silas visited Derbe, but when they visited the city of Lystra, they met a young disciple named Timothy, who would become Paul's most trusted traveling companion and co-worker over the next 15 years. Paul asked Timothy to join him and Silas, then, probably to alleviate conflicts with Jewish believers, had Timothy—whose mother was Jewish but his father Greek—circumcised.

W.W.J.K. (What Would Jesus Know?)

The Timothy who Paul and Silas met in Lystra would later receive two letters from Paul that would be part of the New Testament (1 Timothy and 2 Timothy).

Athens: A Bit Stoic Toward the Message (Acts 17:16–34)

Athens was the very cradle of Greek culture and the most celebrated city in ancient culture. There Paul went to the synagogue to talk with the Jews and with the "God-fearing" Gentiles. In Athens, he was disturbed by the Greek idols he saw all around him, but he also debated with some *Epicurean* and *Stoic* philosophers—who thought he was babbling or simply pushing some new religion on them.

Let's Come to Terms

The Greek **Stoics** and **Epicureans** practiced greatly disparate life philosophies. The Stoics believed in the denial of all personal desires, while the Epicureans devoted themselves to personal happiness based on intellectual pursuits. In time, the Epicurean philosophy degenerated into one of seeking happiness through sensual gratification. Both philosophies had many adherents in the Greco-Roman world.

In Athens, Paul saw an altar dedicated "to an unknown God" and he used what he had seen as an opening to explain the nature of the true God he served. He quoted their own poets and philosophers to persuade them. Some Athenians rejected Paul's message, some said they wanted to hear more later, but very few actually became believers.

Tentmaker–A Preacher Leading a "Sheltered" Life (Acts 18)

Corinth was a Grecian port city on the isthmus that joins the Peloponnesus to the mainland of Greece. It was around 50 miles west of Athens. Here Paul stayed with a Christian couple named Aquila and Priscilla, who also had in common with Paul the profession of tentmaking. Paul worked with Aquila for a while and went to the synagogues on the Sabbath and tried to persuade the Jews and Greeks alike to believe in Jesus.

The Jews in Corinth resisted Paul's message, so he began concentrating on preaching to the Gentiles in the city. He began staying in the home of a godly man named Titius Justus, who lived next door to the synagogue. Paul persuaded many people in Corinth to believe in Jesus, including Crispus, the leader of the synagogue.

After about 18 months in Corinth, Paul and his companions made their way toward Jerusalem—making several other rewarding stops along the way—where he hoped to observe the feast of Pentecost.

Idol Silversmiths Not Wanting to Be Idle (Acts 19:21–41)

Paul spent his first three months in Ephesus preaching boldly in the synagogue. After that, he preached daily to Jews and Greeks alike.

During this time, Paul ran into a "new" kind of religious opposition. A silversmith named Demetrius had been making a handsome living in Ephesus selling statues of the Greek goddess Artemis, an idol for whom a huge temple had been built in the city (the Temple of Artemis was one of the Seven Wonders of the Ancient World).

His Name Is Jesus, a.k.a.

"Lord of lords" (Revelation 19:16). The main message of the disciples was "Jesus is Lord" and was meant to communicate that he had victory and authority over the nations, gods, and spirit beings in the entire universe. The common use of the term "Lord" was mainly related to earthly rulers who were "benefactors" to their subjects because they were seen as the suppliers of every need. Jesus is also portrayed in this light by his followers.

Demetrius feared that Paul's message could cut into his business, or maybe even end it, so he rallied the tradesmen in the city who built the statues and they began marching through Ephesus chanting, "Great is Artemis of the Ephesians!" Soon, the whole city was in an uproar, and the lives of Paul and his traveling companions were in danger. Fortunately, the city's mayor, mindful that a riot could bring Ephesus unwanted attention from the Roman government, got the people to settle down.

Good News Pauline Style

If you're going to take three successful missionary journeys throughout a world full of hostility to what you're trying to do, you certainly need a unique message about Jesus. Paul had just that kind. His message can be found in his writings to the churches he started, known as the Pauline Epistles, and is especially well spelled out in his epistle to the Romans.

While the four gospels recounted the life and work of Jesus, in Romans Paul eloquently spells out the message of Jesus for the Gentiles. This letter, which has been referred to as "The Gospel According to Paul," systematically lays out the Good News of salvation through Jesus:

- The fallenness and sinfulness of humankind in contrast with the perfection and holiness of God.

- How God has freely provided us with that holiness through Jesus.

- How God empowers believers in Jesus to live lives that please him.

In the eighth chapter of Romans, Paul spells out for believers the benefits they receive when they are "in Christ":

- They no longer need to fear condemnation (verse 1).

- They are free from the hold of sin and death and can focus on higher things (2–3).

- They are adopted into God's family and have the right to call God "Abba," a familiar and affectionate term that literally means "Daddy" (15–17).

- They have a future in heaven that surpasses any kind of earthly suffering (18).

Romeward Bound (Acts 21:37–28)

When Paul arrived in Jerusalem, he and the apostles started trading stories about the things that had happened surrounding their ministries. During this conversation, they warned Paul that a rumor had been going around about him—namely that he was telling people to disobey the Law of Moses.

In an effort to dispel these rumors, Paul went through a purification ceremony with some other Jewish men. But that didn't solve all of Paul's problems with some of the Jews in Jerusalem. They believed that Paul was associating himself a little too closely with Gentiles, making him a traitor to his own people.

Aren't You That Egyptian Terrorist?

About that time, things started turning ugly. A riot broke out and Paul was nearly killed. Only the intervention of the Roman authorities saved his life. The Roman soldiers, believing they had in their custody an Egyptian terrorist who had earlier started a riot in Jerusalem, took Paul to their the barracks. But Paul told the authorities that he wasn't an Egyptian at all but a Jew from Tarsus.

With the accusations and threats to Paul's life still coming, the Roman commander was about to have the truth beaten out of Paul. But when Paul mentioned his Roman citizenship, he was put in prison and chained to a Roman guard. That night, Paul had a vision of Jesus, who encouraged him and promised him that he would have a chance to preach in Rome.

A Plan That Was Not Shipshape

Later, Paul was transferred to the city of Caesarea, and after two years of delays he was on his way to Rome. The trip itself wasn't without some trials of its own, most notably a horrendous shipwreck near the Mediterranean island nation of Malta. Miraculously, Paul and the others on the ship made it to shore alive, and they stayed in Malta for three months before continuing on to Rome.

Paul remained in Rome for at least two years. He was a prisoner, but he was allowed some privileges. He was allowed to have his own residence (although he was under guard the whole time) and was allowed to meet with his fellow believers and to write epistles, or letters, to churches and individuals with whom he had associated. There is circumstantial evidence that Paul was martyred along with Peter in Rome during the reign of the emperor Nero.

In the final chapter we'll look at what happened to the apostles, how the message of Jesus "conquered" the Roman Empire, and what Jesus intends for himself and us in the future.

The Least You Need to Know

♦ Ten days after Jesus returned to heaven, the believers in Jerusalem received the Holy Spirit.

♦ Peter led the apostles as they evangelized the city of Jerusalem, then the out-lying areas.

♦ One of the church's harshest opponents, a Pharisee named Saul, was converted to the Christian faith and became known as "the apostle Paul."

♦ The apostle Paul took three missionary journeys reaching many cities, and spreading Jesus' message mainly to the Gentiles.

Chapter 26

The Triumph of Jesus' Message

In This Chapter

- ◆ The eventual fates of Jesus' apostles
- ◆ The spread of the church in the face of Roman persecution
- ◆ The Romans accept, then embrace, the Christian faith
- ◆ Christianity dominates the world religious scene for several centuries
- ◆ The apostle John's vision of the "end times"

In the previous chapter, we talked about the things that happened in Palestine, and in much of the rest of the Roman Empire, following the departure of Jesus. It was then the apostles obediently began taking the message of Jesus to Jerusalem, to the outlying areas, and to areas such as Asia Minor and Greece.

In this chapter, we want to discuss what eventually happened to the apostles as well as what happened to the Christian faith itself, including what are called the "last days" of the world as we presently know it.

Of Jesus' original 12 apostles, the New Testament tells us of the ultimate fate of only 2: Judas, who betrayed Jesus and then hanged himself in a fit of remorse, and James (the brother of John), who was executed by Herod Agrippa, the grandson of Herod the Great and the king of Judea and Samaria from 41–44 C.E. Other than that, what we know about the eventual fates of the apostles comes from "extrabiblical" history and from ancient church tradition.

Now let's take a look at what that history and tradition tells us about what became of the apostles of Jesus.

A Life That Didn't Just "Peter" Out

The last mention of Simon Peter in the Bible (other than a brief reference by Paul in one of his epistles) appears in Acts 15, in which we read of him taking part in the deliberations of the Council at Jerusalem, which dealt with what it took for Gentiles to be accepted into the kingdom of God, then again at a similar meeting in Antioch.

Eventually, after being arrested and thrown in jail several times, Peter left Jerusalem. From there, it is believed that he traveled to Babylon to minister to the Jewish population there. But as persecution began, Babylon was also a code name for Rome, so this is uncertain. Some also believe that during this time in Peter's life, he wrote his first epistle, 1 Peter.

According to church tradition, Peter eventually made his way to Rome—just in time to face Roman persecution from Emperor Nero, who had started a savage campaign of persecution against the apostles and other believers in the empire. It is believed that Peter was arrested and thrown into a Roman prison called the Mamertine, where he stayed for nine months, enduring horrific torture and degradation.

Finally, around 67 C.E., Peter died by crucifixion at the hands of the Romans. Tradition holds that as Peter was taken out to be killed, he pleaded with his executioners not to crucify him in the same manner as they had his Lord, Jesus. They obliged, crucifying him upside down.

W.W.J.K. (What Would Jesus Know?)

It has long been held that while Peter was preaching in Babylon (or Rome), his right-hand man and interpreter was John Mark, the same young man who spent a short time traveling with the apostles Paul and Barnabas and the writer of the Gospel of Mark. As John Mark interpreted Peter's experiences with Jesus, he committed those things to memory, allowing him to write a clear and accurate account of Jesus' earthly ministry as it was told by an eyewitness, Peter. So, in a way, the Gospel of Mark is really the Gospel of Peter.

Reading Someone's Mail ... for Centuries

When the apostle Paul first arrived in Rome, he did so believing that because he was a Roman citizen he would have a chance to plead his case with Emperor Nero. However, the Acts of the Apostles ends after Paul's two-year stay in Rome—a time when he was more or less under "house arrest"—with no resolution of his situation.

During his stay in Rome, Paul was more or less free to meet with fellow believers and to write letters, or *epistles*, to his associates in ministry and to the churches he had founded throughout Asia Minor. Several of Paul's letters ended up being part of the New Testament.

> **Let's Come to Terms**
>
> **Epistles** are the letters written by the apostle Paul to various churches and individuals under his spiritual care. The epistles of Paul that ended up in the New Testament are as follows: Romans, 1 and 2 Corinthians, Galatians, Ephesians, Philippians, Colossians, 1 and 2 Thessalonians, 1 and 2 Timothy, Titus, and Philemon. Some believe that Paul penned the epistle to the Hebrews.

Two P's in a Very Unpleasant Pod

While the Bible doesn't tell us what became of Paul, it is widely believed that he was eventually released from Roman custody around 63 or 64 C.E. After that, he is believed to have revisited Greece and Asia Minor and perhaps realized his goal of traveling to Spain, then the westernmost part of the known world.

It is also believed that Paul was later brought back to Rome, this time forcibly. This was around the same time that Peter faced his execution at the hands of Nero, a fate Paul shared with his fellow apostle. It is held that Paul was imprisoned for nine months alongside Peter and that he suffered the same kind of abuse Peter had to endure. Church tradition has it that after his arrest, Paul was either beheaded or torn apart by wild animals in the arena as a crowd stood cheering.

A Mandatory Island Vacation

Of the original 12 apostles, the apostle John was the only one not to die a violent death. But that doesn't mean he escaped persecution. As we pointed out in the last chapter, John had been arrested, imprisoned, and punished physically during the early days of the Christian church in Jerusalem.

Just before the destruction of Jerusalem by the Romans in 70 C.E., John moved to Ephesus, where he became the pastor of the Ephesian church. At the same time he established a close relationship with other churches in that area of Asia Minor.

During a wave of Roman persecution of Christians under Emperor Domitian, John was exiled to Patmos, a small, rocky island off the coast of Asia Minor in the Aegean Sea. It was here he reputedly wrote the Book of Revelation, which we'll cover later in the chapter. According to the second/third-century Christian writer Tertullian, before John went to Patmos he was thrown into a caldron of boiling oil, but wasn't injured seriously.

When John was released from exile, he returned to Ephesus, where he continued leading the Ephesian church and working to build new churches throughout Asia Minor. John died a peaceful and natural death around the year 99 C.E.

> **W.W.J.K. (What Would Jesus Know?)**
>
> At the time of Jesus' crucifixion, he charged the apostle John with caring for his mother, Mary. While the time and place of Mary's death aren't known, ancient church tradition holds that Mary spent her last few years living with John in Ephesus.

> **W.W.J.K. (What Would Jesus Know?)**
>
> One tradition about the apostle John is that he often said to his congregation, "Little children, love one another!" After hearing that simple message time after time—and probably wanting to hear something different—some of his disciples asked John, "Master, why do you always say this?" John's reply? "It is the Lord's command. And if this alone be done, it is enough!"

Unique Exploits and Unusual Endings

Here are the fates of the other apostles, according to history and church tradition:

- Andrew—He is believed to have preached in Scythia, Greece, and Asia Minor before being martyred. One ancient writer wrote that Andrew hung on a cross three whole days, but continued telling people about the love of Jesus until he died, which is believed to have happened on November 30, 69 C.E.

- Philip—It is believed that most of Philip's ministry took place in Galatia in Asia Minor. He is believed to have been crucified at the age of 87 in a city called Hierapolis.

- Bartholemew (Nathanael)—He is believed to have traveled with Philip to Asia Minor. Tradition holds that he and Philip healed the wife of a Roman governor, but that he later ordered them crucified. Philip died on a cross, but Bartholomew survived, then served in India and Armenia, where he was beaten to death.

◆ Thomas—He preached in Babylon and is believed to have established the first church there. He also served in Persia and India, where he was killed with a lance. Some tradition has it that he traveled to China.

◆ Matthew—After Jesus' ascension, Matthew wrote the gospel that bears his name. There are several traditions concerning his death, including one that says he was martyred in Ethiopia and another that says he was killed in Egypt after his return from Ethiopia.

◆ James the younger—Tradition has it that he preached in Palestine and in Egypt, where he was crucified.

◆ Jude (Thaddaeus)—He is believed to have preached in Assyria and in Persia, where he died as a martyr.

◆ Simon the Zealot—He is believed to have preached the message of Jesus throughout North Africa and even into what would become Britain. One tradition has it that he was crucified by the Romans in Britain around 61 C.E. Another tradition has it that he was martyred in Persia by being sawn in half.

Obviously, being an apostle in the Roman Empire during the first century was a dangerous occupation. However, it should be noted that just being a Christian wasn't much safer.

Jesus and Other "Gods" Don't Get Along

Everything that happened through and to Jesus' followers in the first two-plus centuries of the church's existence took place against the backdrop of sometimes intense persecution by the Romans. There were times when Christians could live and worship in relative peace and safety, but other times just being a Christian could cost someone his or her home, livelihood, family, and even life.

Some provinces of the empire tried a compromise of sorts with the Christians, offering to erect statues honoring Jesus so that they could worship him as well as the Roman idols. But

Let's Come to Terms

Eventually, the Roman Empire instituted a law called *religio illicita*—or "illegal religion"—which banned the Christian religion altogether. This was largely because the Greco-Roman world of that time practiced the worship of literally hundreds of pagan gods. Roman laws and customs didn't allow for the worship of only one god, and refusal to pay homage to these "gods" put people in defiance of Caesar himself.

that wasn't good enough for Jesus' followers, who saw him and him alone as being worthy of their worship.

Further complicating matters for the Christians was the fact that citizens of the Roman Empire were expected to see Caesar not just as their political leader but as one who was worthy of worship. In fact, every city in the empire erected statues in honor of Caesar, and people were expected to worship the statue by placing incense at its base.

Of course, the Christians refused to worship Caesar or any of Rome's pagan Gods. Because of that, many of the Romans came to believe that when something bad happened in the empire—such as a natural disaster—it was because the gods were angry at Jesus' followers for not worshipping them.

This brought accusations that the Christians were antisocial, anti-empire, and anti-human. What's more, because they often met in private, horrible misunderstandings began circulating about Jesus' followers, some of which suggested abhorrent behavior such as cannibalism, drunkenness, and—incest. The charge of cannibalism and drunkenness related to their eating the body and blood of Jesus; their calling each other "brother" and "sister" prompted the charge of incest. Yet no historical evidence even remotely supports these accusations.

Hot Time in the Old Town Tonight

Persecution against Christians first took on an "official" feel in 64 C.E.—during the reign of Emperor Nero—following a horrible fire and the suffering and hardship that followed in the city of Rome.

It's human nature to want to find someone to blame for a tragedy like that, and at first some of Nero's enemies began circulating a rumor that Nero himself was responsible for the fire, a charge that many even today believe may have been true. Of course, Nero wanted to deflect the blame onto someone else, and that someone else was the Christians in Rome. The general population in Rome bought into Nero's accusations, and the result was a great wave of persecution. Many Christians were crucified, fed to wild animals, or burned at the stake.

The second great wave of persecution against Christians began in 95 C.E. under Emperor Domitian. In a way, this persecution was a matter of "guilt by association." It was directed at Jews, who refused to pay taxes earmarked to fund a pagan temple in Rome, but since the Romans saw Christianity as a sect of Judaism, the Christians were also victims of the violence.

Being a "Yes Man" Has Consequences

Eventually, the persecution of Christians became not just a widespread practice of the Roman Empire but one of its official policies. Pliny the Younger, who served as governor of the Roman provinces of Bithynia and Pontus (both in Asia Minor) from 111–113 C.E., was faced with a problem: Christianity was spreading so quickly in his provinces that Jesus' followers soon outnumbered the pagans.

Pliny's approach to dealing with this "problem" was to bring Jesus' followers to trial and ask them three times if they were Christians. If they answered "yes" all three times, they were taken out and executed. However, Pliny wasn't sure if he was handling the situation correctly, so he wrote to Emperor Trajan (who reigned from 98–117 C.E.) and asked for some advice. Trajan replied that the Roman government shouldn't be in the business of hunting down Christians but that if they were brought

before the authorities, they would be given a chance to renounce their allegiance to Jesus and make a sacrifice to the Roman gods. Many thousands of Christians lost their lives under this policy.

The Roman persecution of Christians, which included some unspeakable acts of brutality, continued until early in the fourth century C.E., when Emperor Constantine put a stop to it. However, prior to Constantine, a long line of Roman emperors made it very dangerous to be a Christian living in the empire.

Eventually, things would get easier for the Christians living in the empire. In fact, under Emperor Constantine and those who followed him, it became downright advantageous to follow Jesus.

> **W.W.J.K. (What Would Jesus Know?)**
>
> There was intense and brutal persecution against Christians under most of the Roman emperors during the first, second, third, and early fourth centuries. However, many historians consider the worst of those persecutors to be Emperor Diocletian Galarius, who ruled from 303–311 C.E. Under his rule, churches were destroyed or shut down and Bibles were burned. If you were a Christian under his rule, you could forget about any kind of "due process" or civil rights.

Now a Sign of Victory, Not Defeat

Early in his life, Constantine—like the other Roman emperors before him—believed that Sol, the Roman sun god, was the visible revelation of the invisible "Highest God" and that Sol accompanied him in everything he did.

That changed on the eve of the Battle of Milvian Bridge, when Constantine looked toward the setting sun and saw emblazoned on it a cross and the words "Under this sign, you will conquer." Constantine entered Rome soon after the battle, crediting the Christian God for his success. Not long after that—in January of 313—he issued the Edict of Milan, which lifted the imperial ban on Christianity and made it a legal religion.

From the time of the Edict of Milan forward, persecution of Christians in the empire not only ended but was replaced with what can only be described as favoritism on the part of the emperor. Church buildings, which had been seized by authorities and shut down under previous emperors, were restored and reopened everywhere. New churches sprang up throughout the Roman provinces.

But that was just the beginning. In 380 C.E., Emperor Theodosius I declared the Christian faith the official religion of the empire. Public support shifted away from the pagan religions to this relatively new religion, Christianity. Although pagan worship and sacrifices were still tolerated, government sanctioning of those practices came to an end and was replaced by the official sanctioning of Christianity.

Mixing Politics and Religion

Over the coming centuries, there would be a close relationship between the church and the government. But it was also a volatile relationship, one that went through sometimes wrenching change over time.

From the time of Emperor Constantine on, the church exerted more and more control. During what is known as the Dark Ages and medieval era—the long periods following the fall of the Roman Empire and before the Renaissance—the church had more than just spiritual authority over nations and their leaders. The Pope, or Bishop of Rome, affected the outcome of wars, royal marriages, and financial dealings in the nations under his pastoral care.

This all led to periods of incredible corruption in the power-hungry church leadership, but also to a series of world-changing events—events that helped shape the culture we live in today. The most important of these events are the Protestant Reformation of the sixteenth century and the Catholic Counter-reformation that followed, both of which would profoundly change the world for centuries to come.

Let's Come to Terms

Christendom is a big, religious-sounding word that means "the Christian world." Prior to the Protestant Reformation in the sixteenth century, Christendom meant the world dominated by the Catholic Church, which had been established over a period of several centuries. After the Reformation, Christendom included both the Catholic and Protestant world.

We Blew It ... but God Isn't Finished

The history of the Christian faith isn't always pretty. In fact, it is a history filled with internal conflicts, wars, reformations gone awry, and some well-intentioned but misguided missionary efforts. But the problems within the Christian faith have never been with Jesus himself or with the message of salvation he came to bring. His was a message of eternal life, love, justice, and compassion, and it was a message, as far as we can see, that he practiced as well as preached.

But Jesus left his legacy in the hands of imperfect human beings, and there have been many times in the history of the Christian faith when an impure humanity has mishandled the pure message just described. There have also been many times when the "Mother Theresas" (and there are many hidden ones) have transformed the world for good and shown the face of Jesus to the world.

But that's not the end of the story of Jesus as far as the church is concerned. Christians believe that one day Jesus will again take his legacy into his own hands and that when he does the good he came to bring will permanently triumph over the evil he came to defeat.

Jesus' Final Chapter

The gospel accounts of Jesus give us a picture of the Messiah as the "Suffering Servant" many of the Old Testament Messianic prophecies had predicted he would be. But, as you have already seen in this book, there was another side of Jesus, one that was also recorded in the Old Testament prophecies of the Messiah, and that was the one of the conquering King.

These predictions of the Messiah as a conquering King, one who would ultimately and eternally defeat evil and replace it with not just good but perfection, didn't end in Old Testament days. On the contrary, this picture of the Messiah is reflected in the writings of the apostles Paul, Peter, and (especially) John. The best known of these "end times" writings in the New Testament is the book of Revelation, which, as we pointed out earlier, was written by the apostle John after he was exiled by the Roman emperor to the island of Patmos.

In John's New Testament epistles—1 John, 2 John, and 3 John—the apostle paints a warm and comforting picture of Jesus as the Messiah who came to bring the rule of love and compassion. But John's vision of Jesus as recorded in the book of Revelation is one that is at the same time frightening *and* encouraging and comforting for his followers.

Crashing Symbols to a Grand Theme

Probably no book in the Bible has been interpreted in as many different ways as Revelation. That's simply because the book incorporates so many symbols of conflict—horsemen, trumpets, golden bowls, seals, and even a seven-headed beast—making it very difficult to decipher with certainty what they mean. There is also disagreement as to what order the events described in Revelation take place.

We don't have time or space to discuss the whats, whens, and wheres of the prophecies in the Revelation. As we close this book, we want to focus on the two themes of Revelation that most people agree on: 1) Jesus will one day return to earth and 2) Jesus will bring his eternal kingdom, where those who follow him faithfully will live with him forever.

His Name Is Jesus, a.k.a.

"Faithful and True" (Revelation 19:11). The second coming of Jesus is not similar to the helpless infant in a stable. Here he is graphically and symbolically portrayed as a mighty warrior on a white horse. He is named Faithful and True because he judges fairly and goes to war against evil on behalf of his followers. He comes with a sharp sword and will rule the nations (in the new heaven and earth) with an iron rod. To know he is faithful is actually comforting to his followers, who at the time seem to be losing the battle on earth and are being martyred by the score in many places.

It's Not over 'til the White Horse Appears

John recorded some really disturbing visions in the book of Revelation. He wrote of horrible wars, devastating famines, and cataclysmic natural disasters. He also wrote of "the Beast," who is also known as the Antichrist (although John never uses that name), who will become the primary source of hostility toward God's people.

But John also had a spectacular vision of the return of Jesus to earth to save his followers. John wrote, "I heard the sound of a vast crowd in heaven shouting, 'Hallelujah! Salvation is from our God. Glory and power belong to him alone. His judgments are just and true'."

John then saw heaven opened, revealing a white horse whose rider was called "faithful and true." The rider had eyes like blazing fire, and he wore many crowns on his head. He led the armies of heaven, who were also riding white horses and dressed in clean white linen. He was dressed in a robe dipped in blood, and his name was "the Word of God." On his robe and thigh was another of his names: "King of Kings and Lord of Lords."

Beasts and Their Burdens

At the time of Jesus' return, he leads the armies of heaven against a vast army led by "the Beast." But this battle is no contest. The beast and his false prophet are taken and thrown into a lake of fire that burns with sulfur. After that, an angel descends from heaven and seizes the devil and throws him into the Abyss, where he will be held for a thousand years. At the end of that thousand years, the devil is released from the Abyss, then begins wreaking havoc on earth again. But that will be short-lived, as the devil will be taken up and thrown into the lake of fire, where he, the beast, and the false prophet will remain.

John records that with the devil out of the way, Jesus will bring the dead before "a great white throne," where they will be judged according to what they have done. At that point, a series of books will be opened, including one called "the Book of Life," which apparently contains the names of those who faithfully followed Jesus. Those whose names aren't found in the Book of Life are thrown into the lake of fire.

Happily (For)ever After

While many of the things recorded in the book of Revelation are at best hard to understand—as well as more than a little scary—one thing is very clear *and* very encouraging: It has a happy ending!

When everything is said and done, there will be a new heaven and a new earth, for the old heaven and earth have passed away. The Holy City—also called the New Jerusalem—will come down from heaven "like a beautiful bride prepared for her husband" (Revelation 21:2). At the same time, a voice from the throne of heaven will announce that God is now among his people, that he will live with them forever. Then, he will take away all sorrow, all pain, all death, and all weeping for all of eternity.

See You at the Pearly Gates!

John had an incredible vision of the magnificence of the Holy City of God. Its gates were made of pearl (hence the term "pearly gates") and its main street was made of pure gold. The city measured 1,400 miles wide, long, and high, and it needed no temple, no sun, and no moon, because God Almighty and the Lamb (Jesus) themselves were the city's Temple, and they illuminated the city.

Around six decades before John saw this vision, as Jesus hung dying on a cross, he assured a repentant criminal that on that very day he would be with him in paradise. The apostle John viewed this as the paradise Jesus was talking about. This is heaven, the place Jesus said he came to give to those who heard and believed his message of salvation; and the place where he would be their King and friend forever.

The Least You Need to Know

- The apostles spread the message of Jesus throughout the known world and sometimes paid for it with their lives.

- During the first three centuries after Jesus' death and resurrection, Christians faced horrible persecution at the hands of the Romans.

- The emperor Constantine issued the Edict of Milan, which ended Christian persecution in the empire.

- The church thrived, grew, struggled, and changed in the centuries following Rome's adoption of Christianity.

- Jesus' story will be "completed" when he comes to bring his kingdom to those who faithfully follow him.

Appendix A

Bibliography

Bibles and Books Recommended by the Authors

Holy Bible, New Living Translation. Wheaton, Illinois: Tyndale House Publishers, 1996.

NIV [New International Version] *Harmony of the Gospels*. Grand Rapids, Michigan: Zondervan Publishing House.

Allen, Tom, et. al. *A Guide to the Passion: 100 Questions About the Passion of the Christ* [the movie]. West Chester, Pennsylvania: Ascension Press, 2004.

Brown, Fr. Raymond. *The Death of the Messiah: From Gethsemane to the Grave*. New York: Doubleday, 1994.

Gibson, Mel, and Ken Duncan. *Passion: Photography from the Movie The Passion of the Christ*. Wheaton, Illinois: Tyndale House Publishers, 2004.

Habermas, Gary R. *The Historical Jesus: Ancient Evidence for the Life of Christ*. Joplin, Missouri: College Press Publications, 1996.

Lucado, Max. *Just Like Jesus*. Nashville, Tennessee: Word Publishing, 1998.

Manning, Brennan. *The Signature of Jesus*. Sisters, Oregon: Multnomah Press, 1996.

Moore, Beth. *Jesus, the One and Only*. Nashville, Tennessee: Broadman & Holman, 2002.

Rhodes, Tricia McCary. *At the Name of Jesus: Meditations on the Exalted Christ*. Minneapolis, Minnesota: Bethany House Publishers, 2003.

Strobel, Lee. *The Case for Christ: A Journalist's Personal Investigation of the Evidence for Jesus*. Grand Rapids, Michigan: Zondervan Publishing House, 1998.

Van Voorst, Robert E. *Jesus Outside the New Testament: An Introduction to the Ancient Evidence*. Grand Rapids, Michigan: W.B. Eerdmans Publishers, 2000.

Witherington, Ben III. *The Jesus Quest: The Third Search for the Jew of Nazareth*. Downers Grove, Illinois: Inter-Varsity Press, 1995.

Wright, N.T. *Who Was Jesus?* Grand Rapids, Michigan: W.B. Eerdmans, 1993.

Yancey, Philip. *The Jesus I Never Knew*. Grand Rapids, Michigan: Zondervan Publishing House, 1995.

Internet Resources

BBC World Service
www.bbc.co.uk/worldservice/people
Interesting facts on Jesus and his times

Biblical Archaeology Society
www.bib-arch.org
Relates to archaeological finds in the times of Jesus

Campus Crusade for Christ International: Who Is Jesus?
www.ccci.org/whoisjesus/interactive-journey
Discovering more about the person and work of Jesus

Daily Bible Study
www.keyway.ca/htm2002/christ.htm
Becoming a better follower of Jesus (discipleship)

Encarta
www.Encarta.msn.com
An encyclopedic resource on Jesus

Gospelcom
www.gospelcom.net
General Christian website with a variety of topics related to Jesus

JesusFilm.com
www.jesusfilm.com
Relates to the film "Jesus" by Campus Crusade for Christ

LifeOfChrist.com
www.lifeofchrist.com
Overview of the life of Christ

The Passion of the Christ website
www.thepassionoftheChrist.com
Relates to the film *The Passion of the Christ*

Southern Baptist Convention: How to Become a Christian
www.sbc.net/knowjesus/default.asp
Devotionally oriented website fostering a relationship with Jesus

ChristianAnswers.net
www.christiananswers.net/jesus/home.html
Summary of Jesus Christ's story

Scriptural Prophecy Regarding Jesus

The Pre-Existence of the Messiah

Subject	Prophecy	Fulfillment
The Messiah would be eternal.	Psalm 102:25–27a	Colossians 1:17
The Messiah would be from everlasting.	Proverbs 8:22–23	John 17:5

The Messiah Would Be God in the Flesh

Subject	Prophecy	Fulfillment
The Messiah would be the creator of all.	Psalm 102:25–27b	John 1:3
The Messiah would be Lord.	Psalm 110:1a	Matthew 22:41–45
The Messiah would be holy.	Daniel 9:24b	Luke 1:35
The Messiah would be God.	Zechariah 11:10–11b	John 14:7

The Messiah Would Be the Son of God

Subject	Prophecy	Fulfillment
God would have a Son.	Proverbs 30:4b	Matthew 3:16–17
The Messiah would be the Son of God.	Isaiah 9:6b	Luke 1:35

The Time of the Messiah's Coming

Subject	Prophecy	Fulfillment
The Jews' authority to administer capital punishment would be gone when the Messiah arrived.	Genesis 49:10c	John 18:31
The Messiah would be announced to his people 483 years, to the exact day, after the decree to rebuild the city of Jerusalem.	Daniel 9:25	John 12:12–13
The Messiah would be killed before the destruction of the temple.	Daniel 9:26c	Matthew 27:50–51

The Genealogy of the Messiah

Subject	Prophecy	Fulfillment
The Messiah would be a descendant of Abraham.	Genesis 12:3	Matthew 1:1
The Messiah would be a descendant of Isaac.	Genesis 17:19	Luke 3:23–34
The Messiah would be a descendant of Jacob.	Genesis 28:14a	Luke 3:23–34
The Messiah would be a descendant of Judah.	Genesis 49:10a	Luke 3:23–33
The Messiah would be a descendant of Boaz and Ruth.	Ruth 4:12–17	Luke 3:23–32
The Messiah would be a descendant of David.	2 Samuel 7:16	Matthew 1:1

The Birth and Childhood of the Messiah

Subject	Prophecy	Fulfillment
The Messiah would be born of the "seed" of a woman.	Genesis 3:15a	Luke 1:34–35
The Messiah would be born of a virgin.	Isaiah 7:14a	Luke 1:34–35
The Messiah would be Immanuel, "God with us."	Isaiah 7:14b	Matthew 1:21–23
The Messiah would be called by his name before he was born.	Isaiah 49:1c	Luke 1:30–31
The Messiah would be born in Bethlehem.	Micah 5:2a	Matthew 2:1–2
The birth of the Messiah.	Isaiah 9:6a	Luke 2:11
The Messiah would be protected by God.	Isaiah 49:2b	Matthew 2:13–15
The Messiah would grow up in a poor family.	Isaiah 11:1b	Luke 2:7

The Attributes of the Messiah

Subject	Prophecy	Fulfillment
The Messiah would be a Prophet.	Deuteronomy 18:15–19a	John 6:14
The Messiah would be a Priest in the order of Melchizedek.	Psalm 110:4	Hebrews 6:17–20
The Messiah would be a King.	Genesis 49:10b	John 1:49
The Messiah would be the "Prince of Peace."	Isaiah 9:6f	Colossians 1:20
The Messiah would be the subject of angels' worship.	Deuteronomy 32:43	Luke 2:13–14
The Messiah would be a witness.	Isaiah 55:4	John 18:37
The Messiah would be as a shepherd.	Isaiah 40:11	John 10:11
The Messiah would speak in parables.	Isaiah 6:9–10b	Matthew 13:13–15
The Messiah would speak with a message of grace.	Psalm 45:2	Luke 4:22
The Messiah's words would be as a sharp sword.	Isaiah 49:2a	Revelation 2:12–16
The Messiah would speak with words of authority given to Him from God.	Deuteronomy 18:15–19b	John 12:48–50
The Messiah would minister in Galilee.	Isaiah 9:1–2a	Matthew 4:12–17
The Messiah would have the full Spirit of God upon him.	Isaiah 11:2a	Matthew 3:16–17
The Messiah would have the Spirit of Wisdom.	Isaiah 11:2b	Luke 2:40
The Messiah would have the Spirit of Might.	Isaiah 11:2e	Matthew 8:27
The Messiah would place his trust in God.	Isaiah 50:8–10	John 11:7–10
The Messiah would be just.	Zechariah 9:9c	John 5:30
The Messiah would not judge on the basis of external representations.	Isaiah 11:3b	John 7:24
The Messiah would have compassion for the poor and needy.	Isaiah 42:3	Matthew 11:4–5
The Messiah would be responsible for the judgment of mankind.	Isaiah 49:2c	John 5:22–29

Subject	Prophecy	Fulfillment
The Messiah would be humble.	Zechariah 9:9e	Matthew 11:29
The Messiah would have the appearance of an ordinary man.	Isaiah 53:2b	Philippians 2:7–8
The Messiah would be the cornerstone.	Zechariah 10:4	Ephesians 2:20
The Messiah would be as the "light of the morning."	2 Samuel 23:2–4b	Revelation 22:16
The Messiah would say the Scriptures were written of him.	Psalm 40:6–8b	Luke 24:44
The Messiah would have the key of David.	Isaiah 22:22	Revelation 3:7

Events During the Messiah's Ministry

Subject	Prophecy	Fulfillment
The Messiah would preach the Good News.	Isaiah 61:1–2b	Luke 4:17–21
The Messiah would declare that he was the Son of God.	Psalm 2:7b	John 9:35–37
Infants would give praise to the Messiah.	Psalm 8:2	Matthew 21:15–16
The Messiah would be beheld as King.	Zechariah 9:9b	John 12:12–13
The Messiah would be presented to Jerusalem riding on a donkey.	Zechariah 9:9f	Matthew 21:6–9
The Messiah would make a sudden appearance at the temple.	Malachi 3:1b	Mark 11:15–16
The Messiah would be ministered to by God.	Isaiah 42:6b	John 8:29
The Messiah would ask God for His inheritance.	Psalm 2:8a	John 17:4–24

The Messiah Would Perform Miracles

Subject	Prophecy	Fulfillment
The Messiah would heal the blind.	Isaiah 35:5a	Mark 10:51–52
The Messiah would heal the deaf.	Isaiah 35:5b	Mark 7:32–35

continues

The Messiah Would Perform Miracles (continued)

Subject	Prophecy	Fulfillment
The Messiah would heal the lame.	Isaiah 35:6a	Matthew 12:10–13
The Messiah would have a healing ministry.	Isaiah 53:4a	Luke 6:17–19

The Messiah Would Come to Do God's Will

Subject	Prophecy	Fulfillment
The Messiah would be called to God's service from the womb.	Psalm 22:10	Luke 1:30–33
The Messiah would be sent by God.	Isaiah 48:16b	John 7:29
The Messiah would come to do God's will.	Psalm 40:7–8	John 5:30
The Messiah's work would glorify God.	Isaiah 49:3b	Matthew 15:30–31
The Messiah would not conceal his mission from the congregation.	Psalm 40:9–10	Luke 4:16–21
The Messiah would steadfastly set his face toward his mission.	Isaiah 50:7	Luke 9:51–53
The Messiah would be God's servant.	Isaiah 42:1a	John 4:34
The Messiah would bear reproach, for God's sake.	Psalm 69:9b	Romans 15:3
God would be fully satisfied with the suffering of the Messiah.	Isaiah 53:11a	John 12:27
The Messiah would speak with knowledge given to him from God.	Isaiah 50:4	John 12:49

The Messiah Would Come for All People

Subject	Prophecy	Fulfillment
The Messiah would come for all nations.	Genesis 18:17–18b	Acts 3:24–26
The Messiah would be a light to the Gentiles.	Isaiah 9:1–2b	Luke 2:28–32

The Messiah Would Come to Provide Salvation

Subject	Prophecy	Fulfillment
The Messiah would be the messenger of the new covenant.	Malachi 3:1c	Luke 4:43
The Messiah would come to make an end to sins.	Daniel 9:24a	Galatians 1:3–5
The Messiah would give up his life to save mankind.	Isaiah 53:12b	Luke 23:46
The Messiah's offering of himself would replace all sacrifices.	Psalm 40:6–8a	Hebrews 10:10–13
The Messiah's blood would be shed to make atonement for all.	Isaiah 52:15	Revelation 1:5
The Messiah's sacrifice would provide peace between man and God.	Isaiah 53:5b	Colossians 1:20
The Messiah's atonement would enable believers to be his brethren.	Psalm 22:22	Hebrews 2:10–12
The Messiah would come to provide salvation.	Isaiah 59:15–16a	John 6:40
The Messiah would have a ministry to the "poor," the believing remnant.	Zechariah 11:7	Matthew 9:35–36
The Messiah would come to Zion as their Redeemer.	Isaiah 59:20	Luke 2:38
The Messiah would reject those who did not believe in him.	Psalm 2:12b	John 3:36

The Messiah Would Be Betrayed

Subject	Prophecy	Fulfillment
The Messiah's betrayer would be a friend whom he broke bread with.	Psalm 41:9	Mark 14:17–18
The Messiah would be betrayed for 30 pieces of silver.	Zechariah 11:12–13a	Matthew 26:14–15
The Messiah's betrayer would have a short life.	Psalm 109:8a	Acts 1:16–18
The Messiah's betrayer would be replaced.	Psalm 109:8b	Acts 1:20–26

The Messiah Would Be Despised

Subject	Prophecy	Fulfillment
The Messiah would be despised.	Isaiah 49:7	John 10:20
Political and religious leaders would conspire against the Messiah.	Psalm 2:2	Matthew 26:3–4

The Messiah Would Be Judged

Subject	Prophecy	Fulfillment
The Messiah would be accused by false witnesses.	Psalm 109:2	John 18:29–30
The Messiah would be silent before his accusers.	Isaiah 53:7b	Matthew 27:12–14
The Messiah would be innocent and have done no violence.	Isaiah 53:9b	Mark 15:3

The Messiah Would Be Rejected

Subject	Prophecy	Fulfillment
At the time of the Messiah's coming, Israel would have unfit leaders.	Zechariah 11:4–6a	Matthew 23:1–4
The Messiah's brothers would disbelieve him.	Psalm 69:8b	John 7:3–5
The Messiah would be the "stone" rejected by the Jews.	Psalm 118:22	Matthew 21:42–43
The Messiah would be distressed over the Jews' unbelief.	Isaiah 49:4a	Luke 19:41–42
The Messiah would be rejected in favor of another king.	Zechariah 11:4–6c	John 19:13–15
Israel would be scattered as a result of rejecting the Messiah.	Zechariah 13:7d	Matthew 26:31–56

The Messiah Would Suffer Greatly

Subject	Prophecy	Fulfillment
The Messiah would have great sorrow and grief.	Isaiah 53:3c	Luke 19:41–42
The Messiah would be oppressed and afflicted.	Isaiah 53:7a	Matthew 27:27–31
The Messiah's face would be beaten and spit upon.	Isaiah 50:6b	Matthew 26:67
The Messiah's back would be whipped.	Isaiah 50:6a	Matthew 27:26
The Messiah's face would be disfigured from severe beatings.	Isaiah 52:14	Matthew 26:67–68

The Crucifixion of the Messiah

Subject	Prophecy	Fulfillment
The Messiah would be sacrificed upon the same mountain where God tested Abraham.	Genesis 22:14	Luke 23:33
The Messiah would be grouped with criminals.	Isaiah 53:12c	Luke 23:32
The Messiah's hands and feet would be pierced.	Psalm 22:16c	Matthew 27:38
The Messiah would pray for his enemies.	Psalm 109:4	Luke 23:34
The Messiah would be offered gall and vinegar.	Psalm 69:20–21a	Matthew 27:34
Lots would be cast for the Messiah's clothes.	Psalm 22:18b	John 19:23–24
The Messiah would be thought to be cursed by God.	Isaiah 53:4c	Matthew 27:41–43
Mockers would say of the Messiah, "He trusted God, let him deliver him."	Psalm 22:8	Matthew 27:41–43
The Messiah would cry out to God.	Psalm 22:1a	Matthew 27:46
The Messiah would be forsaken by God.	Psalm 22:1b	Mark 15:34
The Messiah would thirst.	Psalm 22:15a	John 19:28
The Messiah would die a violent death.	Zechariah 13:7b	Matthew 27:35

continues

The Crucifixion of the Messiah (continued)

Subject	Prophecy	Fulfillment
None of the Messiah's bones would be broken.	Psalm 22:17a	John 19:32–33
The Messiah's heart would burst, flowing with blood and water.	Psalm 22:14a	John 19:34
The Messiah would be buried in a rich man's grave.	Isaiah 53:9	Matthew 27:57

The Resurrection and Victory of the Messiah

Subject	Prophecy	Fulfillment
The Messiah's body would not be subject to decay.	Psalm 16:8–10b	Acts 13:35–37
The Messiah would be resurrected and live forever.	Isaiah 53:10c	Mark 16:16
Others would rise to life at the resurrection of the Messiah.	Isaiah 26:19	Matthew 27:52–53
The Messiah would defeat death.	Isaiah 25:8	Revelation 1:18
The Messiah would defeat Satan.	Genesis 3:15b	1 John 3:8
The Messiah would be exalted to the presence of God.	Psalm 16:11	Acts 2:25–33
The Messiah would be resurrected and crowned as King.	Psalm 2:7c	Acts 13:30–33
The Messiah would be at the right hand of God.	Psalm 80:17	Acts 5:31
The Messiah's throne would be everlasting.	1 Chronicles 17:11–12b	Luke 1:32–33
The Messiah would be given authority over all things.	Psalm 8:6	Matthew 28:18
A vision of the Messiah in a glorified state.	Daniel 10:5–6	Revelation 1:13–16

Index